WARPLANES
& AIR BATTLES
OF WORLD WAR II

PHOEBUS, LONDON

WARPLANES
& AIR BATTLES
OF WORLD WAR II

PHOEBUS, LONDON

Introduction

In the long summer days of 1940, the war in the sky appeared to those below as an affair of high gallantry, of laughing youth going gaily to battle, and white vapour trails in a clear blue sky.

These elements were certainly present. But behind them was the industrial effort which gave Britain the Spitfire, and the inventive genius which gave us radar. Wars have always been decided more by the quality of weapons and equipment than popular opinion has allowed—and the Battle of Britain was eventually won largely by the ability to climb higher and faster than the antagonist, and to be in the right place at the right time.

As the war developed, the performance of the aircraft themselves became more and more important, and in this book we have tried to encompass the full range of aircraft development between 1939 and 1945 : from the Bristol Blenheim to the Superfortress, and from the Gloster Gladiator to the jet aircraft that came too late to make a difference.

Of course, the most sophisticated aeroplanes are useless without skilful and courageous men to fly them, and their story is here too; the lonely dedication of the fighter pilots, the cold bravery of the bomber crews, even the heroic self-sacrifice of the kamikazes, told by the men themselves and illustrated by drawings of their planes and photographs of their work.

Edited by Bernard Fitzsimons

Phoebus, London.

This edition © BPC Publishing Ltd. 1973

First published in Purnell's History of the Second World War

First published in this form 1973

ISBN 0 7026 0001 6

Printed in Belgium - H. Proost & Cie p.v.b.a. Turnhout - Belgium

Contents

After the Armistice in November 1918 the greatly expanded armed forces of the Allies were hastily and clumsily demobilized. Improvised war organizations were dismantled, and the watchwords of the British government were economy and retrenchment. The war had been won, there was no visible threat to Allied security, and Great Britain and France were swept by a wave of anti-war feeling, largely induced by the terrible casualties and intolerable conditions of trench warfare.

In 1925 the League of Nations had set up a Preparatory Commission to explore the ground for a general disarmament conference. Progress in this field is never rapid, and for many years the commission was involved in interminable difficulties and arguments. Eventually a Disarmament Conference was convened in Geneva in 1932, at which proposals for outlawing air bombardment and drastically limiting the loaded weight of military aircraft were discussed. Hoping for success in these negotiations, the British government declined to authorize the design and construction of any effective bomber aircraft. In addition, it had introduced in 1924 what became known as the 'Ten-year Rule', which postulated that there would be no major war for ten years. Unfortunately each successive year was deemed to be the starting point of this tranquil epoch, and so the period always remained at ten years.

The Disarmament Conference finally broke up in May 1934 without achieving any result whatsoever. But meanwhile Hitler had come to power in Germany, and was clearly bent on a massive programme of rearmament. In 1933 the British government at last permitted the issue of Air Staff requirements for a high-performance multi-gun fighter, which in due course produced the Hurricane and Spitfire. It is often asserted that these two aircraft, and especially the Spitfire, were forced on a reluctant Air Ministry by a far-sighted aircraft industry and its capable designers. There is not a word of truth in this. Both aircraft were designed, ordered, and built to Air Ministry specifications.

Even after the collapse of the Disarmament Conference in 1934 the British government was reluctant to rearm. Alone among nations the British seem to think that if they rearm it will bring about an arms race. The result of this curious delusion is that they usually start when the other competitors are half-way round the course. The bomber force was therefore given a very low priority, but

John Batchelor

The Gloster Gladiator had been Britain's principal fighter at the time of the Munich crisis in 1938, but even when replaced by the Hurricane and Spitfire, the Gladiator's career was by no means over. Gladiators served with the Allies in Norway, and for a time four Gladiators were the only fighter 'defence' of Malta against Mussolini's air fleet. Gladiators, flown by the Finnish air force and Swedish volunteer pilots, had fought the Red Air Force in the Winter War. For the RAF Gladiators, however, their last theatre was the Middle East, which was a backwater in the air war for both Axis and Allies alike. Last of the British biplane fighters, the Gladiator enjoyed the biplane's manoeuvrability; but in terms of speed and fire-power the Gladiator was no match for the monoplane fighters. **Max speed:** 246 mph; **Armament:** four ·303 Browning machine-guns

development of the fighters was allowed to proceed, though without any undue haste.

In 1935 two British ministers, Mr Anthony Eden and Sir John Simon, visited Germany. They reported that Hitler's rearmament in the air had proceeded much farther and faster than the British government had believed possible. This was because the Germans had made a secret agreement to train the Soviet air force, which enabled them to keep in being a sizeable corps of expert pilots and technicians. The government was alarmed, and ordered quantity production of the Hurricanes and Spitfires before the prototype had even flown— the so-called 'ordering off the drawing-board'.

Lord Trenchard, chief of the Air Staff from 1919 to 1928, had always believed that in air defence the bomber was as important as the fighter. He maintained that the air war should be fought in the skies over the enemy's territory, and he therefore advocated a bomber force powerful enough to take the offensive, and attack an enemy's vital centres from the outset. He argued that this would rob an enemy of the initiative and throw his air force on to the defensive.

Eventually Trenchard's views were accepted by the British government, and in the air defence of Great Britain two-thirds of the squadrons were to be bombers and one-third fighters. But because it was thought that the bombers were offensive while the fighters were defensive in character, it was judged that the building up of fighter strength would not be liable to trigger off an arms race. The seventeen authorized fighter squadrons were in existence by 1930, but at that date no more than twelve of the thirty-five authorized bomber squadrons had been formed, most of them equipped with small short-range day bombers. In 1935 the alarm caused by German rearmament in the air occasioned a further shift of emphasis in favour of the fighters. A system of radio-location, later called radar, which would provide invaluable early warning and make it possible to track incoming raids, was pioneered by Robert Watson-Watt, and given all possible encouragement.

At the outbreak of war in September 1939 the odds against the RAF, in terms of modern aircraft, were about four to one. Although money had been poured out like water during the years since the Munich crisis, it had been too late to redress the balance. Only time—as much time as possible— could do that.

The Germans had a numerical
superiority of two to one, and in almost
every department German aircraft
were technically superior to their
Allied counterparts

THE BALANCE IN THE AIR

Fairey Battles,
Britain's light bomber.
Ten squadrons of this
highly rated aircraft
went to France in 1940.
Few came back.

Tested during the Spanish Civil War, the Dornier 'Flying Pencil' (above) took part in the terror bombing of Guernica. A few years later it was used to raze Rotterdam (right), where 30,000 civilian casualties were suffered

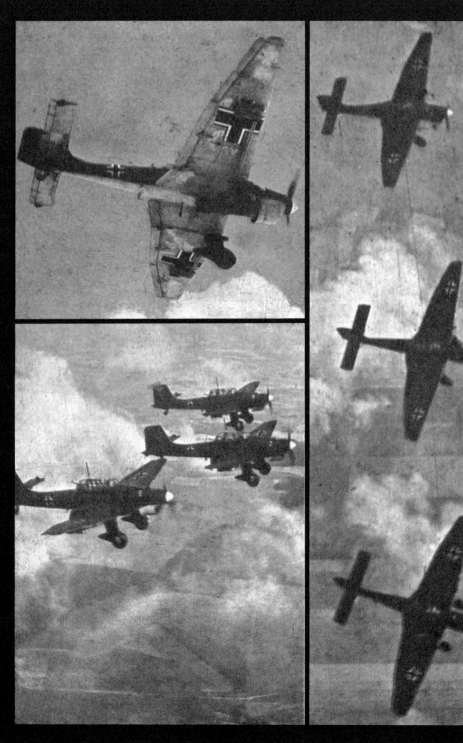

A New Factor: Air Power

One key to Germany's quick victory over Poland was her air power: by the second day of battle, the Luftwaffe had gained complete control of the sky. For the first two days of the campaign German bombers attacked Poland's airfields and struck at her road and rail network, her administrative centres, and her industrial targets. Then their Stukas (shown here) began their close support of the ground forces. During the first week of the fighting, 1,634 sorties were sent out to support one tank corps alone. Up against such efficient aggression, Poland's two air brigades lost half their aircraft by the end of the first week

▲ Blenheims — the standard British bomber used in the campaign in France
◄ French MS-406's — completely outclassed by the German Me-109E

BATTLE OF BRITAIN

Hitler's plan was to soften up Britain for the proposed invasion.
But he was not dealing with the same Britain that signed away
Czechoslovakia at Munich. Fortified and inspired by their war
leader, the British knew that the fate of the West could very well
hinge on their courage on land, and on their aggressive spirit
in the skies

In its element: the Spitfire, symbol of the battle

The moment drew near for the Luftwaffe's great assault

From the very outset of the war a great German air assault had been expected in Britain. It was for fear of this that mothers and children had been evacuated from the big cities, the blackout enforced, gas masks and Anderson shelters distributed, thousands of beds held vacant in the hospitals. But no 'knock-out blow' from the air, or indeed any kind of blow at all—other than minelaying and raids on Scottish naval bases and east coast convoys—had disturbed the uncanny peace of the British Isles during the autumn and winter of 1939-40.

This quiet remained unbroken even when, in the spring of 1940, the war in the west came abruptly to the boil. Strange as it seemed at the time, there were in fact good reasons for Britain's unexpected immunity. Britain herself had not launched a strategic bombing offensive against Germany during the 'Phoney War' for fear of retaliation while the Allies were still the weaker side in the air. Germany had not launched any such offensive against Britain because she did not think she could achieve decisive results from German bases and because the Luftwaffe was largely cast for the role of military support. This support the Luftwaffe had given, with exemplary effectiveness, during the campaign in Poland; and now, as the Germans struck in the west, it operated in similar fashion in Norway, the Low Countries, and France. Meanwhile, it did not waste its strength in irrelevant activity against England.

This self-imposed restriction lasted until the German army entered the smoking ruins of Dunkirk. Within less than 48 hours, on the night of June 5/6, the Luftwaffe began to show a more lively interest in the British homeland. Some 30 German bombers—far more than on any previous occasion—crossed the east coast to attack airfields and other objectives; and the following night similar forces repeated the experiment. Then came a lull while the German armies in France struck southwards, again supported by the Luftwaffe. It lasted until the French sought an armistice, whereupon within a few hours German aircraft resumed night operations over Britain. From then on until the opening of their full daylight air offensive in August, the Germans repeatedly dispatched bombers—70 of them on the busiest night—against widely separated targets in England. Their intention was to give their crews experience in night operations and the use of radio navigational aids, to reconnoitre, and to maintain pressure inexpensively (their usual losses were one or two aircraft each night) until captured airfields in France and the Low Countries could be made ready for operations of a more intensive kind.

Meanwhile there was always the chance—or so it seemed to Hitler—that such operations might not be necessary. The Führer accordingly put out 'peace-feelers', at the same time encouraging preparations for the next stage of hostilities. This next stage, the invasion or occupation of Britain, was not one to which the Germans had already devoted long thought. The speed and completeness of the German victory in France had taken even the optimistic Hitler by surprise; and though his armed forces had given some casual attention in the autumn of 1939 to the general problems of invading Britain, it was not until German troops actually reached the Channel coast on May 20, 1940, that the project really came to life. From then on the German navy, anxious not to be caught out by Hitler, began serious planning; but the German army showed comparable interest only after the total defeat of France. On July 2 Hitler formally directed his services to proceed with this invasion planning, though on a purely provisional basis. On July 19 came his public peace offer; on the 22nd, its rejection.

If the Germans were to take advantage of the 'invasion season' in the Channel that year, their three services would now have to formulate and agree plans with extraordinary speed. This difficulty struck the German naval and military chiefs more forcibly than it did Hitler, who declared to his paladins that only the rapid elimination of Britain would enable him to complete his life's work by turning against Russia. On July 31 he accordingly disregarded the fast-waning enthusiasm of the German navy and army and ordered that an attempt must be made to prepare the invasion operation, to which the code-name 'Seelöwe' ('Sea Lion') was given, for September 15. The following day, August 1, he issued a directive concerning the only part of the venture on which all three German services were thus far agreed. It was for the preliminary stage, which must consist of the subjugation of the RAF. 'The German air force is to overcome the British air force with all means at its disposal, and as soon as possible.' With these words, Hitler finally decreed the Battle of Britain.

600 RAF sorties a day

While the plans for Sea Lion and the preliminary air battle were taking shape, the Luftwaffe was not of course idle. From its captured airfields it continued to harass Britain by night, and from July 10 onwards it waged increasing war by day against British shipping in the Channel. The German bombers were usually detected by the British radar stations, but since the attacks were delivered at the periphery of the British defensive system they set the Fighter Command a difficult problem. In such circumstances it was highly creditable to the command that the British fighters inflicted more casualties than they themselves suffered: between July 10 and August 10, as we now know, the Germans lost 217 aircraft, Fighter Command 96. On the other hand the German attacks, though sinking only a modest tonnage of British shipping, imposed a severe strain on Fighter Command, which was compelled to fly some 600 sorties a day at extended range at a time when it was trying to build up resources for the greater trials clearly soon to come. As Air Chief Marshal Sir Hugh Dowding, Air Officer C-in-C of the Fighter Command, pointed out to the Air Ministry and the Admiralty, if constant air protection was to be given to all British shipping in home waters, the entire British fighter force could be kept fully employed on that task alone.

These German attacks on shipping, however, were only a prelude to the air battle which the Luftwaffe had now to induce. The prerequisite of Sea Lion was that the Germans should gain air supremacy over the Channel and southern Britain. Only if the RAF were put out of business could the Germans hope to cross, land, and maintain communications without an unacceptable rate of casualties; for the destruction of the RAF would not only obviate British bombing attacks, but would also enable the Luftwaffe to deal, uninterrupted from the air, with the Royal Navy. And beyond this there was always the hope, ever present in the minds of Hitler and his service chiefs alike, that the Luftwaffe's success alone might be so great as to bring Britain to submission, or very near it. In that case, an invasion about which neither the German navy nor army was really happy could become something much more to their liking—a virtually unresisted occupation.

As the moment drew near for the Luftwaffe's great assault, the forces arrayed stood as follows. On the German side there were three Luftflotten, or air fleets. The main ones were Luftflotte II, under Field-Marshal Kesselring, in northern Germany, Holland, Belgium, and in north-eastern France; and Luftflotte III, under Field-Marshal Sperrle, in northern and western France. By day, these two air fleets threatened the entire southern half of England, up to and including the Midlands; and by night they could range still farther afield. In addition, to disperse the British defences and to threaten Scotland and north-eastern England there was also a smaller force, Luftflotte V, under General Stumpff, based in Denmark and Norway. Between them, the three air fleets on August 10 comprised over 3,000 aircraft, of which about three-quarters were normally serviceable at any one time. Roughly 1,100 of the 3,000 were fighters—for the most part Messerschmitt 109E's, virtually the equal of the opposing Spitfires of that date, but handicapped in a protective role by their limited range.

To escort bombers to the more distant targets, including those to be reached across the North Sea from Norway, there were some 300 Messerschmitt 110s; but these twin-engined fighters, though sturdy, could not compare in manoeuvrability with the single-engined Spitfire or Hurricane. The remaining 1,900 German aircraft were almost entirely bombers, mainly the well-tried if slow Heinkel 111, the slim, pencil-like Dornier 17, and the fast and more recent Junkers 88, but including also about 400 Junkers 87s—the Stukas, or dive-bombers. These had established a legendary reputation on the battlefields of Poland and France, but their range was very short and they had yet to face powerful and sustained opposition.

On the British side, the situation was a great deal better than it had been a few weeks earlier. On June 4, following the heavy losses of Hurricanes in France, Fighter Command had been able to muster only 446 modern single-engined fighters—Spitfires and Hurricanes—with another 36 ready in the Aircraft Storage Units (ASUs) as replacements. But on August 11, on the eve of the main air battle, Fighter Command had 704 of these aircraft in the squadrons and 289 in the ASUs. Its fighting strength had been virtually doubled during those ten critical weeks since Dunkirk, thanks to the fruition of earlier Air Ministry plans and the tremendous efforts of the aircraft industry under the stimulus of the newly appointed Minister of Aircraft Production, Lord Beaverbrook.

Strengthening the shield
During those same ten weeks the British air defence system, built up against an enemy operating from Germany and possibly the Low Countries, had also been extended, thanks to schemes already worked out and in progress, to deal with forces operating from France and Norway. To the existing groups within Fighter Command – No. 11 Group, guarding the south-east, No. 12 Group, guarding the east and Midlands, and No. 13 Group, guarding the north-east up to the Forth – had been added another: No. 10 Group, guarding the south-west. The intermittent defences of the north-west, including Northern Ireland, had been thickened, as had those of Scotland.

This was not only a matter of providing more fighter aircraft and the pilots to fly them. It was also a matter of extending the main coastal radar chain, adding special radar stations to detect low-flying aircraft, extending Observer Corps posts for inland tracking over the south-western counties and western Wales, adapting more airfields for fighter operations, installing guns, searchlights, balloon barrages. All this was the concomitant, on the air defence side, of the gun-posts and the pill-boxes, the barbed wire and the dragon's teeth, that the inhabitant of southern England, enrolled perhaps in the newly formed Local Defence Volunteers and on watch at dawn and dusk for the arrival of German paratroops, saw springing up before his eyes along his familiar coasts and downlands.

The island's air defences had grown stronger and more extensive, but many grave deficiencies remained. Of the 120 fighter squadrons which the Director of Home Operations at the Air Ministry considered desirable in the new situation created by the German conquests, Dowding had less than 60 – and eight of these flew Blenheims or Defiants, no match for the Me-109s. Of the 4,000 anti-aircraft guns deemed necessary even before the German conquests, Anti-Aircraft Command still had less than 2,000. The early warning and inland tracking systems were still incomplete in the west and over parts of Scotland. There was a shortage of fighter pilots: new planes could be produced quicker than new skilled men to fly them. But whatever the deficiencies of the air defence system by day, they were as nothing compared with its alarming weaknesses by night, when ordinary fighters were useful only in the brightest moonlight, and when the men of the Observer Corps had to rely on ineffective acoustical detectors instead of their clear eyesight and a pair of binoculars.

Britain, however, had assets not yet mentioned. Among others, there was RAF Coastal Command, prepared both to carry out reconnaissance and to help in offensive operations; and there was RAF Bomber Command. Most of the latter's aircraft could operate safely only by night, and by night it was by no means certain that they could find and hit the more distant targets. The daylight bombers – about 100 Blenheims – were capable of much greater accuracy; but they needed fighter support, which could be supplied only at short range (assuming the Hurricanes or Spitfires could be spared). Against targets near at hand – airfields, ports, and shipping just across the Channel

– the British bombing force was capable of playing a vital part. Against distant objectives, its effectiveness at that date was more problematical.

In sum, the opposing forces, disregarding reconnaissance aircraft and units still stationed in Germany, consisted of about 1,900 bombers assisted by 1,100 fighters on the German side, and of about 700 fighters assisted to a limited extent by 350 bombers on the British side. The Germans had the advantage not only of numbers but of the tactical initiative – of the fact that they could strike anywhere within their range – while the British defences could react only to the German moves.

The British air defence system, however, though incomplete, was the most technically advanced in the world. The early warning supplied by the radar stations (which in the south-east could pick up enemy formations before they crossed the French coast), the inland tracking by the Observer Corps, the control of the British fighters from the ground in the light of this information and the continuous reporting of the fighters' own position – all this, designed to obviate the need for wasteful standing patrols, meant that the British fighters could be used with economy and could take off with a good chance of making interception.

One other factor, too, helped the British: the Luftwaffe's offensive against Britain was largely an improvised one; and Luftwaffe C-in-C Göring, though an able man, was also a vainglorious boaster who in technical proficiency was not in the same class as the opposing commander. The single-minded Dowding, in charge of Fighter Command since its formation in 1936 – the man whose obduracy had preserved Britain's fighter resources against the clamour to squander them in France – knew his job. Göring, as much politician as airman, scarcely knew his; while theoretically controlling and co-ordinating the entire offensive, in practice he was incapable of more than occasional acts of intervention. On the next level of command, Kesselring, in charge of the main attacking force – Luftflotte II – was for all his successes in Poland and France a novice in the forthcoming type of operation; while Air Vice-Marshal Keith Park, commanding the main defending force – Group 11 – had earlier been Dowding's right-hand man at Headquarters, Fighter Command. Unlike their opposite numbers, the two principal British commanders had lived with their problem for years. Their skill, experience, and devotion, like those of their pilots, offset some of the British inferiority in numbers.

Operation Eagle
By August 10 the three Luftflotten stood ready to launch the major assault – Operation Eagle ('Adler') – which would drive the RAF from the skies of southern Britain. Four days, in the opinion of the German Air Staff, would see the shattering of the fighter defences south of the line London-Gloucester, four weeks the elimination of the entire RAF. Allowing for the ten days' notice required by the German navy for minelaying and other final preparations before the actual D-Day, the date of the invasion could thus be set for mid-September.

August 11 was a very cloudy day, and the Germans confined their activity to bombing Portland and some east coast shipping. On the following day came what seemed to the British to be the beginning of the main attack: five or six major raids and many

minor ones, involving several hundred aircraft, including escorted Ju-87s, struck at airfields and radar stations along the south coast and at shipping in the Thames Estuary. Of the six radar stations they attacked, the raiders damaged five but knocked out only one – that at Ventnor on the Isle of Wight. It could not be replaced until August 23 – a sharp blow. Among the airfields, they hit Lympne, a forward landing ground, and Manston and Hawkinge, two important fighter stations in Kent, but all were back in action within 24 hours. Fighters from No. 11 Group challenged all the major raids, and frustrated completely one aimed at Manston. In the course of the fighting the Germans lost 31 aircraft, the British 22.

According to the German records, the next day, August 13, was Eagle Day itself – the opening of the Eagle offensive proper. The attack went off at half-cock in the morning, when a message postponing operations till later in the day failed to get through to some of the German squadrons. In the afternoon the main assault developed with a two-pronged thrust, Luftflotte II attacking over Kent and the Thames Estuary, while Luftflotte III, challenged by No. 10 Group, attacked over Hampshire, Dorset, and Wiltshire. The raiders hit three airfields severely – Eastchurch, Detling, and Andover – but none of these belonged to Fighter Command; their attacks on fighter stations such as Rochford were beaten off.

In the whole day's operations – which witnessed 1,485 German sorties and ended with a successful night attack on a Spitfire factory at Castle Bromwich, near Birmingham – the Germans lost 45 aircraft, Fighter Command only 13 (with six of the British pilots saved). This was a poor sort of Eagle Day for the Germans, but they were nevertheless well satisfied with their progress. They calculated that between August 8 and 14, in addition to successful attacks on some 30 airfields and aircraft factories, they had destroyed more than 300 British fighters in combat. In fact, they had destroyed less than 100.

After lesser activity on August 14 – a matter of some 500 German sorties, directed mainly against railways near the coast and against RAF stations – the Luftwaffe on August 15 attempted the great blow with which it had hoped to open the battle some days earlier. In clear skies the Germans sent over during the day no less than seven major raids, using all three Luftflotten in a series of co-ordinated attacks on widely separated areas. The first clash came at about 1130 hours, when some 40 escorted Ju-87s of Luftflotte II struck at Lympne and Hawkinge airfields in Kent. Then, about 1230 hours some 65 He-111s escorted by 35 Me-110s of Luftflotte V, operating from Stavanger in Norway, headed in to the Northumberland coast in an attempt to bomb airfields in the north-east. These formations were barely retiring when at 1315 hours another force of Luftflotte V, consisting of about 50 unescorted Ju-88s operating from Aalborg in Denmark, approached the Yorkshire coast on a similar mission. Little more than an hour later at 1430 hours, and once more at 1500, Luftflotte II struck again, on the first occasion north of the Thames Estuary against Martlesham airfield and on the second against Hawkinge and Eastchurch

▷ **Seen through German eyes: a British fighter pilot bales out of his stricken Hurricane; his parachute canopy is about to open (top)**

A seat in the sun—but both sides are at instant readiness for take-off. On RAF and Luftwaffe bases, the youth, the pipes, and the flying-kit were much the same. There is little to distinguish these pilots except the national markings on their aircraft

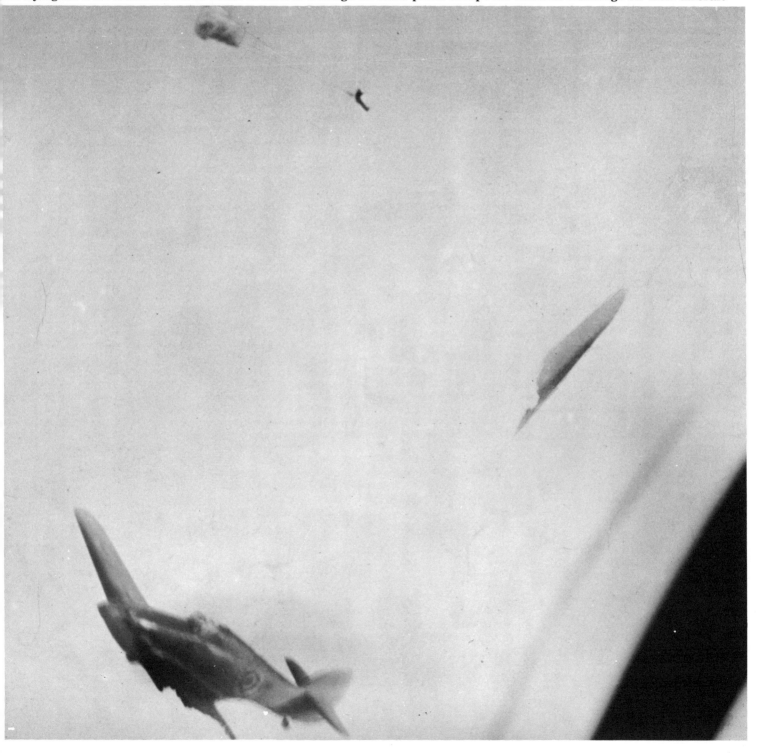

airfields and aircraft factories at Rochester.

Next it was the turn of Luftflotte III: at 720 hours some 80 bombers, heavily escorted, came in to the south coast at Portland, bombed the harbour, and then attacked airfields at Middle Wallop and Worthy Down. Finally, at 1830 hours, 60 or 70 aircraft of Luftflotte II again penetrated over Kent, hitting West Malling airfields and the airfield and aircraft factories at Croydon. To round off the day's work, another 60 or 70 bombers made sporadic attacks during the hours of darkness.

All this German effort was fiercely challenged. Though the bombing had its successes, notably at Middle Wallop, Martlesham, and Driffield (Yorkshire) airfields and at Croydon, in no case did the British fighters allow the raiders to operate unmolested, and in many cases the primary objectives escaped unscathed. Especially significant was the fighting in the north-east, where No. 13 Group, involved for the first time in the battle, intercepted the formations from Norway well out to sea, and with the help of the anti-aircraft guns on Tyne and Tees destroyed eight He-111s and seven Me-110s, with no British losses. A little farther south, too, No. 12 Group and the local guns, tacking the formations from Denmark, brought down eight of the enemy with no loss on the British side. The Germans thus failed in their main hope – that Dowding, in his anxiety to protect the vital and heavily threatened south-east, would have left the north almost undefended. Instead, they discovered, to their cost, that their attacks across the North Sea were met before they reached the British coast, and that the Me-110s in a long-range escorting role were useless against Spitfires and Hurricanes. The lesson was sufficiently expensive to convince the Germans not to launch any further daylight attacks from this area.

The fighting on August 15 was the most extensive in the whole Battle of Britain. With 520 bomber and 1,270 fighter sorties, and attacks stretching from Northumberland to Dorset, the German effort was at its maximum. But so too was the German loss – 75 aircraft as against 34 British fighters. This did not prevent an effort of almost equal magnitude on the following day, when the Germans sent across some 1,700 sorties, attacked a number of airfields (with particular success at Tangmere), and lost 45 aircraft in the process. With Fighter Command losing 21, the balance remained in the British favour.

The Luftwaffe switches strategy

The four days of intensive attack calculated to clear the skies of southern England were now over, and the Germans took stock. In the opinion of their Intelligence, Fighter Command, if not exhausted, was down to its last 300 aircraft. This appreciation was very wide of the mark, for Dowding still had nearly twice that number of Hurricanes and Spitfires in the front line, in addition to another 120 or so Blenheims, Defiants, and Gladiators. However, it encouraged the Germans to believe that another day or two of major effort might see the end of British opposition. On August 18 the Luftwaffe accordingly struck again in full force, chiefly against airfields in Kent, Surrey, and

A Ju-87: the legendary Stuka, the terror of Europe – now, matched at last by comparable fighter opposition, now the hunted and not the hunter ◁

Sussex; but in doing so they lost 71 aircraft while the British lost no more than 27. Clearly Fighter Command was still unsubdued. After a few days of minor activity owing to bad weather, the Germans therefore made their first great change of plan.

Up till then, the main German objectives had been airfields fairly near to the coast; after August 12 they had given up intensive attacks on radar stations – fortunately for Fighter Command – because they found them difficult to destroy. The airfields and other coastal targets they had continued to attack, partly to deny the airfields to the British during the proposed invasion period, but still more to force Fighter Command to join battle in their defence. The German theory was that by such attacks they might, without severe losses to themselves, inflict heavy losses on the RAF – for raids on coastal targets or those not far inland did not involve prolonged exposure to the British defences – while at the same time the Me-109s would be free from worries on the score of endurance and accordingly able to give maximum protection to the German bombers. Such was the German strategy when the battle began. It had not disposed of Fighter Command, so it was now changed in favour of attacks farther inland.

The first phase of the battle was thus over. So far, Fighter Command had more than held its own: 363 German aircraft had been destroyed between August 8 and 18, as against 181 British fighters lost in the air and another 30 on the ground. The period had also seen what proved to be the last daylight attack by Luftflotte V, and the last attempt by Luftflotte II to make regular use of its Ju-87s – both notable successes for the British defences.

At the same time, however, there was one aspect of the struggle which gave Dowding and the Air Ministry acute anxiety. During the same ten days, when Fighter Command had lost 211 Spitfires and Hurricanes, the number of replacements forthcoming from the aircraft industry had fallen short of this total by at least 40. In the same period, Fighter Command had lost 154 experienced fighter pilots: but the output of the training schools had been only 63 – and those less skilled than the men they replaced. Fighter Command, while inflicting nearly twice as many casualties as it was suffering, was thus in fact being weakened – though not, as yet, at anything like the speed desired by the enemy.

It was to increase the rate of destruction of the British fighter force – which unchanged would have left Fighter Command still in existence in mid-September – that the Germans now switched to targets farther inland. They reckoned that by making their prime objective the fighter airfields, and in particular the sector airfields of No. 11 Group from which the British fighters in the south-east were controlled, they would not only strike at the heart of the British defences, but would also compel Fighter Command to meet their challenge with all its remaining forces. In the resulting air battles, they hoped to achieve a rate of attrition that would knock out Fighter Command within their scheduled time: though they also knew that in penetrating farther inland they were likely to suffer greater losses themselves. To guard against this, and to destroy as many Hurricanes and Spitfires as possible, they decided to send over a still higher proportion of fighters with their bombers.

The sector stations of No. 11 Group stood

in a ring guarding London. To the south-west, in a forward position near Chichester, lay Tangmere. Nearer the capital and south of it there were Kenley in Surrey and Biggin Hill in Kent, both on the North Downs. Close to London in the east lay Hornchurch, near the factories of Dagenham; and round to the north-east was North Weald, in metropolitan Essex. Farther out there was Debden, near Saffron Walden. The ring was completed to the west by Northolt, on the road to Uxbridge, where No. 11 Group itself had its headquarters – which in turn was only a few minutes' drive from that of Fighter Command at Stanmore. All the sector stations normally controlled three fighter squadrons, based either on the sector station itself or on satellite airfields.

Strikes at the source

The Germans had already severely damaged two of the sector stations – Kenley and Biggin Hill – on August 18. Now, on August 24, they struck hard at North Weald and Hornchurch. On August 26 they attempted to bomb Biggin Hill, Kenley, North Weald, and Hornchurch, were beaten off, but got through to Debden. On August 30 they hit Biggin Hill twice, doing great damage and killing 39 persons. The following day – the most expensive of the whole battle for Fighter Command, with 39 aircraft lost – they wrought great damage at Debden, Biggin Hill, and Hornchurch.

On September 1 Biggin Hill suffered its sixth raid in three days, only to be bombed again less than 24 hours later; and on September 3 the attack once more fell on North Weald. On the 5th the main raids again headed towards Biggin Hill and North Weald, only to be repelled, while on the 4th and 6th the attacks extended also to the Vickers and Hawker factories near Weybridge. The Hawker factory, which produced more than half the total output of Hurricanes, was a particularly vital target. Its selection showed that the Germans, perplexed by the continued resilience of Fighter Command, were also trying to cut off the British fighter supply at its source.

Between August 24 and September 6 the Germans made no less than 33 major raids, of which more than two-thirds were mainly against the sector and other stations of Fighter Command. This assault imposed on the command a still greater strain than the preceding one, against targets in the coastal belt. The fighting was more difficult for the British pilots, in that the proportion of German fighters to bombers became so high, and sections of the fighter escort so close; and over the whole fortnight a daily average of something like 1,000 German aircraft, of which 250 to 400 were bombers, operated over England. Twice, on August 30 and 31, the number of intruders was nearer 1,500.

In the course of the combats and the ensuing night operations the British defences destroyed 380 German aircraft, as against a Fighter Command loss of 286: but many other British fighters were seriously damaged, and no less than 103 fighter pilots were killed and 128 wounded out of a fighting strength of not much more than 1,000. In addition six of the seven sector stations of No. 11 Group sustained heavy damage: and though none was yet out of action, Biggin Hill could control only one squadron instead of its normal three.

So Fighter Command was being steadily worn down, and at a faster pace than in the opening phase. The wastage, both of fighters

◁ **A Dornier in action: a stick of bombs streams from its bomb-bay**

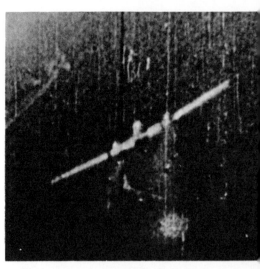

▷ **Target and tracer-fire: camera-gun film from a British fighter records the end of a Me-110 fighter. The 110, at full throttle, streams smoke trails from its twin engines (top); tracer fire misses the starboard wing, then the first hit glows on the port engine which explodes (bottom)**

◁ **Two Dorniers fly over fires started by the first wave**

▽ **The Luftwaffe strikes at Fighter Command: on an RAF fighter base, a Spitfire in its bomb pen survives a low-level strafing run**

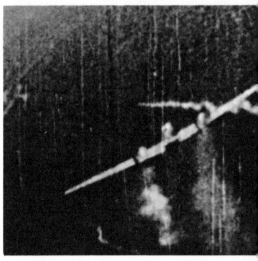

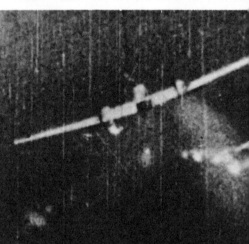

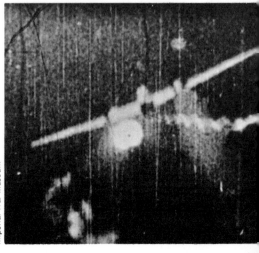

and of pilots, was far exceeding the output. In one sense the command was winning the battle; in another – if the Germans could maintain the pressure long enough – it was losing it.

The Germans, however, were not intending to fight a prolonged battle. They, too, could not afford heavy losses indefinitely – as may be seen from their decision after August 18 to hold back most of the vulnerable Ju-87s for the actual invasion, from their caution in employing Me-110s, and from their increasingly closer and more numerous fighter escort. Their attack, as we have seen, was meant to be a brief one, geared to Operation Sea Lion; and for Sea Lion they were now running short of time. This Hitler recognised at the end of August when he agreed that D-Day, provisionally set for September 15, should be postponed to September 21. For this date to be kept the German navy had to receive the executive order by September 11: and Göring's Luftwaffe had thus to administer the *coup de grâce* to the British fighter forces within the next few days. The attack on sector stations and other inland targets might be doing well, but in itself it was not proving decisive. On September 7 the Germans accordingly switched to another target, farther inland than most of the sector stations and, as they believed, still more vital – London.

Target London

The German decision to attack London was inspired by three beliefs. In the first place, operations against London could be expected to bring about still greater air battles and so – the Germans hoped – still higher wastage in Fighter Command. It was for this reason that Kesselring, though not Sperrle, strongly supported the change of plan. Second, an assault on the capital, if reinforced by attacks during the night against other main cities as well, might paralyse the British machinery of government in the final period before the invasion, or even terrorise the British people into submission. Third, an attack on the British capital would be, as the Germans saw it, an act of retribution. On the night of August 24/25, during the course of the Luftwaffe's usual scattered night operations, some badly aimed or jettisoned bombs had fallen on central London – the first of the war. Churchill and the War Cabinet had immediately ordered retaliation against Berlin; and during the following nights RAF bombers had found and hit the German capital – an occurrence which Göring had assured Hitler could never happen. The enraged Führer promptly vowed revenge and with Göring's eager concurrence unleashed the Luftwaffe against its supreme target.

On the night of September 4 German bombers laid flares over London; on the following two nights small numbers of aircraft dropped bombs on Rotherhithe and other places near the docks. These were the warming-up operations.

In the late afternoon of September 7 some 300 German bombers escorted by 600 fighters crossed the Kent and Sussex coasts or penetrated the Thames Estuary in a series of huge waves. A few bombed the oil installations at Thameshaven, still burning from earlier attacks; the rest, instead of bombing the sector stations, which the British fighters were alert to guard, held on until they reached the outskirts of the capital itself. Though nearly all the British

squadrons ordered up eventually made contact, most of the raiders were able to put down their high explosive and incendiaries before they were molested. The attacks fell in full force on London's dockland east of the City. Huge fires sprang up among the dockside warehouses, especially at Silvertown, and these the Germans used as beacons to light their way to further attacks during the ensuing hours of darkness. That night, when 250 German bombers ranged over the capital in a prolonged assault from dusk to dawn, millions of Londoners had their first experience of what they imagined was Blitzkrieg, and what they were soon to call 'The Blitz'.

The climax of the battle was now approaching. Göring took personal charge of operations, and the bombers from Norway and Denmark joined Kesselring's forces for what were meant to be the final and deciding blows. Meanwhile, however, the German invasion preparations had not gone unobserved: since August 31 Spitfires and Hudsons of RAF Coastal Command had been returning with an impressive photographic record of the growing number of barges and other invasion craft in the ports and estuaries across the Channel. On August 31 in Ostend, for instance, there were 18 barges; by September 6 there were 205.

As the concentrations increased, Bomber Command began to attack them, using at first its daylight Blenheims. By September 6 the enemy preparations were sufficiently obvious for the British authorities to order Invasion Alert 2: 'Attack probable within three days.' The following day, when the German bombers turned against London, it seemed that the hour of supreme trial might be at hand. Alert 2 then gave place to Alert 1: 'Invasion imminent, and probable within twelve hours.'

That night, as the German bombs began to crash down on London, the code-word 'Cromwell' went out to the Southern and Eastern Commands of Britain's Home Forces, bringing them to immediate readiness. In the prevailing excitement a few commanders of Home Guard units rang church bells to call out their men, so spreading the impression that German paratroops had actually landed. Meanwhile, forces of the Royal Navy waited at immediate notice, and the Hampdens of Bomber Command – 'heavy' bombers of the time – joined Blenheims, Hudsons, and Battles in intensified attacks on French and Belgian ports.

It was with the British fully alert to what the next few hours or days might bring that the Luftwaffe now strove to repeat the hammer blows of September 7. On September 8 bad weather limited their daylight activity; but at night Luftflotte III was able to send 200 bombers against London in a lengthy procession lasting more than nine hours. The zone of attack now extended from dockland to the capital as a whole, with special attention to railways and power stations, and by the morning every railway line running south of London was for a brief time unserviceable.

On the next day, September 9, clouds again restricted activity in the morning, only for a further assault to develop in the late afternoon. More than 200 bombers with full escort headed for London; but such was the promptness and vigour of the interception that less than half reached even the outskirts of the capital, and the bombs fell widely over the south-eastern counties. No. 12 Group's Duxford wing of four squadrons,

led by the legless pilot Squadron Leader Douglas Bader, enjoyed a notable success. All told, the British pilots shot down 28 German aircraft for the loss of 19 of their own.

Very different once more was the story at night. Again nearly 200 aircraft bombed the capital in attacks lasting over eight hours; this time some 400 Londoners were killed and 1,400 injured – all with negligible loss to the Luftwaffe.

Hitler again shifts D-Day

September 10 was a day of cloud, rain, and light German activity – though at night there was the usual raid on London, while other German bombers attacked South Wales and Merseyside. The next afternoon, while the Germans tried to jam some of the British radar stations, Luftflotte III attacked Southampton, and Luftflotte II sent three big raids against London. Many of the bombers got through to the City and the docks; and the balance of losses – 25 German ones, against 29 by Fighter Command – for once tilted against the British. On their return, some German pilots reported that British fighter opposition was diminishing. But though the Luftwaffe still hoped to complete its task, the date was now September 11, and Fighter Command was still in existence. With the German navy requiring ten days' notice before D-Day, an invasion on September 21 thus became impossible. Accordingly Hitler now gave the Luftwaffe three more days' grace, till September 14, in the hope that a decision could then be taken to invade on September 24.

As it happened, September 12 and 13 were days of poor visibility, unsuitable for major attacks. Even the nightly efforts against London – which was now enjoying the heartening noise of greatly reinforced gun defences – were on a reduced scale. When September 14 came, Hitler could only postpone the decision for a further three days, till September 17. This set the provisional D-Day for September 27 – about the last date on which the tides would be favourable until October 8. The Führer's order was contrary to the advice of his naval chiefs, who urged indefinite postponement – a tactful term for abandonment. Their worries had been sharply increased by the mounting intensity of the RAF's attacks on the invasion barges, large numbers of which had been destroyed the previous evening.

The Luftwaffe now strove to clinch the issue in the short time still at its disposal. Despite unfavourable weather, on the afternoon of September 14 several raids struck at London. Some of the German pilots reported ineffective opposition, and Fighter Command lost as many aircraft as the enemy. The night proved fine, but on this occasion no more than 50 German bombers droned their way towards London. The Luftwaffe was husbanding its efforts for the morrow.

Sunday September 15 was a day of mingled cloud and sunshine. By 11 am the British radar detected mass formations building up over the Pas-de-Calais region. Half an hour later the raiders, stepped up from 15,000 to 26,000 feet, were crossing the coast in waves bent for London. Park's fighters met them before Canterbury, and in successive groups – two, three, then four squadrons – challenged them all the way to the capital, over which No. 12 Group's Duxford wing, now five squadrons strong, joined the conflict. In the face of such opposition, the raiders dropped their bombs inaccurately or jettisoned them, mainly over south London.

Two hours later a further mass attack developed. Again British radar picked it up well in advance: and again—since they had had time to refuel and rearm—Park's fighters challenged the intruders all the way to, and over, the capital. Once more the Germans jettisoned their bombs or aimed them badly, this time mainly over east London, and, as before, further British formations harassed the raiders on their way back. Meanwhile a smaller German force attacked Portland. Later in the day other raiders—some 20 Me-110s carrying bombs—tried to bomb the Supermarine aircraft works near Southampton, only to meet spirited and effective opposition from local guns. When darkness fell, 180 German bombers continued the damaging but basically ineffectual night assault on London, while others attacked Bristol, Cardiff, Liverpool, and Manchester.

So closed a day on which Göring had hoped to give the death-blow to Fighter Command. In all, the Germans had sent over about 230 bombers and 700 fighters in the daylight raids. Their bombing had been scattered and ineffective, and they had lost the greatest number of aircraft in a single day since August 15—no less than 60. Fighter Command had lost 26, from which the pilots of 13 had been saved.

This further German defeat on September 15—combined with the attacks of British bombers against barge concentrations—settled the issue. When September 17 came, Hitler had no alternative but to postpone Sea Lion indefinitely. A few days later, he agreed to the dispersal of the invasion craft in order to avoid attack from the air. The invasion threat was over.

Göring orders more raids

Göring, however, was not yet prepared to admit failure: he still clung to the belief that given a short spell of good weather the Luftwaffe could crush Fighter Command and thereafter compel Britain to submit, even without invasion. Between September 17 and the end of the month his forces strove to attack London by day, whenever weather permitted, in addition to aircraft factories elsewhere. On only three days—September 18, 27, and 30—was he able to mount a major assault on the capital, and on each occasion British fighters prevented intensive bombing and took a heavy toll of the raiders. The loss of 120 German aircraft during these three days (as against 60 by Fighter Command) was not one which afforded Göring much encouragement to continue.

Had the Luftwaffe's corpulent chief known them, he would not have derived any greater encouragement from the casualty figures during the whole three weeks his air force had been attacking London. Between September 7 and 30 Fighter Command had lost 242 aircraft, the Luftwaffe 433. Equally important, though Dowding was still gravely worried by the continuing loss of pilots (on September 7 his squadrons had only 16 each instead of their proper 26), his anxieties about aircraft were diminishing. From the time the Germans abandoned their attack on sector airfields in favour of an assault on London, the wastage of Hurricanes and Spitfires had been more than counterbalanced by the output of the factories.

The prize of victory had thus eluded Göring's grasp. On October 12 Hitler recognised this by formally postponing Sea Lion

until the spring of 1941. In fact, this meant abandonment: Hitler's mind was now fixed on Russia. Until the German war machine could roll east, however, there was everything to be said, from the German point of view, for maintaining pressure on Britain, so long as it could be done inexpensively. During October the Luftwaffe, assisted by a few Italian aircraft, kept Fighter Command at stretch in daylight by sending over fighter and fighter-bombers, which did little damage but were difficult to intercept. At night the German bombers, operating with virtual impunity, continued to drop their loads on London.

The story of the 'Night Blitz' is one of civilian suffering and heroism, of widespread yet indecisive damage—and of slowly increasing success by the British defences. In the battle of wits against the intruders, perhaps the most vital developments were the discovery (and distortion) of the German navigational beams, the provision of dummy airfields and decoy fires, and the advances in radar which made possible accurate tracking overland.

Radar advances resulted in gun-laying radar that gave accurate readings of heights, and so permitted the engagement of the target 'unseen', and in ground-controlled interception (GCI) radar stations which brought night fighters close enough to the enemy for the fighters to use their own airborne radar (AI) for the final location and pursuit. It was only towards the end of the Blitz, however, that the GCI/AI combination emerged as a real threat to the attackers, who began to lose three or four aircraft in every 100 sorties, instead of merely one.

Meanwhile, the Luftwaffe was able to lay waste the centres of a score or more of British cities. After the early raids in August, the weight of attack by night fell for a time almost entirely on London. Between September 7 and November 13 there was only one night on which London escaped bombing, and the number of German aircraft over the capital each night averaged 163. With the final postponement of Sea Lion, the attack then extended also to longer-term, strategic objectives—the industrial towns, and later mainly the ports, so linking up with the blockading actions of the German submarines.

On November 14 the devastation of Coventry marked the change of policy; thereafter Southampton, Birmingham, Liverpool, Bristol, Plymouth, Portsmouth, Cardiff, Swansea, Belfast, Glasgow, and many other towns felt the full fury of the Blitz. In the course of it all, until Luftflotte II moved east in May 1941 and the attacks died away, the Germans killed about 40,000 British civilians and injured another 46,000, and damaged more than 1,000,000 British homes, at a cost to themselves of some 600 aircraft. On the economic side, they seriously impeded British aircraft production for some months, but in other directions the damage they did was too diffuse to be significant.

Hitler's first setback

The 'Blitz' ceased not because of the increased success of the British defences, but because most of the German aircraft were needed elsewhere. Had Russia collapsed within the eight weeks of the German—and the British—estimate, they would doubtless have returned quickly enough, to clear the way for invasion or to attempt to pulverise Britain into submission. As it was, Russia held, and though the British people were

subjected to further bombardments, they were not again called upon to face a serious threat of invasion.

Though the Night Blitz was inconclusive, the daylight Battle of Britain was thus one of the turning points of the war: it was the air fighting of August and September 1940, together with the existence of the Royal Navy and the English Channel, which first halted Hitler's career of conquest. The 1,000 or so pilots of Fighter Command who bore the brunt of that fighting—including the 400 or more who lost their lives—saved more than Britain by their exertions. By earning Britain a great breathing space in which the further progress of events was to bring her the mighty alliance of Russia and the United States, they made possible the final victory and the liberation of Europe from the Nazi terror.

DENIS RICHARDS took a first-class honours degree in history at Cambridge, and before the war taught history at public schools. After serving in the RAF, he was appointed in 1942 to the Air Ministry to write confidential studies on the war-time operations, and from 1942 to 1946 was in charge of all such work within the Air Ministry Historical Branch. In 1950 he returned to education as principal of Morley College, London. He left this position in 1965 to take up his present post, holding the Longmans Fellowship in history at Sussex University. In collaboration with the late Hilary St George Saunders, he wrote the officially commissioned, three-volume war history of the RAF, and he has also written the text for the *Illustrated History of Modern Europe*, books on British history, a history of Morley College, and contributions to encyclopedias and the *Dictionary of National Biography*.

1940

August 1: Hitler decrees the Battle of Britain with the command: 'The German air force is to overcome the British air force with all means at its disposal, and as soon as possible.'
August 13: 'Eagle Day': the Luftwaffe launches its air offensive against Britain, with 1,485 sorties. The Germans lose 45 aircraft, the RAF 13.
August 15: In the most intense attack of the Battle of Britain, the Luftwaffe sends a total of 1,790 sorties over England. They lose 75 aircraft, while Britain loses 34.
August 17: The Germans establish an 'operational area' around Britain; in it, all ships are to be sunk without warning.
August 25: The RAF conducts its first raid on Berlin.
September 3: Britain cedes to the USA bases in the West Indies and elsewhere in exchange for 50 destroyers.
September 7: Some 300 German bombers, escorted by 600 fighters, penetrate the Thames Estuary and bomb London's dockland.
September 13: *Italy invades Egypt.*
September 15: The RAF claims to have shot down 183 German aircraft during daylight Luftwaffe raids on Britain—a figure subsequently found to have been greatly exaggerated.
September 17: Hitler postpones Operation Sea Lion 'until further notice'.
September 23/25: *British and Free French forces attempt to take Dakar.*
October 12: Operation Sea Lion is postponed until 1941.

A formation of the much-vaunted Me-110s; they had long range but rather poor manoeuvrability, and thus they suffered heavy losses in the battle ▷

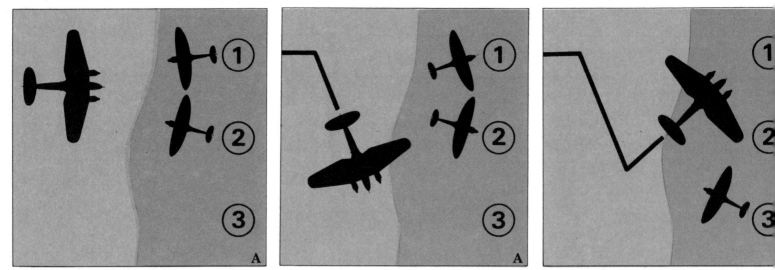

A A

▽ Radar plotted the incoming bomber formations, alerting the AA defences and RAF Headquarters. Fighter Command had to anticipate feints by the incoming bombers in addition to the weight of the German attack itself

■ Fighter reports   ■ Auto radio plots   ■ Radar reports   ■ AA land line   ■ Observer reports   ■ Combat orders

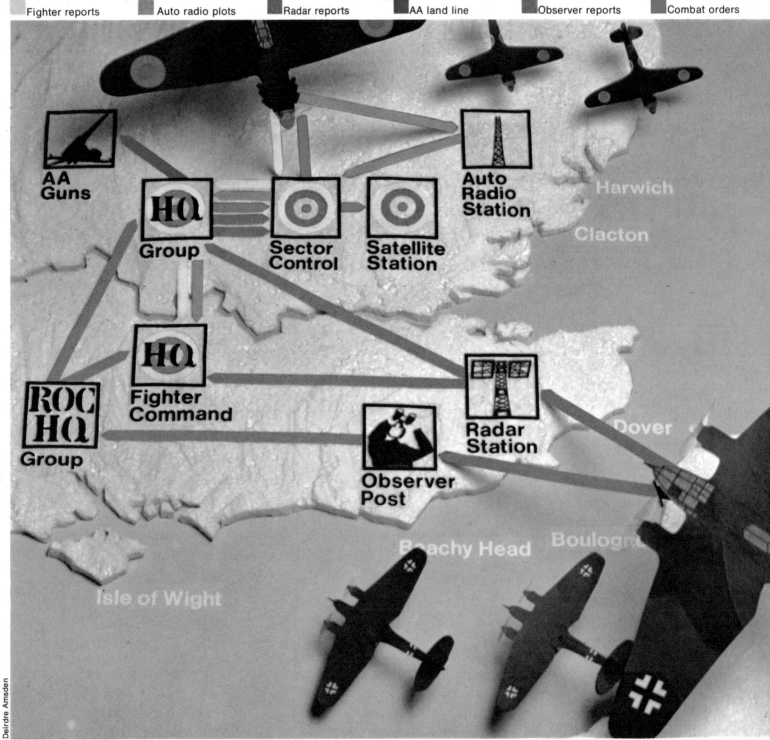

AA
Guns

HQ
Group

Sector
Control

Satellite
Station

Auto
Radio
Station

Harwich

Clacton

HQ

Fighter
Command

ROC
HQ
Group

Observer
Post

Radar
Station

Dover

Beachy Head

Boulogne

Isle of Wight

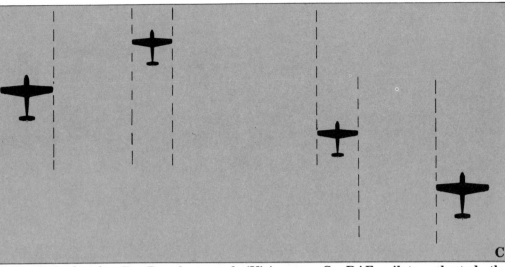

B

C

ighters take off to intercept attack, but land to refuel when it
ls for 3. Attack swings away from fighters at 3, returning to 1
2, where the fighters are still grounded

B: Parade-ground 'Vic' was rigid and inadequate for the needs of modern air fighting

C: RAF pilots adopted the German 'Schwarm': better known as the 'Finger-four'

RAF Commander (X THEATRE OF WAR)	**Luftflotte** (EQUIVALENT OF ARMY GROUP)
Group	**Fliegerkorps**
Wing Fighter Command Bomber Command Coastal Command	**Geschwader** Kampfgeschwader – Bomber Jagdgeschwader – Fighter Stukageschwader – Dive-bomber
(No Direct Equivalent)	**Gruppe**
Squadron	**Staffel**

ial War Museum

Marshal Sir Hugh Dowding

WAAFs plot the battle

Paul Popper

Reichsmarschall Göring (centre), with Luftwaffe officers

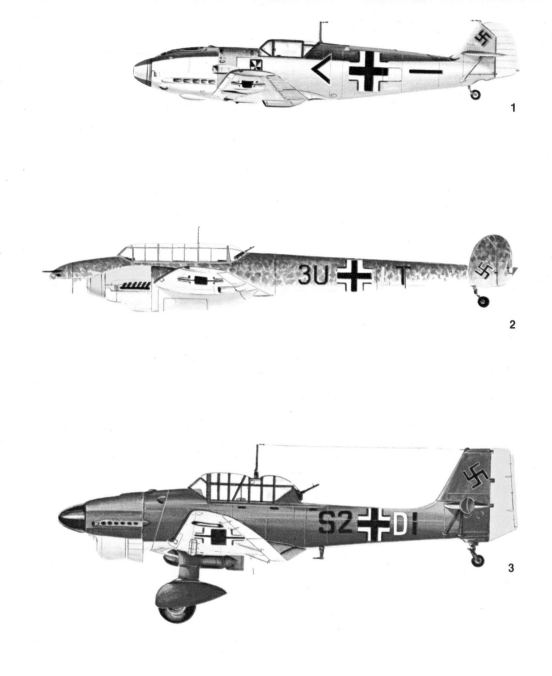

1. Messerschmitt 109E

Known to Luftwaffe pilots as the 'Emil', the 109E was at least as fast as the Spitfire but was found to be less manœuvrable, though more so than the Hurricane. Always handicapped by its short range, its performance as a fighter was further restricted by a bomb load later in the battle, when pressed into service in a fighter/bomber role.

Armament: Two 7·9-mm machine-guns and two 20-mm cannons.

Max speed: 357 mph

2. Messerschmitt 110

Göring's folly: the cream of the Luftwaffe fighter strength was deployed in 'destroyer' units, intended to smash through the fighter defences and provide long-range escort for the bombers. Against the Spitfire and Hurricane, however, the Me-110s had finally to be provided with escorts themselves, for their lack of manœuvrability meant that their powerful armament was all too often useless.

Armament: Two 20-mm cannons, four 7·9-mm machine-guns, one free-mounted 7·9-mm gun.

Max speed: 349 mph

Supermarine Spitfire

The Spitfire fighter was the most agile machine in the battle — it could out-manœuvre even the Me-109E. Another vital superiority was its fire-power: eight wing-mounted Brownings which, though out-ranged by the German cannon, held a decisive concentration of rounds per second. In the Battle of Britain the Spitfire also held the advantage of fighting on home ground, unfettered by the range handicap of the 109E.
Armament: Eight ·303-inch machine-guns.
Max speed: 361 mph

9. Hawker Hurricane

Britain's first monoplane fighter was the numerical mainstay of RAF Fighter Command in the Battle of Britain. The Hurricane's ideal role was that of bomber-interceptor; as a rule, only the Spitfire could tackle the Me-109 on level terms, though the Hurricane scored notable successes against the Me-110. During the battle the Hurricane was already being replaced by the Spitfire as the standard RAF fighter.
Armament: Eight ·303-inch machine-guns.
Max speed: 328 mph

8

9

Junkers 87

The famous gull-winged Stuka was the main weapon which Göring turned against the RAF fighter bases. But the easy victories of past campaigns had been won in the absence of adequate fighter opposition, and RAF pilots found the Stuka an easy prey. Severe losses in operations throughout August destroyed its reputation as the all-conquering weapon of the Luftwaffe, and the Ju-87 was withdrawn from the spearhead of the attack.
Bomb load: One 1,102-lb, four 110-lb bombs.
Max speed: 217 mph

4. Junkers 88

The Ju-88 was the most versatile aircraft in the Luftwaffe's armoury for the entire war, serving as level bomber, dive-bomber, and night-fighter, as well as carrying out valuable reconnaissance duties. It was used by the Luftwaffe as a medium bomber in the Battle of Britain; but neither speed nor its comparatively high number of defending machine-guns was adequate protection from the fire-power of Spitfires and Hurricanes.
Bomb load: 5,510 lb
Max speed: 292 mph

5. Heinkel 111

The standard level bomber of the Luftwaffe at the time of the Battle of Britain, the He-111 suffered from its design as a medium bomber ideal for Continental operations but handicapped — as were all German twin-engined bombers — by the distances to targets in the north of England. Göring was convinced that its use in mass would prove decisive; but the He-111, it was found, was unable to beat off determined RAF fighter attacks.
Bomb load: 5,510 lb
Max speed: 258 mph

6. Dornier 17

The Do-17 was the Luftwaffe's veteran bomber: the type first saw service in the Spanish Civil War. Despite subsequent modifications, it was very weak in defensive fire, especially to attacks from below and to the rear. Known as the 'Flying Pencil' from its slim fuselage, the Do-17 was often confused with the British Hampden bomber, many of which were fired at by their own anti-aircraft guns. Its slender lines dictated a light bomb load.
Bomb load: 2,210 lb
Max speed: 270 mph

7. Dornier 215

This variant was a development of the basic design of the Do-17 with the installation of more powerful Daimler-Benz engines. The Do-215 was faster than the Do-17 — fast enough to tax the lower-rated British engines of the early Spitfires and Hurricanes in a chase. In its light bomb-load and weak defence armament, however, the Do-215 was as handicapped as the Do-17.
Bomb load: 2,215 lb
Max speed: 311 mph

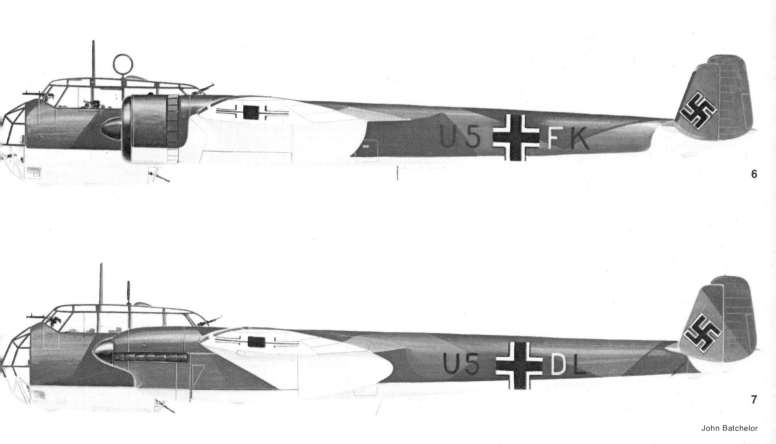

6

7

John Batchelor

BOMBER COMMAND

British Bombing Policy to December 1940

Arthur E. Slater

RAF Bomber Command realised just as clearly as their opposite numbers in the Luftwaffe that war must be taken into the heart of the enemy country. But in 1940 the RAF was limited in action by obsolescent weapons and medium-range aircraft. And even before heavier and more modern aircraft could become available, vital experience had to be gained, often at a cruel price. This is the story of how these lessons were learned

Early in 1940 the new Bomber Command Headquarters, skilfully sited in the woods near High Wycombe, was ready for occupation and the Air Officer Commanding-in-Chief, Sir Edgar Ludlow-Hewitt, moved in. This was the only air force headquarters to be built expressly for that purpose, and it was in direct communication with the bomber groups and stations, with Fighter Command, and with the Air Ministry. Sir Edgar's first preoccupation was to survey the forces at his disposal and to consider how they could best be used to further the war effort.

The quality of his senior staff officers and of the commanders of groups, stations, and squadrons gave him no misgivings. They were a competent and dedicated body of men, proved by up to 20 years' experience devoted to professional flying, most of them hand-picked from the survivors of the First World War. Their counterparts on the German side had not the same advantage. The Luftwaffe was a mushroom growth and its high command was composed mostly of pilots without military experience or of soldiers with little knowledge of the air: though some had seen action through participation in the Spanish Civil War, and their lightning campaign against the Poles had been well planned and ruthlessly executed.

As regards air crews and ground crews there was little to choose between the two sides. The excitement of flying was an attraction for all the most courageous, enterprising, and resolute of the young men of both Britain and Germany, who volunteered for their respective air forces, which were thus well matched in gallantry, skill,

◁ **Bombing-up: on a RAF base, the bomb-load is brought to a Wellington as the ground crew arm the aircraft for a raid**

Western Europe, Aug. 1940.
■ Axis powers
■ German occupied countries

A. W. Gatrell & Co Ltd

There was a wide choice of enemy targets for the RAF; but long-range missions demanded lighter bomb-loads than those intended for the aircraft

and devotion. At this early stage of the war, most of the pilots of Bomber Command had been trained as regular officers; but preparations had been made to receive and train operationally the vast flow of RAF Volunteer Reserve pilots and crews who were undergoing initial flying training in the Dominions under the Empire Air Training Scheme. To meet this operational training commitment, Bomber Command had 'rolled up' 13 squadrons at the outbreak of the war and these were subsequently reorganised as Operational Training Units under a separate Group Headquarters (No. 6 Group at Abingdon).

The relegation of these squadrons to a training role had left Bomber Command with a nominal total of 33 squadrons for operational purposes. But one whole Group (No. 1), armed with Fairey Battles – an obsolescent and hopelessly outmatched aircraft – was sent to France with the British Expeditionary Force and became the advanced air striking force. The remainder were distributed as follows: No. 2 Group, comprising six squadrons of Blenheim light bombers, was stationed in East Anglia from where it could intervene as required in support of army operations; six squadrons of Wellingtons under No. 3 Group in Suffolk; five squadrons of Whitleys under No. 4 Group in Yorkshire; and six squadrons of Hampdens under No. 5 Group in Lincolnshire. All this was the tiny nucleus of the great organisation which Bomber Command was to become.

Excluding the Blenheims which, by reason of their small bomb-load of 1,000 pounds, were unsuitable for strategic bombing, Bomber Command could muster for the attack on Germany a maximum of 17 operational squadrons – nominally 272 aircraft – though availability of crews reduced this to an average (during September 1939) of 140. For comparison, the Luftwaffe had between 1,200 and 1,600 bombers, not including dive-bombers; around 1,000 of these were fully operational. Hence the great disparity between German attacks on Britain in 1940, and British attacks on Germany.

This paucity in numbers was not compensated for by any great superiority in quality, range, or capacity of the aircraft then available in Bomber Command. All of those aircraft mentioned were twin-engined. As early as 1936 it had been realised that the twin-engined bomber would never be an adequate instrument for carrying the war into the heart of Germany, and specifications were issued for a four-engined bomber of long range and high load-capacity, to compose the major part of the striking force. But there was no prospect of such a force being ready until 1942 at the earliest.

The Wellingtons, Whitleys, and Hampdens were good in their day, as good as or perhaps rather ahead of the German aircraft which bombarded Britain. Fortunately for England, the German High Command had given little thought to a possible bombing offensive against England and had concentrated on the production of aircraft designed to facilitate the operations of their army on land. In 1937, for financial reasons, the development of long-range heavy bombers for the Luftwaffe had been suspended. This policy paid them good dividends in the opening phases of the war but was not to their advantage in the long run.

High hopes for the Wellington
On account of their slow top speed, the Whitleys were intended almost exclusively for night operations: Hampdens and Wellingtons were thought to be capable of both day and night missions. In particular, high hopes were placed in the Wellington, by reason of its sturdy 'geodetic' construction of curved sections of pressed metal in short pieces bolted together outlining the frame of the body like a kind of basket. This form of construction had been developed by the aviation firm of Vickers from the experience gained in building the giant airship, the R-100. The Wellington also mounted a formidable armament of six machine-guns in movable turrets, covering the aircraft from front, in rear, and below. With this fire-power, it was thought, tight formations of bombers, affording one another mutual protection, would be able to fight their way to their objective in spite of the opposing fighters' superiority in speed and ability to manoeuvre. This was soon proved to be an illusion, but the Wellington was further developed in a number of marks and variations and remained in service throughout the war.

In terms of capacity, the Wellingtons and Hampdens could carry a useful load of bombs to Berlin, Munich, or Turin but had really been designed to carry much more substantial loads of up to 4,000 pounds within a radius of 600 miles from English bases. The Whitleys could carry as much as 8,000 pounds of bombs for a total distance of 630 miles; with full tanks and a 5,500-pound bomb load they could operate within a radius of 650 miles; with auxiliary petrol tanks and a light load of up to 3,500 pounds, nowhere in Germany and Austria was beyond their reach. But these calculations assumed that the bombers would take the shortest route to and from their targets, which was not possible so long as Holland and Belgium maintained their strict neutrality. In these circumstances, to deliver a really heavy blow against the Ruhr or the Rhineland, advanced bases on the Continent would have been necessary and (as will be seen later) French consent to this was not forthcoming until it was too late.

During the first eight months of the war, these considerations were academic, since by a political decision, bombing attacks were strictly limited to 'military' targets. On September 1, 1939, President Roosevelt had appealed to all the belligerents to refrain from bombing attacks on the civilian population. Such an appeal from such a person amounted almost to a command, and both sides hastened to give their assent, the more readily because at that time it fitted in with their plans. Hitler had made no preparations for a bombing war. No doubt he hoped that when the Allies were confronted with a subjugated Poland, whose fate they had been powerless to avert, they would once more back down, to be tackled in their turn on a more convenient occasion. At this time, unknown to the Allies, the German stock of bombs was sufficient for only three weeks of sustained operations, and two-thirds of these had been expended in the Polish campaign. It was not until October, when his hopes of a bloodless victory over the West were seen to be vain, that Hitler approved a full-scale programme of bomb production; but German industry worked to such good effect that ample supplies were ready for the battles of the summer.

Since the Allies also were unready, the War Cabinet had decided that so long as the Luftwaffe attacked only military objectives, Bomber Command should confine its enterprises to attacking the German fleet and dropping propaganda leaflets over Germany. If bombs had been dropped on land-based objectives some loss of civilian lives and property was inevitable and neither side wished to incur the odium of precipitating a contest in destruction.

The first attacks
Bomber Command was quick off the mark against such targets as were available under this policy. On September 4, German warships in the Heligoland Bight were attacked by ten Blenheims and nine Wellingtons in rain and cloud. The Blenheims dropped their bombs from 500 feet and suffered heavily from anti-aircraft fire from the ships, five being shot down. Several hits were scored on the *Emden* and the *Scheer*, but from this height the bombs failed to penetrate the warships' decks and little damage was done. The Wellingtons were opposed by Messerschmitt fighters and two failed to return. The results of this brush with the enemy were inconclusive, and not

△ **Hampden:** *Max speed:* 254 mph; *Bomb-load:* 4,000 lbs (Max): their raid on Hörnum dropped the first bombs on Germany

△ **Whitley:** *Max speed:* 192 mph; *Bomb-load:* 8,000 lbs (Max): first RAF bomber to be designed solely for night operations

△ **Wellington:** *Max speed:* 234 mph; *Bomb-load:* 4,500 lbs (Max): suffered heavy losses in the raid on the Schillig Roads

encouraging. But German warships kept out of the way until December.

Three successive actions on December 3, 14, and 18, 1939, showed that Bomber Command was in no position to take on German warships when protected by flak and shore-based fighters. On the first occasion, on December 3, honours were easy. Bad weather prevented effective bombing but the fighters were wary of the bombers' tail-guns and all the 24 Wellingtons engaged got home. On the second occasion the weather closed down over the objective, a number of vessels moored in the Schillig Roads. Though unable to bomb, 12 Wellingtons persisted in their patrol in accordance with their orders, exposing themselves for half an hour to heavy anti-aircraft fire interspersed with fighter attacks. Five of them failed to return and a sixth crashed on landing, but whether these losses were due to flak or to the fighters was uncertain. Gallantry at such a cost had to be discouraged.

The third occasion, which took place in cloudless skies with a visibility of 30 miles, was conclusive. Forewarned by radar, the German fighters harried the bombers incessantly during the approach to the attack and on the return. Some used cannon, which far outranged the bombers' machine-guns. Others attacked from abeam, from which direction the Wellingtons had been left undefended: it had been thought that such attacks would be ineffective because they involved aiming ahead of the moving bomber in a no-deflection shot. The Wellingtons caught fire easily, the petrol tanks in the wings being extremely vulnerable. (Self-sealing tanks and armour-plating were subsequently installed to rectify this.) The results were disastrous, for of the 22 Wellingtons engaged only ten returned—a wholly unacceptable casualty rate for such meagre results as four German aircraft destroyed and nine damaged.

The Germans were elated by their success, claiming to have shot down 34 Wellingtons and thinking it 'criminal folly' for the bombers to have pressed on when conditions were all against them. In consequence, daylight raids by heavy bombers in formation were tacitly abandoned, and the Wellingtons and Hampdens were ordered to join the Whitleys in leaflet raids to gain night-flying experience over Germany.

All this while the Whitleys of No. 4 Group had been plodding away, scattering propaganda leaflets on various German towns. Their efforts were derided by friend and foe. Air Marshal Harris, with his usual pungency, has indicated (in his *Bomber Offensive*) what he thought was the probable fate of all this deluge of paper and that in his judgement this fate was all that the leaflets were fit for.

The French acidly attributed the gesture to being part of *'Ce drôle de guerre'*. But it was no joke for the crews involved in these nightly forays. Active German opposition was surprisingly slight and casualties consequently low; but the crews were left to find out the hard way the natural obstacles to putting a bombing policy into practice. The greatest obstacle was the weather. Temperatures could drop to as low as $-30°C$ $(-86°F)$ and in thick cloud this led to severe icing over the wings, airscrews, and cabin windows, obscuring vision and reducing performance. Turrets jammed and, worse still, engines failed and even caught fire. If, to escape the cloud, the aircraft climbed above it, the cold was increased and crews became stupefied to the point of collapse from frost-bite and oxygen shortage.

Apart from these dangers there was a constant struggle to overcome the difficulties of determining position in conditions of darkness and black-out. To set an accurate course for an aircraft by night requires a precise knowledge of the speed and direction of the wind which are liable to change, so that, in a long flight by dead reckoning cumulative errors could take an aircraft miles off its course. At this time the only navigational aids available were an astro-sextant for obtaining position from the stars and a radio aerial which could determine the bearing of wireless signals received from ground stations. But neither of these could be relied upon for accurate results and both required a high degree of skill in operation. Thus, unless navigators could check their calculations by observing a series of identifiable landmarks, they were seldom entirely certain where they were. No serious attempt to improve this situation was made until the winter of 1941, with the development of the radio aid to which was given the code-name of GEE.

Nevertheless, all this groping in the dark to deliver leaflets was not wasted, for it gave the bomber crews a knowledge of what was to be their main battlefield. And though there was perhaps excessive delay in drawing the right conclusions from this experience and in remedying the defects disclosed, the lessons sank home and eventually bore fruit. In the first six months of the war, Bomber Command aircraft made 262 night sorties—all of them over Germany—at a cost of five aircraft missing and eight which crashed. In the same period, 173 aircraft were dispatched on day raids involving little or no penetration of the German defences; 31 of them were lost. From this it was not difficult to draw the conclusion that Bomber Com-

A formation of Bristol Blenheims, the RAF's maids-of-all-work

Air Marshal Lord Trenchard Air Marshal Sir Richard Peirse

mand's most economical mode of operation was to fly by night rather than by day.

Making a policy

Of course, the Air Officer Commanding-in-Chief of Bomber Command had nothing like a free hand in deciding how his forces should be employed. War plans had been prepared in peacetime, covering various contingencies, though surprisingly little thought had been given to relating these plans to the practical limitations of the aircraft available. On top of these the Air Staff issued a sequence of directives in the form of letters to the Commander-in-Chief, prescribing in some detail how the different sorts of bomber should be employed, and what classes of target or even specific objectives should be attacked.

There were other agencies and authorities also seeking to influence bombing strategy, the most important being the Ministry of Economic Warfare and its associated committees. Clearly, bombing attacks on German industry would be most effective if co-ordinated with other means of exerting economic pressure. The MEW's estimates of the economic and industrial situation of Germany were often wide of the mark but they played a significant part in determining the choice of targets. The Admiralty too had its own ideas on how the bombers could be employed to assist in control of the seas; for instance, an unexpected use was found for the Hampdens of No. 5 Group for dropping mines in German coastal waters, which had considerable effect in hampering inshore traffic.

Within the scope of his current instructions, the Commander-in-Chief's function was to plan the detailed operations and to issue the necessary orders to his subordinate formations. It was not his place to advise on policy but naturally his assessment of the capacity of his forces to achieve their set tasks and of the casualties which might be expected from them had an important bearing on the operations actually attempted.

As it had always been confidently expected that the restriction of bombing to military targets would soon break down on Hitler's initiative, attempts were made to reach agreement with the French on the action to be taken in this event. The Air Staff's notion was that, when the German invasion really began, the whole of Bomber Command should be launched on a massive daylight onslaught on the Ruhr. But this was too much for Sir Edgar Ludlow-Hewitt's fatherly care for his crews and his more realistic appreciation of their powers.

He protested that his small force could achieve no worthwhile destruction and that casualties might easily amount to 50%, crippling the force for months to come by depriving it of its experienced leaders. In view of the Wellington losses in December previously described, he had grounds for this apprehension, and the Chief of the Air Staff ruled that the Ruhr plan should be adopted only if the situation became critical. Instead, night attacks on plants producing synthetic oil took front rank in the programme, for the Ministry of Economic Warfare was predicting (quite erroneously) that the Germans were running into a serious fuel shortage.

The French views on bomber strategy were quite different. Their policy was restricted to supporting land operations, and was directed against columns of invading troops, military communications, and airfields—which in the Air Staff's view would be 'to fritter away our striking force on unprofitable objectives'. In reality the French were highly alarmed at what Hitler's bombers might do to French industry if provoked to retaliation. Justifiably perhaps, in view of the sad state into which the French air squadrons had declined, they were sceptical of their own power to cause equivalent destruction.

As France controlled the advanced airfields necessary to carry out the Ruhr plan, the result was a rather muddled compromise.

On April 13, 1940, Air Marshal Portal, who had recently replaced Sir Edgar Ludlow-Hewitt as Commander-in-Chief, was given a fresh directive. If the Germans invaded Holland or Belgium the bombing objectives would be: troop concentrations; communications in the Ruhr such as railway marshalling yards; oil plants in the Ruhr, the principal weight of attack falling on the last-named. The heavy bombers were to operate mainly by night.

Applying the policy

The German invasion of Scandinavia was in full swing and the moment for putting theories to the test of battle was at hand. But meanwhile another incident had occurred which was to have a considerable effect on the new Commander-in-Chief's thinking on night operations. On March 19, as a reprisal for a German attack on Scapa Flow, 50 bombers were ordered to attack the sea-plane base at Hörnum on the island of Sylt, 400 miles across the North Sea.

Dictated by political considerations, this first attack by Bomber Command on a land target was executed under the most favourable conditions. There was complete surprise and, for six hours, 41 of the aircraft dispatched dropped their bombs individually on the air station buildings and slipways, lit by a setting moon. Many direct hits were claimed and two hangars were said to have been left on fire. Great care was taken to avoid endangering civilian lives. The crews were specially selected and all the aircraft but one returned to base.

This was precision bombing at its easiest, yet photographic reconnaissance of the island on April 6 indicated that all the buildings at Hörnum and elsewhere remained outwardly intact. Of course, the damage might have been repaired or camouflaged, but Bomber Command had its doubts:

Our general opinion is that under war conditions the average crew of a night bomber could not be relied upon to identify or attack targets at night except under the best conditions of visibility, even when the target is on the coast or on a large river like the Rhine. Under the latter conditions about 50% of the average crews might be expected to find and bomb the right target in good visibility; if the target has no conspicuous aids to its location, very few inexperienced crews would be likely to find it under any conditions.

In writing thus, Air Marshal Portal displayed the perspicacity and unemotional judgement which were shortly to take him to the highest appointment in the Royal Air Force. But much was to happen before its practical implications were to be accepted.

The situation envisaged in the directive of April 13 was not long deferred. On May 10 the German army and Luftwaffe struck at Holland, Belgium, and France; but for four days Churchill's newly formed War Cabinet still hesitated to unleash the power of Bomber Command.

The mass bombing of Rotterdam turned the scale. On May 15 the Dutch army was forced to surrender: on the same night Bomber Command was out in force over the Ruhr.

In thus challenging Germany to a bombing contest, Britain was taking a great risk. The gauntlet was flung down, and it was not the fault of the bomber crews that they had not yet been given 'the tools to finish the job'. Out of 78 aircraft directed against oil targets on the night of May 15, only 24 even claimed to have found them, for the Ruhr lay concealed by the smog-ridden vapours of its own creation. Much damage was done, however, to railway junctions and marshalling yards at Aachen, Duisburg, and elsewhere. One aircraft failed to return.

During the next five months the bomber effort was more and more diverted from its primary purpose in order to meet the ever growing exigencies of the immediate situation. Britain was on the defensive. The counterattack had to wait.

Bomber operations in this period fall into the 'tactical', rather than the 'strategic', category; they were subsidiary to the course of the war in other fields. During the Battle of France the light bombers (Battles and Blenheims) were sacrificed in a vain attempt to hold up the advancing German columns by daylight attacks on such targets as troop concentrations, airfields, and bridges. In so doing they had to meet the full weight of German fighter strength and concentrated anti-aircraft fire while possessing neither the speed nor the armament to engage the enemy on anything like equal terms. If they kept close formation the bombers offered an easy target to the anti-aircraft guns; if they split up to evade the shell-bursts they were picked off individually by the fighters. In either case, crippling losses were incurred. In 856 day sorties during May, No. 2 Group lost 56 aircraft, with ten more damaged beyond repair—nearly half their total strength. From some missions no aircraft returned.

With the fall of France in June, the strategic situation was completely altered, and vastly to Britain's disadvantage. From a semiircle of airfields, stretching from Stavanger in Norway to Brest in Brittany, the Luftwaffe could raid Great Britain from every direction. A bare 100 miles separated London and other vulnerable points from the main German bases in northern France and Belgium. On the other hand, to reach targets in Germany, Bomber Command aircraft now had to run the gauntlet of 100 miles of German defences in the occupied territories, bristling with searchlights, anti-aircraft guns, and hostile fighters.

In these circumstances the primary objectives of Bomber Command were defined as those which 'will have the most immediate effect on reducing the scale of air attack on this country' (directive of June 20) — such as the German aircraft industry, railways, and canals, but not forgetting the oil plants. As the threat of invasion loomed, the emphasis was shifted to attack by the heavy bombers on enemy ports and shipping, while the medium bombers were directed to watch for and attack concentrations of barges and small craft in the canals and ports of Holland and Belgium. The dropping of mines in coastal waters was intensified.

Luftwaffe policy

The initiative in the air offensive now lay with the Germans and was manifested in the Battle of Britain and in the subsequent Blitz on London and other cities. German strategy was dictated by the necessity for gaining air superiority over the Channel and southern England, without which no invasion of Britain was feasible. It followed the classical lines laid down by the Italian General Douhet. The role of the German bombers was to compel the defending fighters to accept battle in the air so that they might be overwhelmed by the invading fighter escorts.

This policy might well have proved effective if Fighter Command had played it the Germans' way and engaged in an all-out slogging match with the enemy fighters. But no amount of increase in their fighter escorts could save the German day bombers from a rate of loss of aircraft and experienced crews which eventually became unacceptable. To preserve the bomber crews' morale they were increasingly switched to night raids, mainly on London. These produced spectacular results in terms of fire and havoc, but were really a diversion from the supreme aim of gaining air ascendancy as a preliminary to invasion.

This significant change in German policy may have been powerfully assisted by the night raid on Berlin on August 25 by 81 aircraft of Bomber Command as a reprisal for bombs dropped on London (probably accidentally through a navigational error) on the previous night. Again the gauntlet had been flung down and this time Hitler picked it up. Though the damage inflicted on Berlin was slight, it was repeated on successive nights and sent Hitler into one of his rages, so that he ordered reprisal raids on London to begin in early September. It has been argued that the switch in targets to the towns instead of on Fighter Command sector stations (where it was beginning to pay a dividend through loss of operational control) was all part of the German plan. But it certainly took the strain off the hard-pressed Fighter Command when it was most timely.

Bomber Command's attacks on the invasion fleet of barges were also a significant factor in convincing the German High Command of the risks and probable losses of the planned invasion. This was just the task for which the British bombers had been designed and they set about it with gusto. As the barges drawn from all over Germany were collected in Dutch and Belgian harbours they were systematically checked and bombed, causing great confusion.

By the end of September the Battle of Britain had been won by Fighter Command and the threat of invasion had obviously receded, though the German night attacks on cities continued without respite. The results of these were carefully tabulated and certain deductions from them were in due course applied in the counter-offensive.

Time to take stock

It was time to take stock of the position. Though Britain stood alone, the country was resolute that the war against Germany had to be carried on. But how? And with what? The navy was supreme on the seas, but this time its long-term policy of blockade was not applicable, for the Germans controlled most of Europe and could draw upon the rest of the world for supplies. Indeed, the blockade weapon was about to be turned against Britain by the U-boats.

On land Britain had neither the means nor the manpower to invade Europe or even to recross the English Channel unless the RAF cleared the way. The situation was summed up by Winston Churchill to the War Cabinet in these words: 'The Navy can lose us the war, but only the Air Force can win it. Therefore our supreme effort must be to gain overwhelming mastery in the air. The Fighters are our salvation but the Bombers alone provide the means of victory.' So, by the logic of circumstances, Britain turned to the bombing offensive as the only means of carrying on the war in Europe.

The Royal Air Force as a whole was confident that it could achieve the task of winning the war thus thrust upon it, though not perhaps with its existing equipment. It had been moulded as a force by the dominant personality of its first chief, Lord Trenchard, to whom it looked with confidence and respect. His utterances were oracular, based on intuitional rather than on logical thinking, but he had a terrible knack of being right or at least of seeming to be so. The RAF's first article of faith was in the power of the bomb, though there was little actual experience to back it. However, in the constant inter-service disputes between the world wars, when the Admiralty and War Office sought to dismember the Royal Air Force, the assertion of an independent role in the air had been clung to as a matter of self-preservation.

All forms of warfare seek to break down the enemy's will and capacity to resist; but the advent of air power meant that this could now be done by direct assault on the sources of the enemy's will and capacity — his centres of government and production, which were vulnerable to sea and land power only if the corresponding enemy forces had first been overcome. The concept of 'strategic bombing' is that of an offensive directly conducive to winning the war or to gaining some positive advantage leading to speedier victory: as opposed to the 'tactical' use of aircraft arising out of the immediate necessities of conflict when armed forces are in contact.

Such heretics in the Royal Air Force as doubted this faith had been eliminated in the course of its growth, but there was no such unanimity as regards the methods by which the aim of strategic bombing could be achieved.

The concept of an independent air offensive originated in the First World War. Long-range bombers with four engines had been ordered for attacks on Berlin and other industrial cities to commence in 1919, but the first of these had only just been delivered from the makers when that war ended. Between the wars the RAF's experience of bombing was derived from operations against tribesmen in policing the frontiers, for which purpose a simple strategy sufficed and the bombs and bombers currently available proved to be adequate.

Until 1934, after the abortive disarmament talks came to an end, it seemed likely that the heavy bomber would be banned by international agreement, and in the pressure to achieve parity with the growth of German air power, bombers had to take second place to fighters for financial and technical reasons.

Madrid and Barcelona were bombed during the Spanish Civil War of 1936-39 but the conclusions drawn from these operations were distorted by propaganda and led to exaggerated expectations of the damage likely to be caused by strategic bombing and of its effect on civilian morale. Thus it is not altogether surprising that in 1939 the RAF had no clear-cut doctrine as regards the manner of carrying out a bombing offensive against a first-class power, since there was practically no experience on which such a doctrine could be based. In the first years of war, Bomber Command had to feel its way by trial and error with such aircraft as it possessed, while awaiting the delivery of the four-engined bombers which were essential for the strategic offensive.

For the purpose of immediate operations, the Air Staff adhered to a policy of 'precision bombing': that is, they wished precise targets, such as factories, to be selected, the destruction of which would seriously affect the enemy's war effort. The attacks were to be repeated until the target was put out of action.

The damage would not, of course, be vital unless a whole class of similar targets could be eliminated more or less simultaneously. From time to time, a variety of 'target systems' competed for priority in destruction, depending on the current view of Germany's industrial situation. Oil production, transportation, the power supply of industries, aircraft factories, naval vessels, and construction — all headed the list at times, but the favourite was oil. It was realised that civilian lives and property in the vicinity of the targets would inevitably suffer but this was regarded as incidental. Thus the humanitarian feeling opposed to attacks upon civilians, based upon a tradition of right conduct in war developed under very different circumstances, was partially acknowledged. Any so-called 'indiscriminate' bombing was sternly frowned on.

Pragmatic objections

To this idealistic or academic approach there was opposition on pragmatic grounds from those who had to do the actual bombing or order it to be done — that is, most of Bomber Command. The precision bombing concept presupposed:

● that the bombers could be navigated to their targets after penetrating several hundred miles of enemy territory, in the face of possibly adverse weather and the German defences. The navigational difficulties of unopposed flights have been described. They ▷

were intensified when successive changes of course were imposed by the necessity of avoiding the most heavily defended areas;

● that, having reached the target area, crews could identify a precise target among a mass of similar buildings or when skilfully disguised, while they themselves were dazzled by the glare of searchlights or the gaudy firework display of anti-aircraft shells. In such conditions, pilots could fly around for as much as half an hour before their bombing target was identified;

● that the pilot could then turn and fly a perfectly straight and level course, low enough to see the target, for up to 10 miles so as to give the bomb-aimer a chance of successfully releasing the bombs, while physically and mentally disturbed by shell-bursts and hostile fighter attacks.

There were crews in Bomber Command who could do this, but they formed a very small proportion of the whole. Many others thought they could, and did their best, but perished in the attempt. Against a small isolated target, every bomb that fell wide was wasted; in built-up industrial areas there was a chance of hitting by accident some other target of military importance, or at worst the misses would have an effect on the morale of the industrial population.

Since the district surrounding the target was bound to be hit anyway, why not plaster it and make a thorough job at the outset, instead of coming back again and again? So ran the argument of the pragmatists, and it was powerfully reinforced by the simple reaction of the Prime Minister and the bulk of public opinion that what the Germans had done to the British ought to be done to them.

At this time, intelligence reports from agents and neutrals on the Continent gave an exaggerated account of the effects of the bomber offensive on German civilian morale, with wild estimates of the extent of the damage. On October 10, 'well-informed industrialists' estimated that some 25% of the total productive capacity of Germany had been affected by the bombing, and were not wholly disbelieved. Illusions still ran rampant. The British were in the dark and whistled to keep their spirits up.

On October 25 Sir Charles Portal was promoted to be Chief of the Air Staff and was succeeded at Bomber Command by the Vice-Chief of the Air Staff, Sir Richard Peirse. This exchange of roles had less immediate impact on bombing policy than might have been expected. With the exchange of hats, these high-ranking officers appeared to adopt also the standpoint of the organisations whose heads they were. Sir Richard Peirse stressed the tactical difficulties, while Sir Charles Portal came out as an exponent of speedy victory through the precision bombing of German oil plants. Nevertheless there was one significant change in the directive of October 30. Oil plants were still the primary targets for moonlit nights, but, as an alternative, 'regular concentrated attacks should be made on objectives in large towns and centres of industry, with the primary aim of causing very heavy material destruction which will demonstrate to the enemy the power and severity of air bombardment and the hardship and dislocation which will result from it'. The target was now to be the will of the German people to continue the war.

Heavy cost

Some selected incidents will illustrate how Bomber Command endeavoured to comply with their instructions. On August 12 five Hampdens were dispatched to bomb the Dortmund-Ems canal, an important link in industrial communications and high on the list for attack. The target, a canal crossing a wide river, was easily identified but heavily defended by anti-aircraft guns. The first two aircraft were shot down before reaching the target; two others scored near-misses but were hard hit themselves. At last the leader, Flight Lieutenant Learoyd, made a direct hit on the canal bank, for which feat he was awarded a well-deserved Victoria Cross. The canal was drained of water so that no boats could pass for 12 days. Precision bombing *could* succeed, but at a heavy cost in trained and experienced crews.

Bomber crews continued to claim an unexpected degree of success in identifying and hitting precise targets, even at objectives as distant and confusing as Berlin. They may have been encouraged in their optimism by the Station Intelligence Officers charged with their debriefing, many of whom were without operational experience and anxious to put forward a good story for the edification of their superiors and of the general public. For instance, the report of a Berlin raid on October 7 contained a most circumstantial account of individual buildings recognised and hits observed, which is difficult to reconcile with the limitations in night vision which other raiders experienced.

Doubts were beginning to creep in, particularly after a raid on Krupp's at Essen on November 7 by a force of Wellingtons, Hampdens, and Blenheims had resulted in conflicting and incompatible reports from the various groups involved. It seemed possible that none of the aircraft had been where they thought they were, but that they had been deceived by artificial fires, started by the enemy, into dropping their bombs on open country. Cameras were installed in some of the aircraft to photograph the surroundings of the target at the time of bombing as a positional check; but these were in short supply and were not welcomed by the crews. A more effective check was obtainable from photographs of the bomb damage taken after the event by the special Photographic Reconnaissance Flight of Coastal Command. This unit was formed on November 16 and equipped with unarmed Spitfires, whose height and speed enabled them to escape enemy flak and fighters and to bring back on clear days extensive pictures of the target area.

The raid on Mannheim on December 19 by 134 aircraft was something of a new departure for Bomber Command. Following the tactics used in the German raid on Coventry on November 14/15, the attack was begun by a fire-raising force of Wellingtons with the most experienced crews available. These were to set light to the centre of the town to serve as a beacon and aiming point for subsequent waves of attackers with high-explosive bombs. In full moonlight, 100 aircraft claimed to have dropped their bombs on the target area, leaving the town centre in flames. On these reports the raid was at first thought to have been a spectacular success, but photographs brought back by a reconnaissance Spitfire a few days later disclosed a wholly different picture. Though considerable damage had been done, it was widely dispersed. Obviously, many of the fires had been started well outside the target area and subsequent aircraft had unloaded their bombs on these in accordance with their orders, but without the material destruction of industrial capacity which had been expected.

Very soon afterwards, disillusionment was increased by photographs of two oil plants at Gelsenkirchen in the Ruhr. Though 196 aircraft in successive raids had recently dropped 260 tons of bombs on them, as well as incendiaries, neither had sustained any major damage. Evidently most of the attackers had not got within miles of their objective, and whatever else the bombs had hit, the vital oil plants had escaped.

The resulting inquest in Bomber Command failed to produce any encouraging suggestions for remedying the unsatisfactory state of affairs disclosed by the reconnaissance photographs. Obviously the bombers had to be given more effective aids for navigation and target location; some of these were already in course of development, but there was no early prospect of their becoming available.

The Ministry of Aircraft Production was pressed to produce more cameras for bomber aircraft. The use of the more experienced crews to find the target for the benefit of the less experienced was mooted but not immediately followed up, though eventually it produced the Pathfinder Force—aircraft to blaze a bright trail of flares for the bombers. There was an obvious need for better bombs. British bombs were manifestly much less effective than the German ones; their explosive content was only half for a corresponding weight of bomb and it was composed of the old-fashioned amatol, a relatively inefficient explosive; many failed to detonate. Steps were taken to produce better bombs of ever increasing size but it was a long while before these were available in any quantity. The effects of the German raids on Britain showed that, against built-up areas, incendiaries caused far more destruction than an equivalent weight of high-explosive bombs, and they were employed in increasing proportions; but the incendiary could not be used as a weapon of precision.

At the end of 1940, Bomber Command was still groping for ways and means of carrying the war to the German home front. Since the bomber crews were plainly unable to find and hit the ideal targets given to them, the logical course was to assign them larger and easier targets which they could find and hit. For, as Sir Charles Portal was soon afterwards to say: 'The most suitable object from the economic point of view is not worth pursuing if it is not tactically attainable.'

ARTHUR E. SLATER, CBE, was born in Kent in 1895 and was educated at King's College, London University. He was commissioned in the Devonshire Regiment in the First World War and was wounded in the Battle of the Somme. After transferring to the Machine Gun Corps he was permanently disabled at Passchendaele, and in 1919 was invalided from the army with the rank of lieutenant. He then entered the Civil Service, was appointed to the Air Ministry as an Assistant Principal, and edited the King's RAF Regulations and a revision of the Air Force Law Manual. From 1930 to 1935 he served as Private Secretary to Sir Hugh Dowding, then Air Member of the Council for Research and Development. He was promoted to Under Secretary in 1951 and retired in 1956.

NIGHT RAID

Policy into practice: the story of one of the early raids as experienced by a Wellington bomber crew bound for Mannheim in late 1940

After the regular morning air test the aircrews drifted back in ones and twos to their messes to discover the battle order for the night posted on the notice boards. Twelve crews were up—half the maximum effort of the squadron. M for Monkey, a Wellington bomber, was flying tonight.

Her pilot and observer went into the mess together, noted their names on the battle order—and declined pre-lunch beers. They exchanged desultory squadron chat with the other officers. Already, an air of tension lay over the mess.

The Senior Intelligence Officer, wearing 'Mutt and Geoff' ribbons from the First World War under his pilot's wings, came into the ante-room and said: 'Briefing's at three o'clock, chaps.' Almost at once his words were confirmed by the metallic voice of the Tannoy system blaring out over the airfield: 'All crews on the battle order are to report to the briefing room at fifteen hundred hours.'

After lunch, followed by a nap in an easy chair, the two officers from M for Monkey walked slowly in the misty autumn sunlight to the long briefing room attached to one of the hangars. At the door an armed service policeman examined identity cards and cheerfully wished them good luck as they passed inside to where several rows of chairs stood facing a raised platform. Behind the platform a large map of northern and western Europe completely covered the wall. A white dust sheet hid most of Holland and Germany, and a red ribbon, stuck through with large-headed map pins, led from the Lincolnshire airfield across the North Sea to disappear behind the sheet.

The room was noisy with the babble of 72 men as they cloaked their nervousness with catcalls and banter. Suddenly it was hushed as flood-lights illuminated the stage and a group of officers, including the station and squadron commanders, mounted it. Amid the preceding hubbub nobody had mentioned—or even in jest hazarded a guess—as to where the target for tonight would be.

The squadron Commanding Officer, a young Wing Commander with a DFC ribbon gleaming beneath his brevet, stepped up to the map and, watched with bated breath by the crews, ceremoniously pulled off the white sheet. There was a silence, a pause, then a deep sigh that was almost a groan as the crews saw that tonight's target lay deep in enemy territory.

The Wing Commander spoke. 'OK, chaps, Mannheim again. Now you know the worst—it's a hell of a way but the flak there's not too bad. At least it wasn't, the last time I went. The intelligence officer will put you in the picture about aiming points, flak, etc.'

A young intelligence officer stepped forward, a pointer in his hand. 'Yes, sir—well, chaps, Mannheim is a port on the Rhine, population . . . .' The intelligence officer's voice sounded high and clear in his effort to make himself sound superior—but he wasn't and he knew it: fortunately, the crews knew he knew it, too.

His briefing finished, the intelligence officer stepped from the stage to be followed by the observer leader who explained the suggested route, the armaments officer who described the bomb load, and the wireless officer who dealt with the various codes to be used during the night's operation. Then came the meteorological officer, who interspersed his slides of weather charts with others of scantily dressed ladies which were greeted with ribald cheers.

A pep talk from the station commander, a Group Captain, concluded the briefing and, as the senior officers left the briefing room, the crews filed out into their changing room, where they leisurely changed into flying kit, collected their flying rations—chocolate, chewing gum, and barley sugar—and moved into the high room next door to collect their parachutes. Left behind in the briefing room, the observers plotted their routes on Mercator charts.

By 1700 hours all except the observers had piled into open 3-ton trucks and were shuttling out to their aircraft, dispersed around the airfield in the grey Lincolnshire dusk.

M for Monkey stood squat and black against the skyline waiting for her crew to mount the short metal ladder which disappeared into the nose of the fuselage. There were a few caustic exchanges with the ground staff—hanging around pretending to attend to odd bits of equipment but in reality to wave 'Good Luck' to their own special aircrew—then the crew disappeared up the ladder and out of sight. The observer, his arrival delayed by the route planning, arrived after the others in a small van and, laden with a large green canvas satchel and a sextant, was the last of the crew to enter the 'Wimpey'.

Two members of the ground staff at a thumbs-up sign from the pilot slowly rotated the large airscrews, and stood back while the pilot pressed the port-engine starter. A high-pitched whine, a puff of vapour, a splutter, and the big engine started, making surprisingly little noise as it did so. The ground crew wheeled the starter battery on its trolley round to the other side of the plane where the same routine was run through with the starboard engine.

While the pilot and second pilot completed their cockpit check, checking and cross-checking each item on the long list together, the observer pinned his chart to the green-painted navigator's table. He carefully adjusted the light over the table and placed his various instruments in handy places, wedging them behind wires or into joints in the cockpit furniture. Above his head, tied to the header tank of hydraulic fluid, he hung a small teddy-bear—the crew's mascot.

Satisfied that all was well with the aircraft, the pilot switched on his intercom and called up each member of the crew in turn, checking that they were ready to go. When they had all replied he called up the control tower over the radio telephone link and informed the Duty Officer that M for Monkey was ready for take-off. An answering green flash gleamed momentarily from the control tower, and the pilot released the brakes. Slowly M for Monkey began her journey to Mannheim.

As she taxied over the grass to where a small van showed the take-off point, the crew strapped themselves in and made final preparations for the journey. A small knot of men standing around the van gave the thumbs-up sign, and the aircraft lined itself up with the row of flickering lights. The pilot switched on his intercom, as did the second pilot. A green Very light soared up from the top of the van, the pilot answered by a flick of the landing light, and M for Monkey had been cleared for take-off.

Inside the aircraft the crew sat tense as the pilot pushed forward both throttles. The fuselage shook and the wings seemed to undulate as he released the brakes and the heavily laden aircraft began rolling slowly over the grass. As it gathered speed the second pilot read off figures as the needle climbed, and when the pilot was satisfied, he hauled back on the control column and the Wellington lumbered slowly into the air.

Safely airborne, and the first course set from over the middle of the airfield, the crew busied themselves with their tasks. The gunners, front and rear, began their long stare into the black night sky, acclimatising their eyes to its emptiness; the wireless operator, at his table behind the observer, slowly twiddled the knobs of his various sets so that they would be set up on the correct ground stations for an emergency call. The observer, illuminated only by the light reflected off his navigation table, was comparing the course drawn across his Mercator chart with unfolded topographical maps spread over his knee.

Side by side in the cockpit the two pilots sat almost motionless as if they were asleep, their heads hunched into the upturned collars of their thick fur-lined flying jackets. Occasionally one or other of them would come to life and point to a dial in front of him, to be answered by a thumbs-up sign or by some alteration to one or other of the many control knobs. After about 20 minutes on their first course, the second pilot broke the long silence on the intercom to tell the observer that he had caught sight of the coastline ahead of them.

The observer came out into the cockpit and stood behind the second pilot, searching for an accurate pinpoint from which to start a dead-reckoning plot. As the pilot could fly whichever route to the target he wished, an accurate air plot was essential in case he decided, for any reason, to alter the route. Satisfied at last, the observer went back to his table and plotted the pinpoint before calling up his captain to give him the amended course across the North Sea to the point near Ostend where they would turn east. Flying this latter course until the Rhine was reached south of Koblenz, he would then map-read their way south to the target area.

Once well away from land the rear gunner, his voice slightly breathless as a result of the cold rarefied air, asked permission to test his guns by firing them into the sea below. The pilot gave his permission and then, his memory jogged by the sound of the rear gunner's voice, told the second pilot to switch on the oxygen. At the same time he checked with the observer that the IFF (Identification—Friend or Foe) was switched off. The crew, even behind their oxygen masks, could smell the cordite from the gun test and were reminded of the dangers of their mission. From that moment on a new height of tension pervaded their actions.

As they passed over Ostend, the land beneath them was covered with low cloud and the plane had to set course for Koblenz without a pinpoint. When, two minutes later, unseen by the observer in the blacked-out cabin, the sky beneath them was filled with a tracery of red, green, and yellow light flak, the pilot switched on his intercom and commented, 'That's

'Then the crew disappeared up the ladder'

'In the cockpit the two pilots sat almost motionless'

Ostend, I reckon—unless it's Ramsgate'. The observer, amused by neither the lack of a pinpoint nor the heavy joke about his navigational prowess, began to haul out the several volumes of almanacks and tables necessary to plot an astro-fix.

M for Monkey forged on, eastward now, over the dark hills of occupied Belgium.

Ninety minutes later, the observer plotted his second astro-fix, gained by sextant observation from the moon and two stars. He switched on his intercom, gave the pilot permission to continue the weaving flight he always liked to perform after the aircraft had crossed the enemy coast, and said, 'We're on track OK—I'm coming up in a minute to see if I can get a pinpoint. If you see anything like a river, sing out.' Picking up the map of the Strasbourg area he unplugged himself from the intercom circuit and the oxygen supply, and went through the cabin door to stand behind the second pilot.

Below the aircraft the cloud had now disappeared, and the landscape of wooded hills showed up clearly in the bright moonlight. All the crew— except for the wireless operator, happily tuned into the BBC Home Service —were staring into the night, searching for the glitter of water. Suddenly the second pilot pointed downwards to starboard. The observer said, 'That's the Nahe, the Moselle, or the Rhine. Let's go and have a look and I'll see if I can fit it on to the map.'

Later, his position satisfactorily fixed, the observer went down into the nose of the aircraft and assumed his second identity as bomb-aimer. Lying on his stomach, a closely-shaded orange light faintly illuminating his map, he map-read the course until the Rhine was directly beneath them. At the same time, working in the dark almost as if by instinct, he began to prepare the bombing panel and bombsight for the bombing run and attack. Telling the pilot to turn south-east and to track along the right bank of the river, he concentrated more and more intently on the ground beneath him.

The south-easterly course took the aircraft over Bingen, and now Mannheim lay only ten minutes ahead of them; the Rhine flowed away to the left, the broad river growing narrower in the distance but still reflecting the moonlight. No one spoke and, apart from the heavy breathing of the rear-gunner who kept his intercom 'live' so that he could give immediate warning of any enemy fighter, each member of the crew silently faced the stress and strain of the next ten minutes.

Suddenly the sky ahead of them, until then a dark and velvety blanket, was punctured with red flak bursts. 'Mannheim!' grunted the pilot over the intercom, and the observer silently prayed he was right; after a previous raid on the city, reconnaissance reports had shown that most of the bombs had fallen in fields near Heidelberg, and that the railway yards that he and the other crews were supposed to have attacked had escaped unscathed.

Still in the distance, over to port, the Rhine gleamed, a welcome reassurance that this time their navigation was correct. Quite suddenly the river appeared to swing towards the aircraft and the observer hurriedly checked the compass in the bombsight to make sure that the plane itself had not altered course towards the river; but just then a large town swung beneath him. 'Worms,' he thought, doubly sure because of the odd-shaped lake south-east of the town. He was now convinced that they were heading for Mannheim with about only 10 miles to go—especially as ahead of them the sky was now full of flak bursts.

Telling the pilot to continue on course until he saw the river divide, the observer looked along the wires of the bombsight. Suddenly the junction of the river appeared—'I've got it!' yelled the observer. The pilot replied, 'I can see it too, but I'll go round a couple of times to make sure it really *is* the right place this time! Keep a good look out for Jerry and watch we don't get too close to any of our bods either.'

As the aircraft swept across the target area white flashes that pocked the darkness beneath them indicated that other aircraft were dropping their bombs. All around flak bursts lit up the sky, in the distance red, but yellow and white when close. Springing up from the ground below, an occasional searchlight waved its silvery finger of light.

Twice the pilot took the aircraft through two slow turns round the aiming point, before flying away to get the moon behind the target and help the observer to identify it more easily. Approximately lined up on the target, the pilot told the crew that he was about to start the bombing run. The tension by now had increased almost to breaking point, but the pilot eased it slightly when he told them that they could throw out their own personal contribution to the raid—empty beer bottles.

The only voice on the intercom now was that of the observer. 'OK, skip —keep her where she is—left, left—a bit more—blast that searchlight— left, left again—OK, skip, steady—steady—steady—bomb doors open—right —right—steady, keep her there.' Suddenly his voice lifted excitedly as he pressed the bomb release button. 'Bombs gone!' he shouted. 'It looks good this time, skip, I could see the docks quite clearly.'

Immediately every member of the crew appeared to be shouting over the intercom, giving their own personal views of the success of the raid. Cutting through their voices the pilot told them to be quiet, the authority in his voice calming them down. The observer, after a cheerful tap on the hanging foot of the front gunner, struggled back through the cockpit to his navigation table and plugged himself back onto the intercom and oxygen.

He asked the pilot what course they were flying.

'Two seven zero. Ludwigshafen right beneath us.'

Satisfied, the observer bent over his log and chart and worked out his course for home.

Now that the excitement and elation of finding and attacking their target had ceased, the pilot warned the crew to be particularly watchful for enemy fighters, and at the same time he asked them—while memory was still recent —for their views on the attack. The observer recorded the crew's comments in his log.

The rear-gunner had seen several bombs exploding in the barge dock area as they flew away from the target, and the second pilot reported that he had seen another Wellington crossing only a few hundred feet above their own aircraft, its silhouette sharp in the bright moonlight. Other reports were confused but optimistic.

The red flak bursts behind them gradually disappeared, and the crew turned their minds to home and the promise of clean sheets and warm beds. They thought of the scene at interrogation, when over cups of Ovaltine laced with navy rum they would tell the intelligence officer of their success. He, piecing together the reports of all the squadron's crews, would make his own estimate of the success of the raid and send it on to Base HQ.

But only the Germans would know for certain if M for Monkey and her companions had struck home.

PHILIP F. SIMPSON was an aircraft spotter at Croydon before the war. After war broke out he filled machine-gun belts and sandbags as a member of the Air Defence Cadet Corps; during the Phoney War he was a full-time volunteer runner for the RAF. In 1941 he became an aircrew cadet and trained as an observer, finally becoming a navigator with Squadrons 100, 138, and 166 of Bomber Command. After spells as teacher and headmaster of handicapped children, he now lectures on the education of the mentally handicapped.

SEA POWER VERSUS STUKA...

THE STRUGGLE FOR CRETE

Major-General J. L. Moulton
Crete was conquered by the German supremacy in the air, a supremacy which was a terrible threat to the British naval forces operating in support of the garrison. Despite the battering received from the Stukas, the British Mediterranean Fleet stood by the retreating land forces to provide their evacuation —but at a heavy cost

1941 **May 15:** The Germans begin intensive bombing of Crete.
May 19: The British withdraw their last fighters from Crete, thus assuring the Luftwaffe of air control.
May 20: The German airborne attack on Crete begins. Admiral Cunningham begins to send British naval sweeps north of Crete by night.
May 20/21: British destroyers bombard Scarpanto airfield to the north-east of Crete. Stukas sink British destroyer *Juno*. Admiral Glennie scatters the light German invasion fleet from Mílos.
May 22: German bombers attack Admiral King's force, damaging British battleships *Warspite* and *Valiant*, and sinking the destroyer *Greyhound* and cruisers *Gloucester* and *Fiji*.
May 23: British 5th Destroyer Flotilla bombards the German troops in control of Máleme airfield. Stukas sink British destroyers *Kelly* and *Kashmir*.
May 24: British minelayer *Abdiel* and destroyers supply British land forces at Suda Bay.
May 25: British battleships *Queen Elizabeth*, *Barham*, and the aircraft-carrier *Formidable* sail from Alexandria with eight destroyers.
May 26: Stukas surprise and damage the *Formidable*.
May 27: German bombers damage the *Barham*. Admiral Cunningham prepares the British naval forces for the evacuation of Freyberg's troops.
May 28/29: Admiral Rawlings embarks 4,000 men from Heráklion. German bombers cause the loss of British destroyers *Hereward* and *Imperial*, and damage the cruisers *Dido* and *Orion*. Captain Arliss lands supplies at Sfakía and embarks 700 men.
May 29: Admiral King embarks 6,000 men from Sfakía. German bomber damages British cruiser *Perth*.
May 30: Captain Arliss embarks 1,500 more troops from Sfakía.
May 31/June 1: Admiral King embarks 4,000 men from Sfakía, leaving 5,000 on the beaches. Cruiser *Calcutta* bombed and sunk.

The battle of Crete was to the Royal Navy the culmination of a period of continuing strain and heavy losses. At the turn of the year, the Italian fleet, crippled at Taranto in November 1940, had seemed willing enough to leave the British unchallenged in the Mediterranean, while the high-level bombing and torpedo attacks of the Regia Aeronautica had been more of a nuisance to the British fleet than a threat to its strength. Then the Germans had come to the rescue of their allies, and all had been changed.

First, X Fliegerkorps had appeared in Sicily. In the previous year, its Ju-88 and He-111 aircraft had been rather ineffective against warships off Norway. The Ju-87, the Stuka dive-bomber— intended primarily for the close support of the army—had proved far more formidable. Tenth Fliegerkorps now included a large force of Stukas, and its skilful and determined pilots were ready to press home their attacks.

The Mediterranean Fleet met them on January 10 and 11, 1941, as it escorted a convoy to Malta. The German pilots hit the aircraft-carrier *Illustrious* six times with heavy bombs, and only her armoured flight-deck saved her to limp into the Grand Harbour for temporary repairs, after which she left for more extensive repairs in America. The cruiser *Southampton* was sunk, and the *Gloucester* damaged. Admiral Sir Andrew Cunningham, Commander-in-Chief of the Mediterranean Fleet, reported to London that a serious situation had developed off Malta, and called for a greater degree of air support.

Next had come the German threat to Greece and the decision to send there a British and Commonwealth expeditionary force. The convoys from Egypt had started to run on March 5, and ran every three days for three weeks. Urged on by the Germans, the Italian fleet came out to attack, only to find Cunningham and the Mediterranean Fleet ready for them, and to return to harbour after losing three large cruisers in the night action off Cape Matapan on March 28. The British suffered no losses, but two days earlier the cruiser *York* had been attacked by Italian 'naval assault machines' in Suda Bay, where she was eventually lost.

In February, Rommel and the Afrika Korps had arrived in Tripoli. Their counteroffensive against the weakened British desert army opened on March 24. On April 3, they entered Benghazi, and on April 12 they reached the Egyptian frontier at Sollum, having besieged Tobruk. The emergency to the British army demanded intensive effort by the inshore forces of the Royal Navy, and the Luftwaffe took its toll of them. Malta became the base for destroyers, submarines, and aircraft attacking Rommel's convoys on the Tripoli run and drew upon itself heavy air attack from Sicily.

The intensive activity called for logistic support and for fighter reinforcements, and, with Cyrenaica in German hands, convoys had to be fought through to Malta and fighters ferried there by aircraft-carrier. Force H from Gibraltar and the Mediterranean Fleet from Alexandria co-operated in the task, and on April 21 the battleships of the latter bombarded Benghazi harbour.

On April 7 the Germans had crossed the Bulgarian frontier to invade Greece, and in the next three weeks had forced the withdrawal of the British and Commonwealth force. The evacuation took place between April 24 and April 29. Six cruisers, 19 des-

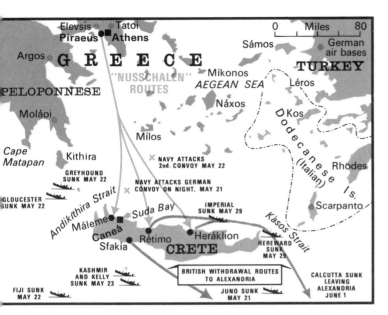

troyers, numerous smaller naval craft, transports, and merchant ships embarked over 50,000 men; and under the attacks of the Luftwaffe four transports and two destroyers were lost. On May 4 the Mediterranean Fleet reassembled in Alexandria; then, after a short period of rest and refit, sailed for Malta to re-supply the island and to bring through the vital 'Tiger convoy' carrying tanks for the 8th Army, which Force H was escorting from Gibraltar.

On May 13 Cunningham informed the British Admiralty that since April 20 his fleet had expended between one-third and one-half of its anti-aircraft ammunition; and that remaining stocks of 5·25- and 4·5-inch shells were down to three-quarters of the amount required to fill the magazines. With Crete in mind and without fighter cover, he looked forward to the future with great anxiety.

Crete – the liability

When, in October 1940, the Italians invaded Greece, the British welcomed the Greek invitation to occupy Crete, where they hoped to establish an advanced fleet base at Suda Bay, and airfields along the coast. In May 1941, with Suda Bay and the landing strips at Máleme, Rétimo, and Heráklion open to Luftwaffe attacks from Greece, and with no adequate fighter defence, Crete was a liability. Ships entering Suda Bay were at the mercy of air attack; and after fighting gallantly against hopeless odds, the last fighters were withdrawn from the island on May 19. In the Mediterranean Fleet, the *Formidable* had replaced the *Illustrious*, but in operations off Benghazi and Malta her aircraft had been reduced to a mere four serviceable machines. So, at sea off Crete, it was to be a straight fight between the guns of the British fleet and the Luftwaffe.

Cunningham realised that the main German attack would be airborne. The task of the fleet, therefore, could only be to prevent any accompanying seaborne invasion, to cover supply and reinforcement of the garrison, to bombard in its support – and, if the worst came to the worst, to evacuate the island. Thus the fleet had to be risked in what could only be a secondary role in the defence of Crete.

Cunningham could not, however, ignore the possibility that the Italian fleet would come out to escort a seaborne attack on the island. When the bombing of Crete began in earnest in mid-May, his battleships took station west of the island, and light forces swept northward at night, watching for invasion.

After reliefs for refuelling, the dawn of May 20 found Rear-Admiral Rawlings with the battleships *Warspite* and *Valiant*, one cruiser, and ten destroyers, 100 miles west of the island. Rear-Admiral Glennie, with the cruisers *Dido* and *Orion*, was, after a night sweep, withdrawing through the Andikíthira Strait to join Rawlings. Rear-Admiral King, with the cruisers *Naiad* and *Perth*, and four destroyers, was withdrawing to the east through Kásos Strait; and Captain Rowley with the cruisers *Gloucester* and *Fiji* was coming north from Alexandria. Cunningham himself, with his widespread responsibilities, had decided to control events from Alexandria.

Under General Löhr, Luftflotte IV had been pushing forward its preparations for the attack on Crete since May 15: improvising airfields, stocking fuel and bombs, assembling troops. Road and rail communications in Greece were poor, and had been damaged in the recent fighting; and much of the heavy supply came by sea. Airfields were inadequate, and flying was much hampered by dust. Available

airfields had to be shared between XI Fliegerkorps – the transport force – and VIII Fliegerkorps, comprising the fighters, bombers, and reconnaissance aircraft.

The responsibilities of General von Richthofen, commanding VIII Fliegerkorps, were:
● To cover the mounting of the attack, and sea movements in the Aegean necessary for it;
● To destroy British air forces in Crete and to silence the ground defences while the attack went in;
● To support the troops landed, by bombing and machine-gunning;
● To destroy enemy shipping off the island and to cover the sea movement of troops and heavy weapons. planned to support the attack.

As one would expect, the short-range Stukas and single-engined fighters were based forward, in the Peloponnese and the nearby islands, with the bombers and twin-engined fighters farther back. Intensive bombing of Crete started on May 15, and reached its peak on the 20th, covering first the air landing on Máleme and Caneá, then shifting east to cover the afternoon landings at Rétimo and Heráklion.

That night British cruisers and destroyers swept north of Crete, finding no signs of German sea movement, although they had a brush with Italian motor-boats. Three British destroyers bombarded Scarpanto airfield, and the next morning Stukas sank the destroyer *Juno*.

A German convoy of 25 motor/sailer caiques, carrying a mountain battalion and heavy-weapon groups – 2,300 men in all – from Piraeus, was due to land west of Máleme on the afternoon of May 21. A second light convoy – 38 caiques with 4,000 men – was to reach Heráklion on the 22nd. German accounts refer to this 'cockleshell invasion' as the *Nusschalen* ('nut-shells') and the *Mückenflotilla* ('midge flotilla'). A heavy convoy of steamers with artillery and a few tanks was to wait at Piraeus until ordered forward. At dawn on May 21, when the first convoy was well on its way to Máleme, it was recalled to Mílos on overnight reports of British naval forces north of Crete. In the afternoon it was ordered to sea again. Thus it approached Crete not, as intended, by daylight – when the Luftwaffe could protect it – but at night, when British ships swept the waters it must traverse.

Overwhelmed by the British

At 2330 hours that night, the convoy was intercepted by Admiral Glennie with *Dido, Orion, Ajax*, and four destroyers. As the alarm was given and the mountain soldiers stumbled on deck, they saw their frail craft caught in the beams of British searchlights and heard the first salvoes. A caique loaded with ammunition blew up, others began to burn, and yet another was rammed and sliced in two. The Italian torpedo-boat *Lupo*, their only escort, faced the overwhelming odds gallantly, and in seeking to protect her charges was hit 18 times. After two-and-a-half hours the British ships turned south, believing that they had destroyed the convoy and drowned about 4,000 men – but in fact the *Lupo* and nearly two-thirds of the caiques remained afloat, and picked up survivors before returning to Mílos. After air-sea rescue operations had been carried out, the German loss was only 297 men drowned.

Next morning Admiral King – with *Naiad, Perth, Carlisle, Calcutta*, and four destroyers – was ordered to sweep north. ▷

STUKA VERSUS SEA POWER

▷ May 22, 1941: the third day of the Crete battle. The cruiser *Gloucester* circles desperately as Luftwaffe bombs score a near-miss, but she is fatally low on anti-aircraft ammunition and is doomed

In the fighting for Crete, the Ju-87 Stuka, which had suffered a severe mauling in the Battle of Britain, won new laurels as a destroyer of enemy shipping. Once again, the superiority of the air arm over enemy shipping was plainly demonstrated: Stukas of the 'Immelmann' *Stukageschwader* (dive-bomber wing) caused tremendous damage to the Mediterranean Fleet: not even the faster destroyers were safe from their attack. Specifications of the Ju-87 B-1: **Max speed:** 217 mph. **Armament:** two fixed 7·9-mm machine-guns firing forward, and one movable 7·9-mm machine-gun mounted in the rear cockpit. **Max bomb-load:** one 1,110-lb bomb and four 110-lb bombs

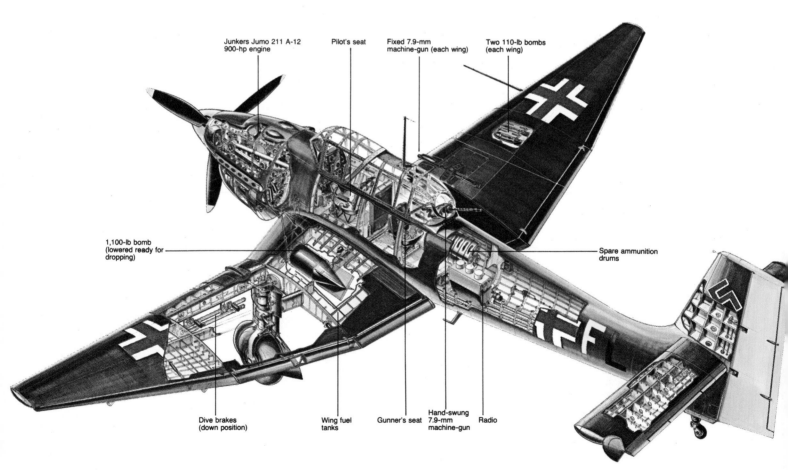

Junkers Jumo 211 A-12 900-hp engine

Pilot's seat

Fixed 7.9-mm machine-gun (each wing)

Two 110-lb bombs (each wing)

1,100-lb bomb (lowered ready for dropping)

Spare ammunition drums

Dive brakes (down position)

Wing fuel tanks

Gunner's seat

Hand-swung 7.9-mm machine-gun

Radio

John Batchelor

◁ This sequence of the *Gloucester* sinking was taken by a Luftwaffe pilot. *(Above)* Dead in the water and listing to port; note the smoke from her internal fires *(centre)*. *(Below)* The end of the *Gloucester*

He found a couple of surviving ships from the first convoy, which he sank; and then, at about 1000 hours, and 25 miles south of Mílos, he sighted the second convoy. A group of Ju-88s from Elevsís saw far below them the helpless caiques turn north at their best speed of 5 or 6 knots, while south of them the Italian torpedo-boat *Sagittario* zig-zagged at high speed, making smoke; beyond her steamed the British cruisers and destroyers in chase, guns firing. The Ju-88 group turned to attack, and as the first attack began their shallow dives the flak came streaming up at them.

On this same day King had already been under air attack for three hours, and with ammunition seriously depleted and the *Carlisle's* speed down to 20 knots, he decided to turn south. Stukas, Ju-88s, and Do-17s continued to engage his ships for the next three-and-a-half hours, during which the *Naiad* was seriously damaged and the *Carlisle's* captain was killed.

Luftwaffe reconnaissance aircraft had found Admiral Rawlings' ships on May 21. On the 22nd, with the critical first two days on Crete over, the urgency of supporting the German paratroops was less, and VIII Fliegerkorps eagerly took up the challenge, long awaited by the German airmen. In the fine weather of an early summer forenoon in the Mediterranean, dive-bombers and bombers had attacked the British cruiser forces. Glennie and Rowley had joined Rawlings some 20 to 30 miles west of Kíthira, and now Rawlings turned east to support King as he came south under air attack. They met in the Kíthira Channel early in the afternoon, and almost at once the *Warspite* was hit by a heavy bomb, putting out of action her starboard 6- and 4-inch batteries.

This was the opportunity for which the Luftwaffe had been waiting. Refuelling and bombing-up after their earlier attacks, and now reinforced by two fresh groups transferred from X Fliegerkorps, the German aircraft converged on the British fleet. Stukas, bombers, and fighters—with no British fighters to consider—made rough and ready formations as aircraft became ready and returned to the attack. At first the concentrated fire of the British ships held them off, but, 30 minutes after the *Warspite* was hit, two bombs struck the destroyer *Greyhound* and sank her. King ordered Rowley back to pick up survivors, and then, realising that *Gloucester* and *Fiji* were very short of anti-aircraft ammunition, ordered them to rejoin the main fleet, and turned back to meet them. The move came too late. As she came in sight, the *Gloucester* was hit, flames spread along her deck, she lost way, and drifted in a circle. At 1600 hours there was an internal explosion and she sank. The *Fiji*, now isolated and under continuous air attack, had to keep going, throwing overboard her life-saving floats as she passed the *Gloucester's* survivors. A little later the *Valiant* was hit and damaged.

The *Fiji* and her two attendant destroyers had missed the main fleet, and now steamed south. At 1845 hours, a lone Me-109 at the limit of its range found her and dropped a single bomb. It exploded close alongside, and with singular good fortune succeeded in crippling the cruiser's engines. Half an hour later a few other aircraft appeared, called up by the lone Messerschmitt—a bomb exploded above a boiler room, and at 2015 hours the *Fiji* turned over and sank.

That night Cunningham, due to a mistaken report that the battleships had expended all their light anti-aircraft ammunition, recalled them to Alexandria. The 5th Destroyer Flotilla, however, had arrived during the afternoon from Malta—Captain Lord Louis Mountbatten in the *Kelly*, with the *Kashmir, Kipling, Kelvin,* and *Jackal.* Now it was their turn to sweep north of Crete. They sank two caiques carrying Germans and bombarded Máleme airfield, which was now in German hands. Next morning a formation of 24 Stukas found the *Kelly* and *Kashmir* south of the island and sank them. Under heavy air attack, the *Kipling* rescued 279 survivors.

The nightly sweeps to the north of Crete continued. Destroyers and the fast minelayer *Abdiel* landed forces and ammunition for the troops around Suda Bay and a destroyer evacuated the King of Greece from the island. Under pressure from London, Cunningham embarked a battalion in the converted merchant ship *Glenroy,* but she was damaged and set on fire by bombs and forced to turn back on the morning of the 26th.

At last a dozen serviceable Fulmar fighters had been mustered for the *Formidable,* and escorted by the *Queen Elizabeth,* the *Barham,* and eight destroyers, she left Alexandria on May 25.

Triumph for the Stukas
At dawn next morning four Fulmars and four Albacores, flown off 100 miles away, attacked Scarpanto airfield, destroying or damaging grounded aircraft and shooting others down; but at 1325 hours, 25 Stukas appeared from the south, two bombs hit the *Formidable's* flight-deck, and she had to return to Alexandria severely damaged.

The II Group from *Stukageschwader* (Dive-Bomber Wing) 'Immelmann' of X Fliegerkorps had been an early arrival in Sicily, and on January 10 they had attacked and severely damaged the *Illustrious.* Later, the group had gone to Africa to support Rommel. On May 26 it was patrolling northwards from the African coast, hoping to catch British ships returning from Crete. It was this group that found the *Formidable,* and as she turned into wind with her fighters starting up on deck, the Stukas screamed down to hit and damage her as they had the *Illustrious.* The next day aircraft hit and damaged the *Barham.*

On May 26 Freyberg reported that the situation in Crete was hopeless, and at 1500 hours on May 27, after approval had been received from London, the decision to evacuate was taken. Now the battered ships and their exhausted crews had to expose themselves again to the Luftwaffe, this time to rescue their comrades of the British, Australian, and New Zealand armies. Cunningham needed no persuasion to take the risk, but warned Wavell that the moment might come when loss of life among troops embarked would force him to end the evacuation. All embarkation would be by night, as far as possible between midnight and 0300 hours, which would allow the ships about three hours' start before full daylight. The troops from Heráklion would be embarked in one lift direct; the remainder would withdraw across the mountains to embark at Sfakía on the south coast.

Rawlings, with the *Orion, Ajax, Dido,* and six destroyers, was given the task of taking off the Heráklion garrison. At 1700 hours on May 28 the Luftwaffe found them about 90 miles south of the Kásos Strait, and attacked until dark. The *Ajax* was damaged and returned to Alexandria, and the destroyer *Imperial* was 'near-missed', without apparent damage. Between 2330 and 0320 hours, some 4,000 were taken off from Heráklion, and the force started back. Half an hour later the *Imperial's* steering failed. Rawlings ordered the *Hotspur* to take off her troops and crew and to sink her, and as she steamed south at full speed after doing so—with 900 troops on board, 50 miles from Scarpanto, and dawn breaking—the *Hotspur's* position was desperate.

Rather than desert the *Hotspur,* however, Rawlings had waited; now he had to face the Stukas. They appeared at 0600 hours. At 0625 the *Hereward* was hit and her speed reduced, so she had to be left, and was last seen making for the Cretan coast; the Stukas sank her, but Italian motor-boats rescued most of the men on board.

Hits and near-misses reduced the speed of the squadron to 25 knots, then to 21. First the *Dido* was hit, then—repeatedly—the *Orion,* and the bombs bursting in the crowded ships did terrible damage. Stuka attacks ended about 1045 hours; but later high bombers appeared, though their bombs failed to hit the ships. Cunningham saw the ships entering Alexandria that evening, guns awry or broken off, decks crowded with troops, the mess decks reduced to shambles. Of the 4,000 men embarked, 800 had been killed, wounded or, like the survivors from the *Hereward,* were prisoners. Meanwhile Captain Arliss with four destroyers had landed ammunition and supplies at Sfakía and had taken off 700 men without loss.

Long-range fighters from Egypt had attempted to cover Rawlings's withdrawal, but missed his ships owing to his reduced speed. During the rest of the evacuation they gave useful cover to ships returning from Sfakía, which were moreover far less exposed to air attack. On the night of May 29 King took the *Phoebe, Perth, Glengyle, Calcutta, Coventry,* and three destroyers to Sfakía and brought out 6,000 men; but the *Perth* was damaged by a Ju-88 on the way back. On May 30 two of Arliss's four destroyers were damaged, but the other two took off another 1,500 men, and then Wavell asked for a final effort to bring off 3,000 on the night of the 31st. King was sent with the *Phoebe, Abdiel,* and three destroyers. They embarked 4,000 men, but then at 0300 hours on June 1 they were forced to sail from Sfakía, leaving another 5,000 on the beach—and the *Calcutta,* coming out from Alexandria to meet them, was bombed and sunk.

Early on June 1 Major Garrett of the Royal Marines found a derelict landing-craft from the *Glengyle* on Sfakía beach. With 137 volunteers on board he sailed for the African coast. He beached 19 miles west of Sidi Barrani at 0230 on June 9, having had to sail his cumbersome craft most of the way using blankets for sails. Another landing-craft reached Sidi Barrani about the same time with 50 men, and a third arrived next day with 37. In all, some 600 men made their way back to Egypt or Syria in the next few months, in Greek fishing-boats or in submarines sent to pick them up.

It was as he risked his battered ships in the evacuation that Cunningham was heard to say: 'It takes the Navy three years to build a ship. It would take three hundred to re-build a tradition.' His total losses off Crete were: three cruisers and six destroyers sunk; three battleships, one aircraft-carrier, six cruisers, and seven destroyers damaged; in the fleet, 1,828 killed and 183 wounded. Cunningham had realised the risks he was forced to run. As shown by the messages Cunningham received, Churchill and the Chiefs-of-Staff were less realistic. Before the year was out, Japanese aircraft off Singapore would ram home the lesson Cunningham drew from Crete: the proper way to fight aircraft is in the air, and if shore-based fighters cannot cover the fleet, it must carry its own fighters with it.

Wing Commander Asher Lee. **The Western Desert in mid-1941 was a backwater for the war in the air. Despite the desperate struggles of both Axis and Allied armies to break each other's control of Egypt and Cyrenaica, the British, Italian, and German desert air forces were astonishingly limited; and as the author comments: 'they were limited because the main strategic interests of the three contenders lay elsewhere'**

In the summer of 1941 the North African air front was, at best, a secondary air front. It might indeed be called the epitome of aeronautical unimportance except, of course, to the limited number of British, Italian, and German air squadrons engaged. They were limited because the main strategic interests of the three contenders lay elsewhere. For the Royal Air Force the three main considerations were to build up the bomber offensive against Germany, to maintain strong fighter forces for the home defences of Great Britain, and for its Coastal Command to play a full part in the Battle of the Atlantic. In this battle German submarines and long-range Focke-Wulf bombers posed a serious threat to the ocean supply life-lines along which the Merchant Navy brought essential food, fuel, and raw materials to a Britain which was still fighting alone against the combined might of Germany and Italy.

The British air forces in North Africa were part of a Middle East Air Command whose resources were, in 1941, stretched to the limit. They comprised some 30 air squadrons totalling just over 300 aircraft. Although in theory they had an aircraft reserve of 100%, in practice replacements and reinforcements from Great Britain were behind schedule, and the repair and servicing of aircraft in the theatre were hampered by the absence of any local aircraft industry or modern large-scale repair facilities.

The aircraft themselves were a remarkably variegated collection of miscellaneous and mainly obsolete types, clearly showing that the command was regarded as a 'Cinderella'—an aeronautical side-show. It is true that by the summer of 1941 the obsolescent biplane Gladiator fighters were being replaced by Hurricanes and United States P-40 Tomahawks, but these were technically far inferior to the new German Me-109F fighters. In order to deal effectively with the new German planes, the Hurricanes and Tomahawks had to hunt them with a numerical advantage which they could not always command.

The British bomber squadrons had recently acquired some long-range twin-engined Wellington aircraft which were rendering yeoman service operating from Malta against Axis convoys and Sicilian targets, or from Egypt against key objectives in Cyrenaica. But there were also some obsolescent Blenheim bomber squadrons.

The 300-350 aircraft of the Middle East Air Command had therefore a vast area of responsibility, and usually little more than half the force was based in Egypt. The geographical commitment of the command extended to the Sudan, Palestine, Jordan, East Africa, Iraq, Cyprus, Turkey, Persia, Yugoslavia, Rumania, Bulgaria, and Greece—not to mention other adjacent territories. Seldom during the Second World War did so few combat aircraft have the responsibility for such a vast area of operations. It was not until the summer of 1942 that the modern Spitfire fighters came to the Mediterranean, and even then they were used not in North African operations but in the air defence of Malta. North Africa remained the theatre of RAF obsolescence, and was desperately short of the kind of aircraft it needed, particularly long-range transport aircraft, to meet the needs of the army's advance and retreat along the North African shores.

1941 had begun as a year of great promise for the British air forces in North Africa but in the next six months there were great changes of aeronautical and military fortune. In January the RAF bombed the Italian-held ports of Derna and Benghazi and the adjacent airfields, carrying out key reconnaissances of enemy positions and minefields around Tobruk, and covering and supporting the Australian attack on Tobruk with intensive air patrol and bombing operations by Hurricanes, Lysanders, and Blenheims. But as the Royal Air Force kept up its pressure on the retreating columns of the Italian army, and as British ground forces moved forward in Cyrenaica, unexpected demands in the Balkan theatre—specifically in Greece and Crete—were to produce months of disaster and disappointment.

The new Royal Air Force Middle East Commander-in-Chief, Air Vice-Marshal A. W. Tedder, was to have all the qualities of his keen intelligence and sardonic humour fully tested by the dangerous situation created when the German army and air force began to move into Bulgaria at the beginning of March. The German attack on Yugoslavia began on April 6 and it was supported by a mobile force of 1,200 Luftwaffe operational planes, a mixed force of fighters, reconnaissance, dive-bombers, and twin-engined medium-range Junkers 88 and Heinkel 111 bombers—a potent force. ▷

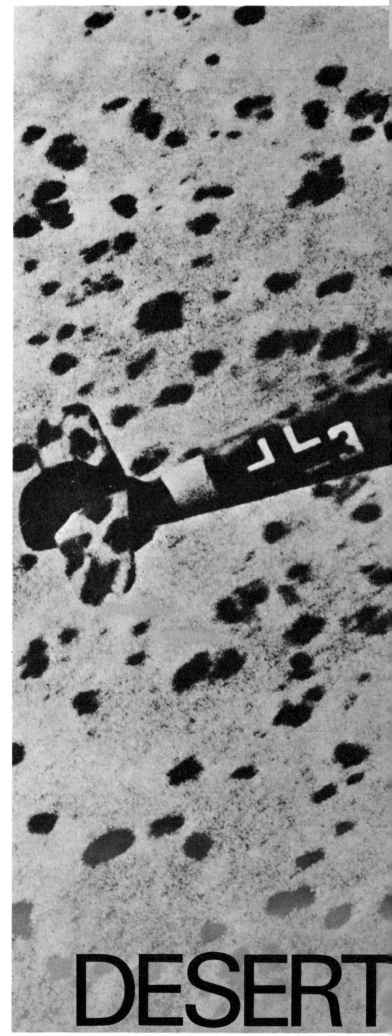

DESERT

AIR WAR

△ British air reinforcements for the Middle East also went out along the 'back-door' route through Takoradi: shipped out to the Gold Coast by carrier, and then the long stages of the flight across Africa to the Nile. ◁ An Me-109E of Rommel's desert air force. ▽ Air Vice-Marshal Tedder, RAF C-in-C Middle East

Keystone

The Italian air force in North Africa, however, like its British opponents, was no more than a rump of its country's main air resources, and it was a rump which had taken a succession of severe batterings. Although the bombing threat to metropolitan Italy was very slight in the summer of 1941, the main strength of Italy's air force fighter squadrons, many of them equipped with modern low-wing monoplane Macchi machines, remained in Italy outside the North African theatre. And yet the latter air front was surely the major one for Italy in the summer of 1941.

1941 had so far been as discouraging a year for the Italian air force as 1940 had been. In the fighting in Cyrenaica, early in the year, they had out-numbered the Royal Air Force by about two to one, but had allowed their British opponents to obtain and secure the initiative and then the ascendancy over the battlefield. Their long-range Savoia S-79 bombers had had little effect in their attacks on Royal Air Force bases in Egypt, and their biplane Fiat CR-42 fighters, though superior in manoeuvrability, had been out-fought by the Hurricanes.

There had been minor successes by Italian torpedo-bombers against British Mediterranean convoys, but these did little to relieve the general gloomy picture of defeat and retreat. Of a total first-line Italian strength of over 1,500 aircraft, some 300 were based in Libya, though these were often easily reinforced by fighter planes which could be flown direct to North Africa inside huge Savoia transport planes. Indeed, one of the great strategic advantages of the Italian air force in North Africa was that they could easily obtain replacements and reinforcements from their main source of supply in Italy. It was an advantage—but not a trump card.

The trump card might have been the arrival of the Luftwaffe in the Mediterranean at the end of 1940, when the Luftwaffe's X Fliegerkorps was sent to Sicily under General Geissler. The first few months of joint German/Italian air operations in the Mediterranean held promise for the future. In January 1941 the British cruiser *Southampton* was hit by German bombers and subsequently sunk, and the aircraft-carrier *Illustrious* was also hit. In January and February Luftwaffe units moved into Tripolitania and pushed along the coast to forward bases in the Gulf of Sirte. Luftwaffe attacks on Malta caused considerable damage to the island's docks and airfields and so eased the passage of Rommel's army to Tripolitania.

All this was promising for the general Axis air picture in North Africa and the Mediterranean. But the bigger picture of German plans, intentions, and strategy made it inevitable that its North African air force was to be a very poor relation, not only in the summer of 1941, but right to the end of the war in the Mediterranean. It totalled less than 10% of the front-line operational strength of the Luftwaffe—and even then its squadrons were liable to be depleted at any time because of the needs of air operations against Malta.

Demands from other fronts
In the summer of 1941 German air planners had two major requirements to meet. The first was the vast need of the new air front against Russia which would open on June 22 when the Wehrmacht attacked the Soviet Union. This initially absorbed about two-thirds of Germany's front-line air squadrons, and as long as Russia was undefeated, the Eastern Front was bound to occupy a high proportion of Hermann Göring's Luftwaffe. To illustrate how unimportant the Mediterranean air front had become in June 1941 it may be worth pointing out that the entire German Luftflotte IV—comprising some 1,200 fighters, reconnaissance, and bomber aircraft which had moved into the Balkans in March and April—was withdrawn in May and early June to bases in Poland and Eastern Germany in preparation for Operation 'Barbarossa', the attack on the USSR.

The second German requirement was the air defence of the Fatherland against the growing weight of Britain's Bomber Command offensive. One-third of Germany's twin-engined fighters in the summer of 1941 were kept back for the night defences of the Third Reich, and the German armies in the field were thus robbed of valuable support from these Messerschmitt 110 squadrons. By the end of 1941, with Russia undefeated and America in the war, the overall prospect of providing adequate German air power in Africa was indeed remote.

The small force of some 350 German planes permanently in the Mediterranean theatre therefore had to split its attentions between air attacks on Malta, attacking convoys, and providing tactical support for Rommel's ground forces. The force included 100 to 150 twin-engined bombers—Junkers 88, and Heinkel 111 machines—a similar number of dive-bomber Junkers 87s, some 40/50 twin-engined Messerschmitt 110s, and about the same number of single-seater Messerschmitt 109s.

Initially the German air force which supported Rommel's ground forces amounted to some 200 aircraft. Rommel was undoubtedly the first German general of the Second World War to fight key ground battles without intensive air support. This he did throughout the long see-saw of the desert warfare of 1941 and 1942. (By 1943 he was no longer unique in this respect: Kleist, Manstein, Kesselring, Bock, and others had come to consider effective support from the Luftwaffe a rare and treasured luxury which was not to be expected as a matter of course.)

Flying under desert conditions had special hazards of its own, apart from the acute shortages of aircraft. The German air force had none of the experience of the Royal Air Force in 'tropicalising' its engines, adjusting them to desert conditions, and keeping them free of sand particles. These problems occurred particularly in the maintenance of the Junkers 88 medium-range bombers. Because of this, the Germans never based a force of more than about 20 of these aircraft on their North African air bases. They did not develop radar facilities in North Africa until the end of 1942, and their interception of British bombers was therefore often a hit and miss affair. They were in any event particularly short of both intercepting and escort fighters. Only the exceptional performance of the Me-109F squadrons enabled them to achieve any kind of parity.

A further problem for the Luftwaffe lay in the supply of ammunition, petrol, and aircraft spares. While Junkers 52 and Italian Savoia 82 transport aircraft flew regular loads to the North African air bases, the numbers of these cargo planes was limited because of the need for transport planes on other fronts. The Junkers 88 was shortly to be pressed into service as an emergency cargo plane, when the battle was joined to stop the supplies from reaching the Axis forces in North Africa by ship. While it is true that a high proportion of Rommel's supply ships was being sunk by the Royal Navy and the Royal Air Force, he would still have faced problems in building up long-term supplies in North Africa even if he had had no shipping casualties at all.

For the airmen, desert air warfare held little romance. The air bases in North Africa have been aptly described as a vast stretch of dust and stones in summer, and of cheerless boggy marsh in winter. The desert airfield amenities were primitive compared with the well-equipped and civilised sites, with their efficient amenities, from which the Royal Air Force had fought the Battle of Britain. The personnel often lived uncomfortably in the desert in little shanties knocked together from empty petrol cans and packing cases and graced by patched bits of tent-cloth.

Beer was warm and rare. The nights were cold, sometimes seeming to approach Arctic temperatures—while the day's sun burnt through your hide after roasting your skin. When rain fell, it did so in torrents, and when it stopped, men floundered in the mud and were badly bitten by insects. Planes stuck in the bog, and as the ground staff struggled to get them off the ground they sank up to their ankles in layers of thick dust which clung like wet flour. The men of the desert air forces of 1941 lived in combat conditions of real hardship. Water was often severely rationed and the corned-beef often fly-infested. The extremes of temperature, the lack of a varied diet, and the prevalence of a form of amoebic dysentery all told on the health of both air and ground crews; it was a miracle that sustained operations could be maintained despite these adverse conditions.

Aircraft also suffered in the desert. Often an engine, after only 30 hours' use, was thoroughly worn out with valves eroded and cylinders pitted with signs of wear. Cables were rotted by the salt in the air; control rods gave way, and the legs of the undercarriages seized up. Tyres had to be specially covered with wet cloths to prevent them bursting in the desert heat; petrol vaporised in the tanks, making them liable to burst at the joints and explode.

Pilots took off in clouds of dust which settled on the perspex glass and obscured all vision. Sometimes they had to land in 60-mph sandstorms which robbed them of landmarks, and set up strange, obscure, thick veils round the air base. Sand was everywhere, in petrol-cans, tool-kits, food, and clothing. Yet even in these conditions men fought air battles with skill and determination, and ground crews kept the squadrons at a remarkable level of serviceability.

WING-COMMANDER ASHER LEE was born in Plymouth in 1909, and educated at London University and the Paris Sorbonne. He joined the RAF Volunteer Reserve in 1939, and served from 1939 to 1945 in Air Intelligence as well as serving in the 1st Allied Airborne Army. He has been decorated with the OBE (Mil), and the US Legion of Merit. His many publications include *The German Air Force, The Soviet Air Force, Blitz on Britain,* and many articles written for *The Economist, The Daily Telegraph, RAF Flying Review,* etc. He has lectured to staff colleges in Britain, the USA, Belgium, and Norway.

Supply and defence for the Afrika Korps: Junkers 52 transports and Me 110 fighters on a Luftwaffe base

The Italian Air Force

◁ **Macchi C-200** was faster than the Fiat G-50 and had better all-round vision. It was undoubtedly the best Italian aircraft of that period.
Armament: two 12·7-mm machine-guns.
Max speed: 312 mph

◁ **Fiat G-50** epitomised two key factors in Italian fighter design: it was highly manoeuvrable but it was also lightly armed.
Armament: two 12·7-mm machine-guns.
Max speed: 293 mph

△ **Savoia SM-79,** like the Luftwaffe's Do-17, had been blooded in the Spanish Civil War and was the standard-long-range bomber of the Regia Aeronautica.
Bomb load: 2,205 lb.
Max speed: 260 mph

△ **Caproni Ca-135** was one of the later Italian designs, but this medium bomber's performance was disappointing.
Bomb load: 2,650 lb.
Max speed: 273 mph

▽ **Fiat BR-20** Cicogna was one of Italy's heaviest bombers and served everywhere in Mussolini's empire except East Africa.
Bomb load: 3,300 lb.
Max speed: 267 mph

▽ **Fiat CR-42** was the last single-seater biplane to be used by any combatant in the Second World War.
Armament: two 12·7-mm machine-guns.
Max speed: 261 mph

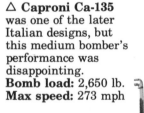

Reggiane RE-2000▷
was one of the
handiest Italian
fighters. In mock
combats it had
outmanoeuvred the
German Me-109E,
but early faults had
caused it to be
neglected.
Armament: two
12·7-mm
machine-guns.
Max speed: 329 mph

△ **Breda Ba-65**
saw service in
Ethiopia in 1935, was
basically a ground-
attack plane. An
observer could be
carried for scouting.
Armament: four
12-mm machine-guns.
Max speed: 267 mph

△ **Cant Z-506B** was one of the most
important of the Cant seaplane
designs. It was used mainly to bomb
French and Greek targets and the
British Mediterranean Fleet.
Bomb load: 3,300 lb. **Max speed:** 217 mph

John Batchelor

DESERT BOMB RUN

One of the most brilliant of the desert war correspondents *(Alexander Clifford)* wrote this account of a normal RAF night raid over the Western Desert, North Africa

I was still in bed at the time of Bardia, and the doctor forbade me to go to Tobruk. But I thought I could do something else. I applied for another operational flight with the RAF, and I was luckier than before. They said I could go on a bombing raid the following night.

The night before it happened I went with the pilots of a Wellington squadron to a sandy, fly-haunted shack beside a remote desert airfield to get the Squadron-Leader's instructions.

'Blitz on tonight,' he told us. 'Take-off after midnight at ten-minute intervals. There are five targets — you can take your choice.'

I looked on rather diffidently while they clustered round maps and photographs and filled in the details, discussing the weather, debating the relative merits of the targets. For them it was pretty nearly routine, but not for me. I felt the sensation I always feel before going on one of those giant racers at fun-fairs — excitement more or less strongly tempered with alarm. I looked through the dirty windows and watched the crews loading up with bombs and petrol, and checking over the guns. I wished strongly that I could do something to help.

As darkness fell everyone trooped in for a noisy, boisterous meal of stew, potatoes, and onions. The atmosphere was less routine now — there was a mood of suppressed exhilaration. The conversation was nearly all shop, most of it over my head, but I felt pleased when I could contribute some bit of gossip I had picked up at another squadron.

Afterwards, for the few intervening hours, we dozed on straw mattresses. Then, booted, helmeted, and very warmly overalled, we walked out to the dimly silhouetted plane.

A moon which looked to my over-excited eye like a luminous slice of melon was just topping the horizon. In a matter of minutes we had climbed aboard, roared down the winking flare-path, and lifted gently into the night. I stood with my head in the little glass bubble which stuck out above the top of the machine, and watched the desert sink away into a misty blur. Little white clouds drenched with moonlight sailed past. A dim white streak was the coastline, and the sea beyond it looked like another desert.

There was nothing to see. I crouched down, trying to keep warm and watching spangles of stars slide past the little glass bubble above my head. Vaguely in my earphones I heard the crew chatting on the 'intercomm' about height, courses, clouds, and navigation signals. As the plane droned on into Libya I fell asleep.

Then someone was shaking me awake and yelling 'Over target!' I fumbled my way forward and peered out of the plane's transparent nose to see earth and sky slashed with flame.

Groups of big yellow flashes were bombs landing. Clusters of incendiaries wove crazy patterns of dazzling white flame athwart the landscape. A parachute flare hung like a great orange star burning steadily above the bay.

To my unaccustomed eyes the ack-ack barrage seemed stupendous. String after string of red tracer-shells spurted up like ruby necklaces. Ack-ack shells bursting splashed the sky with sudden stars and left little balls of smoke hanging aimlessly about.

It was our turn to go in. Just for one second there was icy panic inside me and I wished I hadn't come. I wondered whether I was trembling from cold or fear. Then I grew too excited to be afraid.

I clambered back through the plane's darkened belly, past the bomb-aimer lying flat on his stomach, and over the racks of sleek yellow bombs waiting to be released. Clumsily I eased myself into the rear-gunner's turret — and another, bigger bubble, half filled with intricate gun mechanism. That was my grand-stand seat.

Through my earphones I heard the bomb-aimer's steady monologue: 'Bomb-doors open . . . left . . . left . . . steady . . . right . . . steady . . .' then a pause, and then sharply, 'Bombs gone.'

I swivelled my turret round, manoeuvring to see the bombs land. I had almost given them up when the earth below erupted into five flaming volcanoes.

'Plumb in the target area,' came the bomb-aimer's voice.

Stuff was coming up all round us. The sky seemed filled with coloured tracers, and the heavy ack-ack guns were firing for all they were worth. By now the whole area was picked out in dazzling lights as cluster after cluster of incendiaries sprang into flame.

The pilot called me up on the 'intercomm'.

'We're going in again,' he said. 'Tell me if anything bursts close behind us.'

'Okay,' I said. It was icy cold, and my hands were numb as they manipulated the levers to swing my turret.

Back we turned and plunged again into the fantastic blaze of bursting shells. Another flare was burning, and the bay and promontory showed up like a gigantic thumb sticking out into the sea.

We made straight for the target, but showers of tracers met us and barred the way. The pilot swerved aside and tried from another angle. Again I heard 'Bombs gone,' and this time I saw flame belch up straight across the road junction at which we were aiming.

Two blinding flashes on my left made me rock in my seat. 'Ack-ack shells close behind,' I reported to the pilot, and for a couple of seconds we swerved and twisted, eluding the gunners. Then we jockeyed into position for the third run.

This took us slap through the thickest barrage. An Italian cruiser, half sunk in the harbour, was pumping up stream after stream of tracers. I saw a white one coming straight at me — diamond necklace this time — then it veered off slowly and missed.

Right in the middle of the barrage our bombs fell, and a flare with them. This time the result was spectacular. A large barn-like building flashed into orange flame, and its roof soared gently upward, then fell back in fragments. Swirls of white smoke spiralled up, and as we swung away out to sea I saw two more explosions.

Those were our last bombs. But we still had some leaflets to drop — why I don't know, for the Italians were going to be given no time to read them. We dropped down to a couple of thousand feet well west of the target and shovelled the packets of pamphlets out through a hatchway. Then we made for home, leaving a faint firework display behind us. My first wild exhilaration at having got out of it alive gave way to the flat feeling which follows a moment of high adventure. While dawn was just glimmering in the east we met a squadron of Blenheims on their way to continue the raid. Then we circled down to our airfields again, to a good hot breakfast of fried bread and bacon.

[From Three against Rommel *by Alexander Clifford.]*

'We shall bomb Germany
by day as well as by night
in ever-increasing measure,
casting upon them month
by month a heavier discharge
of bombs, and making the
German people taste and
gulp each month a sharper
dose of the miseries they
have showered upon mankind'
Winston Churchill

THE 1000 BOMBER RAID

Britain and Germany, January 1941/May 1942

Ralph Barker

The first year of the air war—and the sometimes indiscriminate Luftwaffe raids over Britain—had convinced RAF Bomber Command that only a full-scale bombing policy was of any value. In addition to German industry, German morale had to be worn down by heavy, sustained raids. Yet not only were the aircraft lacking for such a full-scale offensive, but it was not until 1941 that the RAF leaders were fully aware of Bomber Command's weakness in finding and hitting its targets. New tactics of saturation bombing were essential—and the first German city singled out for experiment was Cologne

At the beginning of 1941, British hopes of aggressive action against Germany were vested almost entirely in a strategic air offensive, to be mounted by RAF Bomber Command. For the British, still without allies, with their land forces deprived of contact with the enemy following the retreat from Dunkirk, and with their naval blockade largely nullified by Germany's vast conquests in Europe, a bombing campaign offered the only apparent hope of so weakening the industrial and economic structure of Nazi Germany that a landing back on the Continent might one day be contemplated. This situation had been fully recognised by the British War Cabinet in 1940, and when the threat of invasion eased after the Battle of Britain an air offensive—of the greatest possible magnitude—against Germany had been immediately called for, to begin as soon as possible.

Successive directives in the closing months of 1940 had disclosed a twofold aim: the primary object was to be a precision attack on German production of synthetic oil. The secondary object, to be attempted only when the weather was unsuitable for precision bombing, was to be an attack on German morale. This latter aim was to be achieved by the concentrated bombing of Berlin and other large cities, where targets in the middle of industrial areas were to be chosen

as aiming-points. Such raids constituted the first British experiments in area bombing.

From the start of the war the British Air Staff had held to a belief in the efficacy and economy of selective attack on German industrial targets, the most vulnerable of which was believed to be oil. The War Cabinet, on the other hand, believed that the German blitz on British cities ought to be answered by heavy reprisal raids, and some such raids had in fact been carried out. British experience was that morale was toughened rather than weakened by bombing on the German scale, and the German blitz had in any case failed in its intention; but the War Cabinet was led to believe by its economic and political advisers that the situation in Germany was different. Both the German economy and German morale were far more likely, it was thought, to be affected by a bombing campaign.

A compromise between the two viewpoints was not difficult to achieve. Nights when the weather was clear enough for selective attack numbered not more than one in four or five, so if such attacks were to be regarded as exclusive the bombers would remain idle for most of the time. On nights when the weather was unsuitable for precision bombing, the choice of large industrial areas as targets seemed sensible

51

BIRTH OF THE ALLIED BLITZ

After the fall of France, bombing seemed to be the only way in which Britain could strike back at Germany; but the aircraft with which she began the war had too light a bomb-load to be able to mount an offensive which could really hurt the enemy. The Wellington—an incredibly tough machine—formed the mainstay of the bombing force until the new 'heavies' began to arrive during the summer of 1941. The first of these new aircraft—the Stirling, Manchester, and Halifax—all had their teething troubles, but they gave the RAF new power, and the RAF crews vital new experience for the big raids to come

Handley Page Halifax Mk II The successor to the twin-engined Hampden and Hereford designs , the Halifax was the second of the new RAF 'heavies'. It made its first raid against the docks and shipping of Le Havre, in March 1941. **Max speed:** 282 mph. **Range:** 1,030 miles. **Crew:** seven. **Armament:** nine ·303 Browning machine-guns; up to 13,000 lbs of bombs

Vickers Wellington Mk III Its simple but sturdy 'geodetic' (lattice-work) construction enabled the Wellington to endure an astonishing amount of punishment. **Max speed:** 255 mph. **Range:** 1,325 miles. **Crew:** six. **Armament:** six ·303 Browning machine-guns; up to 6,000 lbs of bombs

Short Stirling Mk I The Stirling was the first four-engined bomber to enter service with the RAF; the first raid flown by Stirlings was in February 1941, against oil-storage tanks in Rotterdam. **Max speed:** 260 mph. **Range:** 1,930 miles. **Crew:** seven or eight. **Armament:** eight ·303 Browning machine-guns; up to 14,000 lbs of bombs

Avro Manchester 1A The twin-engined forerunner of the Lancaster had a short and unsuccessful service life, for its Rolls-Royce Vulture engines proved to be underdeveloped and unreliable. **Max speed:** 265 mph. **Range:** 1,200 miles. **Crew:** seven. **Armament:** eight ·303 Browning machine-guns; up to 10,350 lbs of bombs

John Batchelor

and practicable; there was even the likelihood that, if these targets were carefully chosen, attacks on them might assist and be complementary to the more selective bombing of vulnerable industries.

The fact that a new phase in British bombing had been begun in December 1940, with the decision to attack industrial areas, was known to the British people from the official communiqués, publications, and photographs released in the course of 1941; that these raids were partly designed to cause nervousness and apprehension among the inhabitants of the German industrial centres, and ultimately to undermine morale, was also well publicised.

The question of the moral rectitude of such a campaign hardly arose at this time. Germany, by her unprovoked aggression, and by her bombing of British cities, whatever the purpose of that bombing might be — and the British were led to believe, not merely by British exhortation but by German propaganda, that the purpose had been to break their spirit and bring them to the point of surrender — had brought whatever disaster might befall her on herself. And just as the submarine was the natural weapon of the vastly inferior naval power, so the destruction of industrial capacity and national morale by bombing was the inevitable resort of the power out-classed on land.

Aware that they could never defeat a powerful Continental adversary unless that adversary were first fatally weakened by some indirect means, the British people, in the course of 1941, espoused the weapon of aerial bombardment, knowing the weapon from their own experience in the first six months of that year for what it was — an imprecise weapon likely to be most effective against civil populations.

On June 22, 1941, following the German attack on Russia, the British Prime Minister clearly foreshadowed a bombing offensive aimed specifically at the German people. 'We shall bomb Germany,' said Churchill, 'by day as well as by night in ever-increasing measure, casting upon them month by month a heavier discharge of bombs, and making the German people taste and gulp each month a sharper dose of the miseries they have showered upon mankind.' The British people were thus well aware of the plans for the devastation of Germany by bombing, and it was a policy of which they approved. They expected, and indeed were promised, powerful retaliation in kind, and they braced themselves to absorb it, preferring an attritional warfare in which the whole population shared the dangers to the wholesale slaughter of their young men which they imagined was the likely alternative.

As it happened, Bomber Command was far too weak in 1941 to pursue either of its aims with any chance of success. The diversion of scientific and industrial effort from defensive to offensive channels after the Battle of Britain came slowly. Not only was Bomber Command lacking in modern, high-performance aircraft, effective weapons, and scientific aids to navigation and bombing: it had also suffered, in the first few months of the war, one serious defeat and one severe setback, the implications of which were still not fully appreciated. This setback was the loss of the French airfields, which had greatly increased the length of sorties against Germany; the defeat was the inability, through prohibitive losses, to operate

in daylight. The change to night flights of long duration had revealed, in the course of 1940, operating deficiencies which were not easy to evaluate or rectify.

In spite of the confident tone of official communiqués, and the optimistic intelligence estimates of the effects of British bombing on German oil and morale, the C-in-C Bomber Command, Air Marshal Sir Richard Peirse, was not alone in fearing that far too high a percentage of British bombs missed their targets. In the longer-range attacks, indeed, he believed that only one aircraft out of five found its primary target at all. Such photographic evidence as was available in January 1941 — of the area attack on Mannheim of December 17, 1940, and of two precision attacks on the twin Gelsenkirchen oil plants — could only have aggravated his fears. The Mannheim attack, mounted in retaliation for the German raids on Coventry and Southampton, had failed to achieve any effective concentration; the two Gelsenkirchen oil plants, photographed on December 24 after attacks involving nearly 300 aircraft, were found to have suffered no major damage.

Failure to face the facts

The work of damage assessment, however, was still hampered by a shortage of aircraft cameras and a lack of systematic photographic reconnaissance, so that the truth about Bomber Command's inability to hit its targets remained partly obscured. Bigger and better aircraft were coming into the squadrons, among them the Manchester, the Stirling, and the Halifax; and although for the whole of 1941 the command would have to operate without the radar aids it needed and was demanding, it seemed reasonable to expect that bombing results would improve with experience during the year. In any case, unless the offensive was to be abandoned for the time being, the best would have to be made of it. To fail to look the facts of the war in the face, to view Bomber Command's destructive capacity and Germany's economic vulnerability with optimism, was for Britain a psychological necessity at this time.

The precision attack on oil remained, at the beginning of 1941, the foundation of British war strategy, and a further directive of January 15 put additional emphasis upon it, on the assumption that the critical period for Germany would be the first six months of that year. But this new directive had to be put on one side in the months that followed, first through bad weather, and then through the all-out attack by German submarine and surface raiders on British supply shipping in the Atlantic, forcing Britain on the defensive and resulting in Churchill's Atlantic Directive of March 9, 1941.

From that point until July 1941, when the immediate crisis was over, the command was obliged to concentrate on naval targets, beginning with the battle-cruisers *Scharnhorst* and *Gneisenau,* which sought refuge in dry dock at Brest and thus became the Command's primary target. More than 1,100 sorties were flown against them in the next eight weeks, but in all these attacks only four bombs actually hit the ships. Yet in the period from March to July the bombers, with valuable help from Coastal Command, did accomplish their essential task of neutralising the ships and keeping them immobile at Brest.

After conclusive reports that one at least of the ships had been severely damaged,

Bomber Command turned to the precision attack of targets in Germany connected with the Atlantic battle — such as submarine bases and factories producing long-range aircraft — and to the area attack of ports and naval installations. These area attacks were among the most successful yet undertaken. Hamburg, Bremen, and Kiel all suffered severe damage, much of it in the docks and shipyards; in a ten-week period up to the end of May, 900 sorties were flown against Kiel, where the three main naval shipbuilding yards suffered temporary production losses of 60, 25, and 100%.

These targets, however, shared features which made them comparable to coastal targets, which in good weather the bombers had always been able to find. Precision and area attacks on inland targets were no more accurate than before. Nevertheless, British bombing in this period graduated from being a mere nuisance, ridiculed in German home broadcasts, to something calling for stoicism and ultimate retribution, something for which the German High Command would one day have to find an antidote.

Although the pre-occupation with naval targets had tended to obscure the lessons about precision bombing at night that had seemed about to be learned at the end of 1940, enthusiasm for the oil plan had cooled completely by July 1941, when Bomber Command was at last free to resume the strategic offensive. The command's failure to hit precision targets had in fact left it in danger of operating without a clear strategic aim.

The difficulty was to find an alternative target system which offered a real prospect of damaging the German war machine. Eroded by the needs of Coastal Command, diversions of aircraft and crews to overseas theatres, and the formation and succour of its own operational training units, Bomber Command remained much too small to mount an effective attack on morale, which in a country the size of Germany was such a gigantic task that the British had to seek some alternative target system, the destruction or dislocation of which might be within the bombers' power.

The choice this time fell on transport, and particularly on nine specified rail transport targets in the Ruhr area, which were listed in the new bombing directive of July 9. Germany's military adventures in Russia were believed to be putting an unprecedented strain on her transport system, and if this could be upset in the vulnerable Ruhr area, an important contribution might be made to the disruption of the German economy. Such a disruption would also have an effect on morale, especially as the rail targets were chosen not only for their importance in the transport system but also because of their proximity to industrial areas. Once again a compromise had been reached between precision and area bombing.

The transport plan looked and was a makeshift and attritional plan, the choice of a target system to suit the command's operational capability rather than a target whose destruction might win the war. It was a further significant step towards the acceptance of a tenet already propounded by Sir Charles Portal, Chief of the British Air Staff — that the most suitable object from the economic point of view was not worth pursuing if it was not tactically attainable. Bomber Command remained Britain's only offensive striking force against Germany: therefore, if Bomber Command could not hit its preferred targets, other targets had to be found.

Meanwhile, Germany's ability, in June 1941, to mount a land offensive against Russia had shown that in fact Britain's estimates of her economic vulnerability had been entirely misconceived. And despite the claims made – claims which had been well supported by independent intelligence appreciations – the RAF bombing of Germany could have had little or no strategic effect so far. These two misconceptions – of Germany's vulnerability and of the effect of RAF bombing – while not vital in themselves, were to have considerable influence on the future course of the air offensive. The estimates of the Ministry of Economic Warfare, always subject to conjecture, had been discredited, and confidence in such calculations was inevitably shaken. For the British Chiefs-of-Staff, even the attack on rail transport was looked upon as no more than a transitional policy, to be employed until such time as Bomber Command was strong enough to pass to an all-out offensive against civilian morale, still regarded by the politicians as Germany's weakest point.

June 1941: Wasted opportunities

With the opening of the German offensive against Russia, fresh opportunities seemed to present themselves to the Royal Air Force. First, it seemed, was the chance to take tactical advantage of the pre-occupation of the Luftwaffe in the east by stepping up short-range fighter and day bomber operations over France; second, of more immediate importance, and of potential strategic value, was the belief that such operations might compel the Germans to return some of their fighters to the west, thus relieving the Russians. The aim of Fighter Command, together with No. 2 Group of Bomber Command, became to draw the Luftwaffe into combat over France with the idea of destroying the remnant that had been left there, opening the way for the daylight bombing of precision targets in Germany and at the same time compelling the reinforcement of the west at the expense of the east.

The 'Circus' operations, as they were known, foundered for much the same reasons as the German plans had foundered in the Battle of Britain: an efficient radar early-warning system in the hands of the defenders, the short range of the attacking fighters, and the necessity to defend the slow and lightly-armed bombers (in this case the Blenheims of No. 2 Group). British casualties were heavy, various attempts at daylight bombing proved costly, and the wisdom of a night role for Bomber Command was confirmed. Most significant was the reinforcement of the belief that the long-range fighter would always be at a disadvantage when confronted by the short-range fighter operating within the orbit of ground-controlled radar and within easy reach of its base. This belief, much later and almost by chance, was proved to be erroneous.

In the summer of 1941 it seemed that Bomber Command, with a new group operational (No. 1), with new heavy bombers in service, with heavier and more efficient bombs, with a more realistic target system – and with the Luftwaffe pre-occupied elsewhere – could now mount an effective strategic offensive. Yet the continuing inaccuracy of British night bombing was gradually being confirmed as night photography improved and more and more bombers were

fitted with cameras. Scepticism about Bomber Command's effectiveness culminated in the appointment by Lord Cherwell, the British Prime Minister's scientific adviser, of a member of the War Cabinet secretariat, a Mr Butt, to examine some 600 photographs taken by the night bombers in June and July 1941.

The result, on August 18, was the Butt Report, which revealed that matters were far worse than even the sceptics imagined. Only about a quarter of the crews claiming to have reached their targets actually did so, and in raids over the Ruhr, where Bomber Command's major targets under the transport plan were mostly situated, only one bomber in ten dropped its bombs within 5 miles of its target. The problem was thus shown to be not a bomb-aiming problem at all: it was a problem of navigation. Most

Air Marshal Harris conceived the idea of a massive raid on a major German city – a final gamble with a thousand bombers in the air over Germany in a single night

of the crews were failing even to *reach* the target area.

The significance of the change from day bombing to night, and of the long flights over sea and land necessitated by the loss of the French airfields, was at last fully appreciated. The only task that Bomber Command could hope to accomplish at night was the area bombing of cities – and at the moment it was not often capable even of that.

Even more serious for Bomber Command, in the long term, was the discovery in the course of 1941 that fighter defences could not be completely evaded even at night. The German air and ground defences, at first improvised and rudimentary and still a tiny force in terms of pilots and aircraft, were now efficient and well-organised. To reach targets in the Ruhr, British bombers had to make a sea crossing of at least 100 miles, with another 120 miles of occupied territory to cross before they entered the air space of Germany. These defensive advantages were well exploited by General Joseph Kammhuber when he took over the newly-formed German night-fighter division in July 1940. Starting with three coastal fighter zones

in northern, central, and southern Holland, Kammhuber quickly formed a second line of defences to guard the Ruhr, and by 1941 an unbroken line of radar zones stretched right across the Ruhr approaches. In the course of 1941 this line was extended and deepened, so that detours by the bombers to avoid the defences were no longer possible; as the bombers flew across the contiguous radar zones, one night-fighter after another was guided into the attack, and these defences had to be penetrated twice on each sortie – on the way to the target and again on the way back. There remained the formidable flak, searchlight, and night-fighter defences of the main target areas.

These combined defences, although inadequate to meet the developing threat of a concentrated bomber offensive, began to inflict unacceptable losses on the RAF bombers in the summer of 1941, culminating in the destruction of 37 bombers on November 7 – nearly 10% of the total force employed that night. Such casualties, besides being out of all proportion to the potential results, would have wiped out Bomber Command in a matter of weeks, and the result was that the C-in-C was ordered on November 13 to conserve his force, and to build it up for the renewal of the offensive in the spring of 1942. By that time the new radar navigational aid Gee would be available, many more squadrons would have converted from medium to heavy bombers, the Lancaster would be coming into service, and a real chance might exist of damaging targets in Germany without incurring crippling losses.

This policy of conservation was interrupted, towards the end of the year, by renewed calls for attacks on the *Scharnhorst* and *Gneisenau* in Brest.

Bomber Command's weaknesses

Other factors were meanwhile combining to threaten the very existence of Bomber Command. Throughout 1941 the drain to other commands and other theatres had continued: four more squadrons were lent to Coastal Command (a transfer that later became permanent), and the Middle East Air Force was reinforced with both aircraft and crews, largely at Bomber Command's expense. Thus the expansion that had taken place during the year had almost entirely leaked away. The spread of the conflict to global proportions was making increasing demands on British resources and at the same time reducing the flow of arms from America. Overseas defeats and fears of defeat stimulated a further round of demands for the reinforcement of overseas air forces from the British Admiralty and War Office, whose needs were desperate. A bomber offensive which could not be decisive in the foreseeable future was seen as purposeless and a wanton waste if in the meantime the war might be lost elsewhere.

The strongest argument for a British bomber offensive had always been that it was the only means of taking the initiative against Germany; but in the new circumstances obtaining at the close of 1941 it was by no means certain that this argument still held. The whole war situation had become much more complex. With the enormous access of support from Russia, and the tremendous potential of the United States, it was natural that the British government should have its earlier policy under review.

On February 22, 1942, the post of commander-in-chief, Bomber Command, passed to Air Marshal A. T. Harris. The new C-in-C, whose experience of night bombing went back 20 years and who had commanded No. 4 Bomber Group in peacetime and No. 5 Bomber Group for 12 months in wartime, recognised that Bomber Command's chances of being retained as an effective strategic weapon against Germany depended on some early demonstration of its potential power. Otherwise it was doomed to diversion to a variety of other theatres and other tasks.

But the front-line strength of the command was actually less when he took over than it had been two years earlier, although its striking power was increased by its greater bomb-carrying capacity. The Manchester, however, had proved a failure, the Lancaster, developed from it, was only just coming into service, and the Stirling had been a disappointment. The bulk of the command was still equipped with Wellingtons, with only three Halifax squadrons. Thus, in the early months of 1942, the kind of success that might redeem the command's role in British war strategy, and restore its own morale, seemed beyond its grasp.

In pursuing his aim, however, Harris was greatly assisted by two factors: first, a new bombing directive of February 14, 1942, ante-dating his appointment by eight days, authorised him to take up the offensive with the primary object of undermining the morale of the civil population, and especially of the industrial workers. Second, the retreat of the German battle-cruisers from Brest on February 12 had relieved the command of a liability which had absorbed much of its effort in the previous 12 months.

A third factor, of even more importance in the long term, was the introduction, six months before Harris took over, of scientific analysis of the problems affecting night bombing. In August 1941, following the Butt Report, Sir Richard Peirse had asked for the formation of an operational research section at High Wycombe, similar to those already in being at Stanmore and Northwood for Fighter and Coastal Commands. The new section was formed in September 1941 under a scientist named Dr B. G. Dickins, its ultimate purpose being to assist in getting the maximum number of bombers over their targets with the minimum of losses. The lessons of earlier campaigns, and of the German blitz on Britain, were thus incorporated in the tactics of the new offensive.

These tactics would be, first, concentration of the attacking force over a single target in the shortest feasible time-spread, saturating the defences, both active and passive; and second, incendiarism. There was a limit to the damage that could be caused by a given quantity of high explosive, but the German blitz had demonstrated how fire-raising took advantage of the combustible energy within the target itself to spread the area of destruction. Essential to both these concepts was the new radar aid Gee, with which, when Harris took over, between 100 and 150 bombers—about a third of the force—were equipped. These bombers were to be used as an incendiary force, to identify and mark the targets; but complete concentration could not be achieved until the whole force was Gee-equipped.

The Gee campaign opened on March 8, 1942, with the first of a series of raids on Essen, and a complementary technique, involving the use of a flare-dropping force to lead the raid and a target-marking force using incendiaries to follow up, was em-

ployed. The intention was to produce a concentrated area of fire in the centre of the target into which the bombers not equipped with Gee could aim their high explosives. The limitations of this technique were shown in the next few weeks in eight major attacks on Essen, all involving between 100 and 200 bombers: only one bomb in 20 fell within 5 miles of the town.

Essen, powerfully defended and nearly always partly obscured by industrial haze, was the hardest of all area targets to find, but damage everywhere in this period was scanty and scattered, and it was apparent that defences were not being saturated by this scale of attack. Gee could not solve the problem of target recognition unaided, and the bomber force was still much too small.

The best prospect of early success seemed

General Kammhuber took over Germany's night-fighters in July 1940. By 1941 an unbroken line of radar zones stretched right across the approaches to the Ruhr

to lie in fire-raising raids by moonlight against medium-sized targets—important but not vital—where concentration could be achieved and where the defences were not strong enough to escape saturation. The target chosen for the initial experiment was Lübeck, a town the core of which occupied an island site on a river, easily recognisable by moonlight. Because of its age and the congestion of its buildings it was also highly combustible. The raid was carried out by 234 bombers on the night of March 28, 1942, carrying 300 tons of high explosives (including 17 4,000-pounders) and many thousands of incendiaries. For the British it was a resounding success, proving that in conditions of full moon and good visibility a fire blitz by a medium-sized force could knock out a carefully chosen target at small cost.

In releasing an account of the Lübeck raid, the Air Ministry was more outspoken than was usual at this time. The normal pattern of its bulletins would be an announcement that a certain target had been attacked, a description of the target in terms of size and importance, stressing the chief indus-

trial features, and then a list of the specific objectives of an industrial and military nature that were claimed by the bombers as hit. It would then give a description of the raid in a general way. The fact that the town itself had suffered damage and destruction in the course of the raid was often included, but it was not disclosed that, because of the bombers' inability to hit specific targets, this general damage had been the major aim.

The Lübeck raid, however, mounted to test the theories of incendiarism, inevitably fell largely on the civil population, and the Air Ministry bulletin, while carefully parading the military importance of Lübeck as a shipping, submarine, and communication centre, did not shirk mention of the very extensive damage done to the city itself. 'Crews reported fires of great violence and size in the main city area and spreading rapidly,' said the bulletin.

Still no major victory
A month later, in a series of four moonlight raids on Rostock, the experiment was repeated, and this time the area bombing was accompanied by pinpoint attacks on the Heinkel factory on the outskirts of the town, a pattern which was to become standard procedure in an attempt to get the best of both worlds. But much as these raids encouraged the British and shocked the Germans, neither target was a heavily defended industrial centre vital to the German war machine. Two more raids on Essen, on much the same scale as the raid on Lübeck, failed to achieve a comparable concentration, and similar raids on Hamburg and Dortmund were equally disappointing.

Bomber Command had still to demonstrate its ability to inflict serious damage on important and well-defended targets in Germany, and against such targets it had become obvious that a force of 250 bombers could not break down resistance or produce any great degree of devastation. Thus Bomber Command remained without a major victory, and apparently without the means to achieve one.

Yet the necessity for such a victory was becoming, for Bomber Command, more pressing than ever. Disasters in the Far East and setbacks in the Middle East cried out against the continued hoarding of aircraft in the United Kingdom. In the east the Germans were about to develop a spring offensive aimed at overrunning the Caucasus, gaining possession of Russia's main oil supply, and simultaneously opening the way for a link-up with Rommel's advancing Afrika Korps and for the domination of the entire Middle East. Supplies for Rommel's armies were pouring across the Mediterranean, and the only prospect of stopping them seemed to be by massive air intervention. Above all, the entire strategic situation turned on the supply of shipping; in the first two months of 1942, 117 Allied ships totalling over 750,000 tons were sunk in the Atlantic—the heaviest losses of the war so far. The case for applying every unit of air power to avert defeat seemed overwhelming, and the main pressure, as always, fell on Bomber Command. Everywhere the call was for more bombers.

It was in this atmosphere that Air Marshal Harris and his senior air staff officer, Air Vice-Marshal Saundby, aware that if the bombers were once transferred they would never be returned and might never be replaced, conceived the idea of a massive raid on a major German city, something into which they would throw the whole of their front-line strength and all their reserves in what might be a final gamble. The aim of this gamble would be to strike a political and military blow whose effect would be to preserve the one offensive weapon without which they believed the war would never be won—the strategic air offensive against Germany. This was the raid to be known as the 'Thousand Plan'.

It was Harris who first conceived the idea of putting a thousand bombers over Germany in a single night: he mentioned it to Saundby early in May 1942, hardly imagining that it might be possible. In the next few days Saundby checked the figures with many stations and units and was eventually able to report back to Harris that, given the right support, something might be done.

In Bomber Command in May 1942 there were 37 medium- and heavy-bomber squadrons, made up as follows: 16 Wellington squadrons, six Halifax squadrons, six Lancaster squadrons (two of which were still partly equipped with Manchesters), five Stirling squadrons, and two Manchester and two Hampden squadrons. Allowing for an average rate of unserviceability, this gave a front-line strength of about 400 aircraft. Four other squadrons, all Whitleys, were on temporary transfer to Coastal Command, and if these squadrons could be returned for the raid, the total would be close to 450. If operations were suspended for 48 hours to give the ground crews time to work on unserviceable aircraft, a maximum serviceability state might be reached in which virtually 100% of front-line strength would be available. This would bring the total, from 41 squadrons, to approximately 500 aircraft.

All the new heavy-bomber squadrons had their own conversion flights, and if the aircraft in these flights were added, together with the established conversion units, the figure would be nearer 550. If all suitable Coastal Command aircraft could also be called upon—the Hampdens, Beauforts, and Hudsons—and if the Bomber and Coastal operational training units could be drawn on, using instructor crews, the Thousand Plan could become a reality.

But was such a concentration of aircraft over a single target feasible? Clearly there were certain pre-requisites: it would take time to assemble the force, which meant a break in operations of several days; the target must be an easily recognisable one; good weather was essential; so was a full moon. The problems of concentration would certainly be simplified by Gee, but none of the conversion and training aircraft was Gee-equipped, so a similar technique would be needed to that used at Lübeck and Rostock, the Gee-equipped aircraft going in first to mark the aiming point. Whether it was physically possible to put a thousand aircraft over the same target in so short a space of time as one hour, the period envisaged, was just the sort of question that the scientists and statisticians of the operational research section were established to answer, and Harris passed it on.

The compression of the bomb pattern and the saturation of the defences, which were the objects of concentration, would be pointless if the result was that losses increased through mid-air collisions; but, from their studies of earlier raids, the scientists were able to build up a picture of the density of

A Halifax takes off for Germany. The plan to bomb Cologne with over 1,000 bombers called for an unprecedented concentration of aircraft over the target. But on the night of the raid—despite some confusion and the refusal of some crews to leave the city till they had watched the extensive fires—there were only two collisions

aircraft over a given target at any one moment, and they were thus able to estimate the likely spread of the proposed force in time and space and calculate the collision risk. Their final estimate, based on three main assumptions—that the span of the raid would be increased to 90 minutes, that three separate aiming-points would be chosen, and that heights would be staggered—was that collisions would be unlikely to exceed one per hour.

The staggering of heights raised the fear that aircraft might find themselves bombing each other, but this risk too was investigated and pronounced negligible.

Convinced that the raid was at least feasible, Harris went to see Portal, who asked for a workable plan, warning Harris at the same time that the raid might attract reprisals and that the Chiefs-of-Staff would have to be convinced of its usefulness. To forestall political opposition, Harris then went to see Churchill, who was enthusiastic, and the only doubt that remained was the choice of target. Churchill wanted Essen, as the biggest of all military targets. Harris wanted Hamburg, as the most combustible of major targets and therefore potentially the one where the greatest destruction might be wrought and the greatest impact made. The operational research section, however, advised that the force should stay within Gee range and go to Cologne. Essen was ruled out because of the great difficulty of locating aiming-points beneath the haze, and the final choice was left between Cologne and Hamburg, to be decided on the night according to the state of the weather.

On Monday, May 18, Harris went to Portal with details of the workable plan Portal had asked for, and two days later, on May 20, he received Portal's final approval.

Cologne: the guinea-pig
On the same day Harris wrote to Coastal, Fighter, and Army Co-operation Commands and to the five bomber groups and the two training groups, giving details of the plan and asking for a maximum contribution to it. From Coastal Command Harris hoped for a total of 250 aircraft. From Fighter Command and No 2 Group of Bomber Command he asked for intruder attacks on German night-fighter airfields, fighter sweeps over the North Sea to protect the bombers, and special air/sea rescue patrols. In his letter he stated his clear intention of annihilating one of Germany's main industrial centres by fire. There were no euphemisms about factories and military targets. The city of Cologne (or Hamburg) was to be wiped out in one night.

The final operation order was issued on May 26. The raid was to take place on the night of May 27/28 or any night thereafter up to the night of May 31/June 1, by which time the moon would be on the wane. This gave a possible margin, to allow for bad weather, of five days.

Sir Philip Joubert, C-in-C of Coastal Command, had meanwhile promised the 250 aircraft, but had then been overruled by the Admiralty, who sensed the political implications of the raid and ordered that Coastal Command, for whom they were operationally responsible, were not in any circumstances to take part. This, after the initial reaction of the First Sea Lord, was a bitter blow to Harris, bringing his thousand-plus down to about 800.

The defection of Coastal Command had not been entirely unforeseen by either Harris or Saundby, and they set to work to make good the deficiency. By a further comb-out of aircraft, and by making up their minds on a decision they had been reluctant to take, to employ pupil as well as instructor crews, they brought the figure up to 940. Thus to the already considerable hazards were added the requisitioning of every possible aircraft and the employment of pupil crews.

Now came the final frustration—the weather. On the morning of May 27, Harris went down to the underground operations room at High Wycombe for his daily planning conference. Waiting for him were Saundby and his air staff officers, together with Magnus T. Spence, who, as Harris's meteorological specialist, now became his most valued counsellor.

Thundery conditions and heavy cloud

existed over most of Germany, and Harris was forced to postpone the operation for 24 hours. The same thing happened on Thursday the 28th, and again on Friday May 29. Two more nights and the moon would be on the wane. But as the week drew to a close the tally of aircraft mounted, until, on the morning of Saturday, May 30, the total was well over four figures. The Thousand Plan, on paper at least, was a reality.

That morning Spence reported the first signs all week of an improvement in the weather. Thundery conditions were persisting, and Hamburg was still under a blanket of cloud, but there was a chance—a 50-50 chance, according to Spence—that the cloud in the Cologne area would clear by midnight.

To Harris it looked very much like the last chance for Bomber Command. If he waited another month, strategic and political decisions which threatened to break up the force might well have been implemented. Conscious of the decisive influence of the weather on all military and naval adventures, and aware of the penalties that follow when armadas fail, he took the decision to dispatch the force that night to Cologne.

In a personal message to his group and station commanders Harris urged that the whole future course and strategy of the war might be altered by the raid. Calculations from British experience of German attacks, he told them, showed that if the force could reach its objective and bomb it accurately, the weight of the attack would be sufficient to destroy it as an industrial centre and to spread apprehension, despair, and panic throughout Germany. 'At best,' he wrote, 'the result may bring the war to a more or less abrupt conclusion owing to the enemy's unwillingness to accept the worst that must befall him increasingly as our bomber force and that of the United States of America build up. At worst it must have the most dire moral and material effect on the enemy's war effort as a whole and force him to withdraw vast forces from his exterior aggressions for his own protection.'

By 1700 hours Spence had forecast that conditions over the bases at take-off would be clear except for local thunderstorms. Thick cloud was likely up to 15,000 feet along the route to Cologne, with more thunderstorms, and the icing index would be high, but conditions would tend to improve for the return flight. Over Cologne itself the cloud would begin to disperse by midnight, and large breaks were hoped for in the target area. Visibility would deteriorate over eastern England during the night, but only about a quarter of the bases would be affected.

A small miscalculation, either about the time or extent of the cloud dispersion over Cologne or the timing of the deterioration over the bases, could still wreck the raid. But Harris did not rescind his order.

At 1800 hours, at 53 different bases scattered down eastern England and across the Midlands, the briefing of the crews began. The tension in the briefing rooms, already heightened by the awareness that something unusual was planned, broke into an uproar of enthusiasm when the scope of the raid was revealed.

The bombers were routed from their bases to the Dutch coast via East Anglia. Those actually based in East Anglia were no more than 300 miles from the target. Others, in Yorkshire and the Midlands, were more than 400. The Dutch coast would be crossed south

of Rotterdam, and the route across Holland and into Germany would touch good pinpoints at Eindhoven and München Gladbach. Crews were recommended to pick out the Rhine north of the target and follow it into Cologne. After bombing they were to steer south-south-west for 20 minutes to Euskirchen, then turn for home on a track parallel to their outward track.

The leading crews of the Gee-equipped squadrons of No. 1 and 3 Groups—Stirlings and Wellingtons—were to comprise the incendiary force. These were the 'pathfinders', though they were not yet styled as such. Their aiming-point was to be the Neumarkt, in the centre of the old town, and the success of the raid would depend on their accuracy. Starting at 0055 hours, they would have the target to themselves for 15 minutes. Succeeding aircraft would aim either a mile to the north or a mile to the south of the Neumarkt, spreading the area of devastation. For an hour after the initial marking period the target would be bombed by the main force of aircraft—the Stirling, Manchester, Wellington, and Hampden squadrons and the aircraft of the training groups; the Lancasters and the Halifaxes would bomb in the final 15 minutes.

The first aircraft to take off, at 2230 that evening, were the outriders of the incendiary force, the Stirlings of No. 15 Squadron, based at Wyton in Huntingdonshire. But on their way across the North Sea they were overtaken by the Blenheims, the Bostons, the Havocs, and the long-range Hurricanes of the intruder force, bound for the German night-fighter airfields that lay in the path of the bombers. Some 88 aircraft, including 50 Blenheims, took part in these operations, bombing airfields and attacking what few German fighters they saw. But these raids, hampered by low cloud, did not succeed in grounding or seriously inconveniencing the German fighters. The intruder force suffered from the same inadequacies as had frustrated the main British bomber force so far: no navigation or bombing aids, dispersed targets that were difficult to find and even harder to put out of action, inadequate weapons, inadequate numbers. The bombers would still have to fight their way through to Cologne.

Cologne: triumph and tragedy
Across the North Sea and central Holland the crews of the incendiary force flew above a blanket of thundery cloud. It was not until they were approaching the German border, about 60 miles from Cologne, that the long tongue of cloud was suddenly withdrawn, discovering the ground in great clarity under the floodlight of the rising moon. Magnus T. Spence had been right.

The first crews to break through the Kammhuber Line made their approach towards the city at 15,000 feet from almost due west. At this early stage there was no collision risk, and contrary to their briefing they got their pinpoint south of the city and then turned north, with the Rhine to their right. Ahead of them were the two central bridges, first the Hindenbergbrücke, then the Hohenzollernbrücke. A mile due west of the first bridge was their aiming-point, in the centre of the old town. Below them the intense moonlight was throwing the old city into braille-like relief. Individual streets could be traced their entire length, honeycombed with buildings, while railways ploughed their furrows round the city and in one instance probed deep into the old town

before passing the cathedral and swinging east across the Hohenzollernbrücke. The crews were looking down on a sight that might never be seen again—the intricate fretwork of the old city of Cologne.

The defences as yet were uncertain, and the first few crews dropped their bombs almost unopposed. Their sticks of incendiaries, 4- and 30-pounders, were right on target.

On the ground in Cologne, the sirens had sounded half an hour earlier. The population was accustomed to aerial bombardment; this was their 105th air raid of the war. At first they stood about in little groups in the streets, waiting to see if it was a false alarm. Then came the first thin rumble of aircraft engines, growing in volume every minute. Hundreds of searchlights quartered the sky, hundreds of guns fired almost simultaneously. While the citizens of Cologne hurried into their cellars, or into the vast air-raid shelters that had been constructed for them, the civil defence and fire-fighting forces, uniformed and volunteer, made ready.

As the first Stirlings turned for home, dummy fires sprang up outside the city; but the target was still so brilliantly illuminated by the moon, with the Rhine snaking through the middle, that the air crews could not be misled. At the end of the first 15 minutes the centre of the old city was ablaze and a column of smoke was pouring skywards.

The main force of bombers, together with the instructor and pupil crews, was now converging on the target. Some crews bombed from under 10,000 feet, unable to climb any higher; others crossed the target at more than 17,000. The experience of individual crews differed widely, even those at the same height and with roughly the same time on target; some were hotly engaged by searchlights and flak, others believed that the defences had already been swamped. In fact, the ground defences were confused and over-strained, and much of the firing was haphazard, a barrage for its own sake. Searchlights found difficulty in concentrating on individual aircraft, but when they did, the flak co-operated well.

Little fighter opposition was encountered in the target area, but across Holland and Belgium and the German border the fighter pilots were energetic and numerous. Every two or three minutes a bomber burst into flames and went down.

Many of the crews, unable to break the habits of independence, were making their bombing runs direct, according to their direction of approach to the target, converging from all directions and thus increasing the collision risk. Others, after dropping their bombs, were so attracted by the sight of the burning city, with extensive fires on both sides of the river, and cathedral and bridges illuminated, that they circled the city to take it all in. Yet the light remained so brilliant that collisions were rare; there were only two incidents of collision over the target throughout the raid: they accounted for four bombers lost.

Meanwhile the people of Cologne were undergoing the inevitable succession of miraculous escapes and tragic misfortunes that were characteristic of the aerial bombardment of a great city. Thousands of fires had taken hold and the whole city shook continually with the blast from the growing weight of high-explosive as the heavy bombers went in. Tens of thousands of people were crowding the aid centres, many of them already evacuated from the blitzed

. . . an unpleasant
reminder of Nazi
miscalculation
—and of growing
Allied power

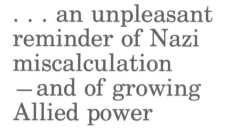

◁ A Halifax comes home: of the 1,046 bombers which took off for Cologne, about 910 reached and bombed the target—but 39 were lost, representing a loss rate of 4%. ▷ Four months after the raid, barges were still clearing rubble from Cologne's dockyard area *(top left)*. Members of a Stirling bomber crew *(top right)* watch while the rear-gun turret is mended. *In colour:* Stirlings in flight: the first RAF aircraft over the target

Imperial War Museum

areas, others bombed out. Water mains in all areas had been breached, power and telephone cables torn up, gas mains punctured. Seventeen major rail centres were reporting severe damage: railway stations, goods depots, locomotives, trucks, and rails were wrecked. Bombs fell with grim impartiality on factories, industrial estates, empty city offices, crowded hospitals, empty churches, hastily abandoned homes, and crowded shelters. Even so, prompt action by individual and group self-protection forces and industrial civil defence units prevented many fires from developing.

All the time the tale of human tragedy and dramatic rescue went on. Hundreds of people were trapped in cellars; scores had already been killed or suffocated in this way. In one cellar where 150 people were trapped, a high-explosive bomb penetrated the cellar ceiling but miraculously did not explode. Rescue work was intensified and the shelterers, women and children among them, had just been evacuated when the bomb went off. Not all incidents had such a merciful ending.

The crews in the final wave of heavy bombers picked out the target by the glow in the sky from a hundred miles distant. The ground defences were badly disorganised by this time, but the fighters were still active.

It seemed, as the raid drew to a close, as though a single immense fire were raging in central Cologne, throwing up a spiral of smoke to 15,000 feet, with hundreds of smaller fires towards the perimeter. Buildings, when recognisable as such, were mostly skeletons in the midst of fires. The frame-work of white-hot joists was visible at high-altitude; aircraft at a lower height could be seen against the flames.

At 0400 hours that morning, long before the last of the bombers had landed back at their bases, a Mosquito took off to photograph the target at first light, but when it reached Cologne a huge pall of smoke covered the city and it was impossible to get photographs. When at last, nearly a

week later, satisfactory photographs could be taken, the damage revealed was on a far greater scale than anything yet seen in a German city. Some 600 acres—including 300 acres in the centre of the city—had been completely destroyed, nearly as much as the total estimated area of destruction by bombing in Germany up till then.

In spite of extensive damage to factories and industrial buildings, and to rail and other public services, throttling the life of the city for many days, the main weight of the attack had inevitably fallen on the civil population in their homes; 13,000 homes were completely destroyed, 6,000 badly damaged, and over 45,000 people rendered homeless. Past experience, good shelters, and the energetic work of the civil defence forces had combined to keep casualties down, but even so they were heavy, more than in any other raid on Germany up to that time. The total was just over 5,000, of whom 469 were killed.

Cologne, however, had not been destroyed, and the main lesson of the raid was that the destruction of German industry and industrial life was not yet within the power of Bomber Command, and that to achieve conclusive results a massive expansion of the bomber force would be necessary, together with improved aids to target-finding and bomb-aiming. The industrial life of Cologne had been paralysed for a week and seriously inconvenienced for from three to six months, but in time it would recover from a raid that was far beyond Bomber Command's normal capacity, delivered on a specially chosen target in exceptional weather. Thus with the weapons and means available to the RAF at this time, large German industrial areas were virtually indestructible.

Of the 1,046 bombers which took off for Cologne, about 910 reached and bombed the target, and 39 were lost. Most of these fell to night-fighters, which retained their effectiveness in spite of the weight of the attack. The loss rate, about 4% of the

effective force, was about as much as the command could withstand over a period. If the raid provoked the heavy reinforcement of German home fighter strength which had been one of its objects, an unacceptable loss rate might follow.

The Cologne raid had failed to support some of Harris's more ambitious claims ('an abrupt conclusion to the war' and 'spread despair . . . throughout Germany'), but a convincing demonstration had been given of what might be achieved if the strength of Bomber Command were doubled and trebled. Serious damage had been done in the short term to the industrial capacity of Germany's fourth largest city, and although the German leaders were satisfied that raids of such strength would for the present be infrequent, they feared the damage, moral and material, that such raids could do and looked forward to the time when they would once again be able to concentrate their air power in the west. The blow to morale would be absorbed, but the raid had provided an unpleasant reminder of Nazi miscalculation and of growing Allied power.

To judge the raid on its immediate material and moral results, however, would be to ignore its main purposes, which were strategic and political; and political vindication, at least, was not long in coming. 'This proof of the growing power of the British bomber force,' wrote Churchill in a signal to Harris that was published after the raid, 'is also the herald of what Germany will receive, city by city, from now on.' It was this unequivocal declaration of the British government's intention of prosecuting a bomber offensive against Germany's principal cities, no matter how hard pressed the Allies might be in other theatres, which, for Bomber Command, justified the gamble.

For the first time in the war so far, Britain stood in the role of attacker, Germany of defender. It remained for attacker and defender to evaluate the lessons of the raid, and to adjust their plans accordingly.

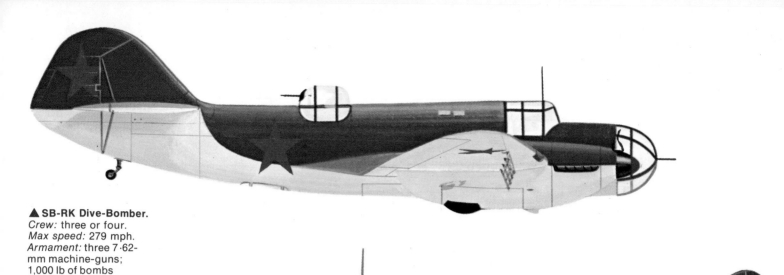

▲ SB-RK Dive-Bomber.
Crew: three or four.
Max speed: 279 mph.
Armament: three 7·62-
mm machine-guns;
1,000 lb of bombs

NEW WEAPONS
FOR THE RED AIR FORCE

During the first eight hours of 'Barbarossa' in June
1941, the Red Air Force had lost over 1,200 aircraft.
But reinforcements were rushed from the east;
and by September the Red Air Force—under
General Novikov, its new leader—began to assert
itself. The new aircraft were equal, or superior, to the
older Luftwaffe designs, but they were in perilously
short supply at first.

Petlyakov Pe-2 ▲
Designed as a light
bomber, the Pe-2
performed a wide
variety of duties. It
had good range and
a useful armament
for close-support
roles, and it also
served as a night-
fighter. **Max speed:**
335 mph. **Range:**
1,200 miles. **Crew:**
two. **Armament:** one
12·7-mm and four
7·62-mm machine-
guns; 2,200 lb of
bombs

Sturmovik Il-2 ▼
This ground-attack and
close-support aircraft w
probably the Red Air
Force's most famous
plane. The Sturmovik
was the German Stuka'
opposite number, and
built up an excellent
record of strafing grou
targets—especially with
rocket projectiles. **Max
speed:** 257 mph. **Crew
Armament:** two 20-mm
cannon, one 12·7-mm,
7·62-mm machine-guns
880 lb of bombs OR
eight 56-lb rocket-
projectiles

▼ Il–4 Medium Bomber.
Crew: four. *Max speed:*
265 mph. *Armament:*
three 7·62-mm machine-
guns; 3,350 lb of
bombs

Hawker Hurricane 11Cs

These were shipped out in the Arctic convoys and arrived in Russia long before they were first delivered to the hard-pressed RAF fighter squadrons in the Far East. Their cannon were invaluable for the tank-busting role. **Max speed:** 329 mph. **Max range:** 520 miles. **Armament:** four 20-mm Hispano or Oerlikon cannon

NEW STRENGTH IN THE AIR

Russia's aircraft production shared top priority with her armour and artillery, and by the end of the first year of the war her aeronautical designers had turned out 14 new types of aircraft and 10 new engines. So effective was the industry's success that a German general was forced to admit: 'After 1943 it was no longer possible to upset the enemy's absolute control in the air.' And at least a part of the credit had to go to Britain, who supplied the Soviet Union with over 3,000 aircraft in the first year of Russia's war alone

Yakovlev Yak-1

The first of Russia's modern monoplane fighters, this was also the first in the series of Yakovlev's celebrated fighter designs. **Max speed:** 364 mph. **Range:** 435 miles. **Armament:** one 20-mm cannon; two 7.62-mm machine-guns: six rocket projectiles

MiG-3

This represented an intermediate phase in Russian fighter design: production ended in November 1941 in favour of superior designs, such as the YAK-1. Although fast, the MiG-3 lacked both the taut manoeuvrability and the high fire-power of the Luftwaffe's FW-190s and Me-109s. **Max speed:** 360 mph. **Armament:** two .50 and two .30 machine-guns

SU-2 (BB-1)

A two-seat fighter-bomber and ground-attack aircraft. As such, it was overshadowed by the 1-2 Sturmovik's prowess, but as an interesting experiment in ground-attack design. **Max speed:** 298 mph. **Armament:** four fixed machine-guns

John Batchelor

Pearl Harbor:

THE ATTACK

Oahu, Hawaii, December 7, 1941   *Captain Donald Macintyre*

The Pearl Harbor air-strike was an act of ruthless, machine-like destruction: never before had air power virtually wiped out an enemy fleet in one action. True, the Japanese victory was not quite complete: two American aircraft-carriers of the Pacific Fleet escaped to play a vital role in the months ahead. But the main Japanese triumph was unalterable: after Pearl Harbor there could be no immediate American challenge to the Japanese battle fleet

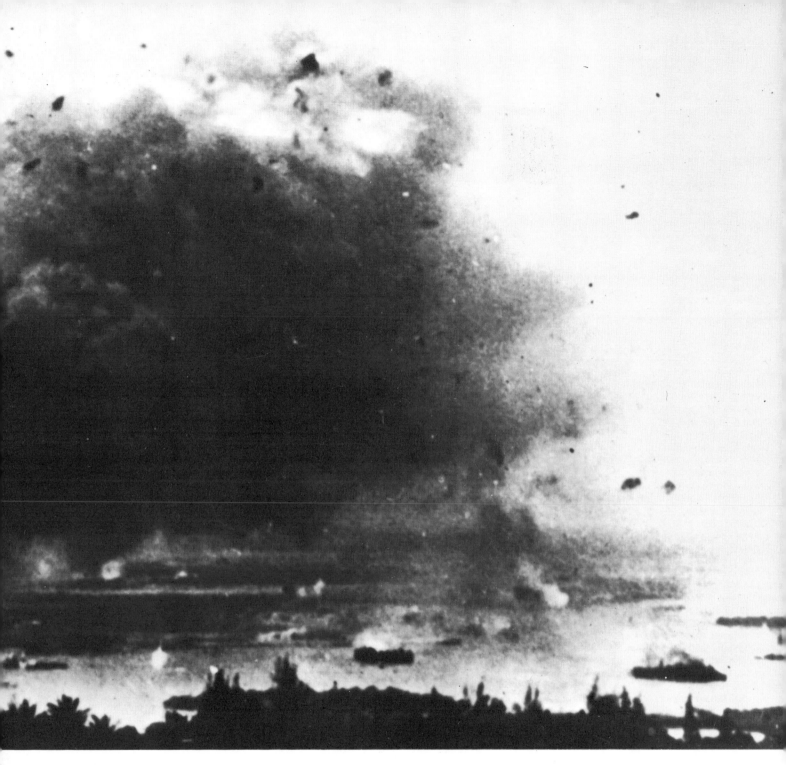

In the original Japanese war plan, the complex multi-pronged southward drive by expeditionary forces to capture Thailand, Malaya, the Philippines, and the Dutch East Indies was to be covered by the whole Imperial Navy. The United States Pacific Fleet, envisaged as hurrying towards the Philippine Sea to the rescue, was to be harried by air and submarine attacks launched from the Marshall and Caroline Islands, before being brought to action by the superior Japanese Main Fleet.

Early in 1941, however, critical eyes had been brought to bear on this plan by the C-in-C of the Japanese Fleet, Admiral Isoroku Yamamoto. Unlike the military faction led by General Tojo, Yamamoto saw clearly that—though the well-prepared Japanese war machine would be able to carry all before it in the initial stages of such a plan—the immense industrial potential of the United States must eventually bring it to a halt. When that time came, a negotiated, compromise peace would be possible only if

Japan had so firmly established herself in her newly-won empire in south-east Asia that eviction would be an insuperable task for the Western Allies. For this, time was needed. Yamamoto wished to gain this time by eliminating the US Pacific Fleet.

An early convert to the decisive role of carrier-borne air power in naval warfare, he had the perfect weapon to his hand in the shape of the six fleet carriers equipped with the most advanced naval aircraft in the world. Rear-Admiral Takijiro Onishi, Chief-of-Staff of the shore-based XI Air Fleet, was instructed to examine the possibility of a carrier-borne air attack on Pearl Harbor. Onishi recruited the best-known hero of such operations in the China War, Commander Minoru Genda. By May 1941, working in great secrecy, Genda had completed a study which promised success—provided that all six fleet aircraft-carriers were committed and complete secrecy imposed.

Put before the Chief of the Naval General Staff, Admiral Nagano, the plan was turned

down on the grounds that the aircraft-carriers were required for the southwards drive, and that an operation depending absolutely on surprise at the end of an ocean passage of 3,400 miles was too much of a gamble. Nevertheless, confident that Nagano's objections would be overcome in time, Yamamoto gave orders for a special training programme to be begun by his carrier air squadrons, concentrating on torpedo, dive-bombing, and high-level bombing attacks on targets in enclosed stretches of water such as Kagoshima Bay in southern Kyushu. Except for a handful of staff officers engaged with Genda in preparing the detailed plan, the object of these practices was revealed to no one.

Technicians at the main naval base of Yokosuka were given the task of adapting airborne torpedoes so that they could be dropped from a greater height than normal and still enter the water in a horizontal attitude, thus avoiding diving deeply at the beginning of their run. The need for such a

Japan's Naval Strike Aircraft

Mitsubishi A6M2 Zero-sen (Zeke)
The Zero outclassed every Allied fighter in the Pacific in December 1941. Light and manoeuvrable, it had a high fire-power, and could also act in a fighter/bomber role. **Max speed:** 351 mph. **Max range:** 975 miles. **Armament:** two 20-mm cannon, and two 7·7-mm machine-guns

Aichi D3A2 (Val)
The *Val* carried home the Japanese dive-bombing attacks at Pearl Harbor. It had been designed in imitation of the pre-war German dive-bombers, and was Japan's first low-wing, all-metal monoplane dive-bomber. **Max speed:** 266 mph. **Max range:** 970 mi. **Bomb load:** 816 lb.

Nakajima B5N2 (Kate)
At the time of Pearl Harbor, the *Kate* was Japan's principal torpedo-bomber, and could also serve as a level bomber. **Max speed:** 235 mph. **Max range:** 1,400 miles. **Weapon load:** one 1,764-lb torpedo

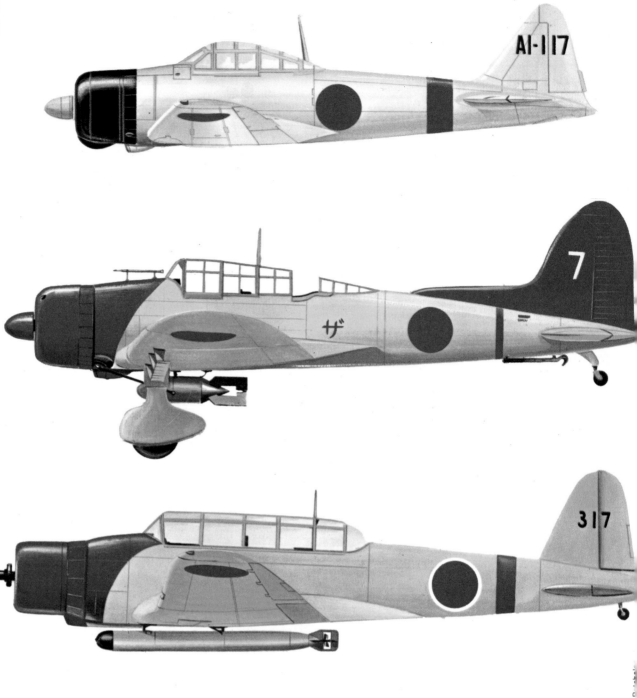

refinement was not revealed; but by September, torpedoes fitted with special fins which would enable them to be effectively launched in the narrow, shallow waters of Pearl Harbor had been successfully tested and production was being feverishly pressed ahead to meet a deadline in mid-November.

The withdrawal of the Japanese aircraft-carriers to home waters resulted in a cessation of radio messages intercepted by the radio traffic analysis units in Hawaii and Manila. The Japanese carrier-force was for a time 'lost' to the American trackers. These correctly assessed the reason and in due course the aircraft-carriers came on the air again; but the accuracy of this appraisal was to lead to a similar and, this time, faulty assumption later.

The Konoye Cabinet fell on October 16, the new Prime Minister being the aggressive General Tojo. Alarm signals, announcing a 'grave situation' went out from Washington to Admiral Kimmel and General Short — heads of the navy and the army commands

in Hawaii. But now these reports were tempered by the continuing Washington belief that an attack on Russia's maritime provinces was the most probable Japanese move. The fact that the Japanese navy had, as long ago as July, finally won the long argument with the army with regard to war plans, and that the southward drive had been agreed upon, had escaped the US Intelligence organisations.

So far as General Short was concerned, this appreciation greatly reduced the probability of any attack on US territory. He was more concerned with the presence of a large local Japanese population in Hawaii and the need to take precautions against sabotage and subversion.

The possibility of an air attack if and when war should break out had been perfunctorily considered, and occasional drills on a peace-time footing had been concerted with the navy. They had not been very impressive. A few primitive, mobile radar sets had been arriving since August and had been set up

at various points round the coast of Oahu. They suffered many teething troubles and breakdowns. Communications between them and a temporary control centre, and between the control centre and the various commands, was by means of the public telephone system. Operators both of the radar sets and at the control centre were to a large degree untrained or inexperienced; the various units were manned only for a few hours each day, principally for training purposes.

Nevertheless, progress towards efficiency seemed adequate to the general who had informed Admiral Kimmel as long ago as August that the aircraft warning system was 'rapidly nearing completion'.

To the navy, however, both in Washington and Hawaii, the new situation seemed more fraught with threatening possibilities. Although a Japanese attack on Russia was considered the most likely, an attack on the United States or Great Britain was by no means ruled out, and the Pacific Fleet was ordered to take 'due precautions including

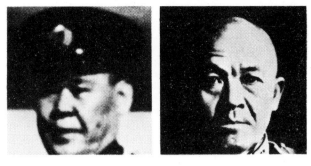

◁ Admiral Kimmel, US Navy commander at Pearl Harbor (far left). General Short, the US Army commander there

▷ Admiral Nagano, Chief of the Japanese Naval General Staff (left). Admiral Nagumo, commander of the Japanese carrier force

such preparatory deployments as will not disclose strategic intention nor constitute provocative actions against Japan'.

In case of hostile action by Japan against US merchant shipping, all vessels in the western Pacific were ordered to make for friendly ports. Instructed to 'take all practical precautions' for the safety of airfields at Wake and Midway (the air staging posts on the route to the Philippines), Kimmel dispatched reinforcements of marines, stores, and ammunition to both islands and stationed additional patrol planes there. Extra precautions were also taken against surprise submarine attack in the exercise areas.

The idea of an air attack on Pearl Harbor or its defences appears to have crossed nobody's mind.

Objective: Pearl Harbor

At about this time, aboard the Japanese aircraft-carrier *Akagi,* flagship of Vice-Admiral Chuichi Nagumo, commanding the Fast Carrier Striking Force, a scale model of Pearl Harbor was unveiled under the eyes of the assembled officer pilots of the air groups and of Yamamoto himself. Now, under seal of secrecy, Yamamoto gave them the electrifying news of their intended objective. Training was thereafter resumed at an even fiercer intensity and with added enthusiasm. On November 1 the C-in-C issued the basic operation order, naming Sunday, December 7 (Hawaiian time) as the day of destiny. Two days later Admiral Nagano was at last won over to give his consent.

Between November 10/18, singly or in pairs, the ships of Nagumo's striking force —six aircraft-carriers, two battleships, three cruisers, nine destroyers, and eight oil tankers—slipped away from their anchorages and, by devious routes, steered for a secret rendezvous in the desolate Tankan Bay on Etorofu, the largest of the Kurile Islands far to the north. Strict radio silence was imposed on all from the moment of sailing while the remainder of the fleet at Kure in the Inland Sea kept up a flow of radio messages for the benefit of American radio intelligence.

At about this time, too, and with the same secrecy, 16 submarines of the 'Advanced Expeditionary Force' left harbour and headed eastwards across the wide Pacific. Five of them carried two-man, midget submarines charged with the task of penetrating Pearl Harbor simultaneously with the air attack. The remainder, besides scouting for the carrier force, were expected to find opportunities for attacking any American ships that escaped seawards.

Signs of some impending major Japanese operation were not lacking in Hawaii or Washington. On November 1 the radio traffic analysis unit had reported that all call-signs of Japanese naval units had been changed. In itself, this was not of outstanding significance: change of call-signs from time to time was a normal procedure. But a second change only a month later, on December 1, could only be an indication of preparations for active operations.

In the interval the radio traffic analysis organisation had managed to re-identify a certain number of units, but had lost all contact with the Japanese aircraft-carriers. Relying upon previous correct assumptions on similar occasions, they decided that the latter were in home waters of the Inland Sea.

From the other source of radio intelligence, the 'Purple' diplomatic code, information of a different sort was obtained, information which, if examined alongside the results of traffic analysis, must have been seen to be of the most sinister import. From November 5 onwards, message after message to the Japanese envoys in Washington warned them that the 25th was a deadline for a successful outcome of their negotiations. On the 22nd, Tokyo extended the deadline to the 29th after which, they said, 'things will automatically begin to happen'. Meanwhile, each side conveyed to the other its final terms for a settlement, the Japanese on the 20th, the Americans on the 26th: neither set of terms was conceivably acceptable by both sides and only deadlock was achieved.

So, by the last week of November, negotiations had finally broken down. War was now clearly imminent; but as the Americans were bound to avoid being the first to open fire, or even to take any provocative action, choice of time and place lay in the hands of the Japanese. Intelligence sources, the deciphering system in particular, had to be relied upon to give advance warning. A steady flow of intelligence had, indeed, been reaching the American government and service chiefs, which clearly indicated preliminary Japanese moves for some southwards expedition.

On November 24 American naval commanders abroad were warned that a 'surprise aggressive move in any direction including attack on Philippines and Guam is a possibility'. Three days later a signal from the Chief of Naval Operations opened with the ominous phrase: 'This dispatch is to be considered a war warning,' and went on to list the possible Japanese objectives as 'either the Philippines, Thai or Kra Peninsula or possibly Borneo.' The Hawaiian Islands or even Wake and Midway were not mentioned.

The day before this signal was sent, from the cold windswept waters of Tankan Bay the anchors of Admiral Nagumo's ships had been weighed to rise, streaming mud and water, and thud home in the hawse pipes. A flurry of white foam round the ships' sterns as their screws pointed them to the harbour entrance and then, one by one, they had gathered way and vanished into the stormy northern sea to head due east along the 43rd Parallel, clear of all regular shipping routes.

Aboard the unlovely, flat-topped aircraft-carriers an atmosphere of excitement prevailed. A few hours earlier all but the privileged few already 'informed' had heard, for the first time, the mission on which they were bound—to strike a devastating surprise blow on the sea power of the nation which stood between Japan and the glorious destiny mapped out by her leaders. A feeling of joyful anticipation could be sensed everywhere, except perhaps on the admiral's bridge of the flagship *Akagi,* where Nagumo contemplated the risks of an operation to which he had only hesitantly agreed under the persuasions of his aviation staff officers and his Commander-in-Chief, Admiral Yamamoto.

An unsuspecting target

Some 3,000 miles away to the south-east lay Pearl Harbor, bathed in its perennial sunshine, all unaware of the approaching blow. The only visible results of the war warning signal was a certain amount of movement of army trucks and soldiers as General Short's troops took up their stations for 'Alert No. 1'—precautions against sabotage by the local Japanese population. In naval units, where a minor degree of alert with a proportion of anti-aircraft guns manned had been in force for some time, no additional precautions were taken. The aircraft-carriers *Enterprise* and *Lexington* had been dispatched to carry Marine fighter planes to Wake and Midway. The remainder of the fleet stayed at sea during the week, returning for leave to Pearl Harbor on weekends.

During the first few days of December, the deciphering system revealed that Japanese diplomatic and consular posts had been ordered to destroy most of their codes and ciphers and all confidential documents.

Though this was an added indication that war was imminent, it did not point at Pearl Harbor as a possible Japanese objective. A series of intercepted reports from the Japanese consul at Honolulu on the berthing of ships of the Pacific Fleet might have done so had it not been that similar reports from consuls elsewhere were also being regularly transmitted. The loss of contact with the carriers by radio traffic analysis was another important straw in the wind—but, as mentioned before, this was misinterpreted to indicate that they were lying peacefully in home waters. No long-range reconnaissance flights were ordered, nor was any alteration made in the fleet training programme which would bring the fleet into harbour at the weekend for rest and recreation.

But the overriding reason for discounting any likelihood of an attack on Pearl Harbor was the clear evidence of a huge amphibious operation in the south getting under way. Japanese troop convoys heading into the Gulf of Siam had been sighted and reported by British and American air reconnaissance planes during December 6, and American opinion simply could not conceive that the Japanese had the capacity—or the imaginative boldness—to mount a simultaneous operation elsewhere involving their carrier force.

Far away to the north-west of Hawaii, the Japanese carrier force had advanced unseen, its concealment assisted by foul weather, storms, and fogs which, however, added to the anxiety of Nagumo, who had to have a spell of fine weather in which to replenish from his tankers. Then, on December 1, came the awaited confirmatory signal for the operation—*Niitaka Yama Nobore* ('Climb Mount Niitaka')—announcing that the die had finally been cast. At last, on the 2nd, the weather moderated, the warships' oil tanks were refilled, and the following evening the force turned south-east, heading for a position 500 miles due north of Pearl Harbor, which it was planned to reach on the evening of the 6th. Now the final decision to make the attack lay with Nagumo, a decision which would depend on last-minute messages from

the Japanese agent in Honolulu as to the presence of the US Pacific Fleet.

Meanwhile, messages in the 'Purple' code, indicating Japanese rejection of the American ultimatum of November 6, were being intercepted and deciphered. The main message was a long-winded presentation of the Japanese case transmitted in 14 parts, only the last of which contained anything new—a formal breaking-off of negotiations. This was in American hands by 0300 hours Washington time on the morning of December 7.

At about the same time (the evening of the 6th by Hawaiian time), emotional ceremonies of dedication were taking place aboard the aircraft-carriers of Nagumo's force. All hands had been piped to assemble on the flight decks, patriotic speeches were made; to the masthead of the *Akagi* rose a historic signal flag used by Admiral Togo before the Battle of Tsushima 36 years earlier; and when the excited ships' companies finally dispersed, the force swung

round on to a southerly course and at high speed steered for the flying-off position arranged for dawn on the morrow.

While the ships raced on into the night, another vital message in the 'Purple' code was being read, deciphered, and translated at the Bainbridge Island radio station, Washington. It instructed the Japanese ambassador to submit the message breaking off negotiations to the US Secretary of State at precisely 1300 hours, December 7 (Washington time). Translated by 0600 hours, it was not until 0915 that this reached Admiral Stark, Chief of Naval Operations, and another 35 minutes passed before it was seen by the Secretary of State. It was pointed out to both that 1300 hours would be about sunrise at Honolulu. Yet a further 70 minutes of inactivity passed before General Marshall, Chief of the US General Staff, saw the message on return from his regular morning ride. He at once proposed to Stark that a joint special war alert should be sent out. When Stark disagreed, Marshall drafted

▽Zeros on the flight-deck of one of Nagumo's carriers. (Bottom) A Japanese *Kate* torpedo-bomber prepares for take-off

his own message to army commanders, concluding: 'Just what significance the hour set may have, we do not know, but be on the alert accordingly.' It was handed in for enciphering and dispatch at 1200 hours. But long before it reached Pearl Harbor, the crump of bursting bombs and torpedo warheads had made it superfluous.

At that moment (0630 hours Hawaiian time) the first wave of Nagumo's striking aircraft had already been launched – 50 bombers, each armed with one 1,760-pound armour-piercing bomb, 70 more each carrying a torpedo, 51 dive-bombers each loaded with one 550-pound bomb, and 43 Zero fighters to provide escort and to deliver ground-strafing attacks.

It had not been without doubts and hesitation that Nagumo had given the final order – for the agent's report on ships in Pearl Harbor had made no mention of the US aircraft-carriers *Lexington* and *Enterprise* which, in fact, were away on their missions to Wake and Midway. The lure of the eight imposing battleships of the Pacific Fleet and their numerous attendant cruisers and destroyers, however, had been sufficient to harden his decision.

Off Pearl Harbor, indeed, the first acts of war were already taking place. The US minesweeper *Condor,* carrying out a routine sweep, signalled the destroyer *Ward,* on night patrol, that a periscope had been sighted, but no alarm was passed to the harbour control station. After the *Ward* had searched fruitlessly for more than two hours, the periscope was again sighted and marked by smoke bomb from a seaplane, and the destroyer then gained contact with a midget submarine and sank it with depth-charges and gunfire at 0645 hours. A message reporting the encounter reached the Port Admiral at 0712 hours, and, after some delay, was passed to Admiral Kimmel.

At 0750 hours, as Kimmel was hurrying to his office, an explosion on Ford Island, the Naval Air Station, in the middle of the harbour, gave the first startling indication that Pearl Harbor was under air attack.

Since 0615 hours the first wave of Japanese aircraft had been winging their way southwards led by Commander Mitsuo Fuchida, the air group commander, in the leading high-level bomber. A pair of trainee radar operators at the mobile station at Opana, practising with the equipment beyond the normal closing-down hour of 0700 hours, saw them appear on the screen at a range of 137 miles and plotted their approach just as a matter of interest: they were told by the information centre, to which they reported, that the contact could be disregarded as it was probably a flight of Fortresses due to arrive that morning from the mainland.

Fuchida led his swarm of aircraft down the western coast of Oahu, watched with idle curiosity by the many service and civilian families living along the shore, who took them for the air groups returning from the *Lexington* and *Enterprise*. By 0750 hours Fuchida could see across the central plain of the island to Pearl Harbor, its waters glint-

▽The US destroyer *Shaw* vanishes as its magazines explode. (Right) A *Val* dive-bomber, just after releasing its bomb   US Navy

△ Wrecked navy seaplanes after a raid: the Japanese disposed of any American challenge to their command of the air over Oahu

ing in the early sunshine of a peaceful Sunday morning, and through binoculars he was able to count the seven capital ships moored two by two in 'Battleship Row' on the eastern side of Ford Island

Surprise was complete: he gave the order to attack.

From endlessly repeated practice and meticulous study of maps and models of Oahu and Pearl Harbor, every Japanese pilot knew exactly what he had to do. While the squadrons of dive-bombers split up into sections which were to swoop simultaneously on the several army, navy, and marine airfields, the high-level bombers settled on to their pre-arranged approach course, bomb aimers adjusting their sights, and the torpedo-bombers began the long downward slant to their torpedo launching positions abreast the battleships. A few minutes before 0800 hours, to the scream of vertically plummeting planes, bombs began to burst among the aircraft drawn up, wing-tip to wing-tip in parade-ground perfection on

the various airfields. Simultaneously the duty watch aboard the ships in 'Battleship Row', preparing for the eight o'clock ceremony of hoisting the colours, saw the torpedo-bombers dip low to launch their torpedoes and watched, horror-stricken, the thin pencil line of the tracks heading for their helpless, immobile hulls. Not an American gun had yet opened fire. Not an American fighter plane had taken off.

The absolute surprise achieved by the attack on the airfields, where the bursting of bombs was followed by the tearing chatter of cannon-fire from diving Zero fighters, eliminated any posibility of an effective fighter defence. In the harbour, five of the battleships—*West Virginia, Arizona, Nevada, Oklahoma,* and *California*—were rent open by torpedo hits in the first few minutes; only the *Maryland* and *Tennessee,* occupying inside berths, and the flagship *Pennsylvania* which was in dry dock, escaped torpedo damage. Other ships torpedoed were the old target battleship *Utah,*

and the light cruisers *Raleigh* and *Helena.*

Nevertheless, although to the shudder and shock of underwater explosions was soon added the rising whine of dive-bombers and the shriek and shattering detonation of bombs from them and from the high-flying bombers, the American crews, for the most part, went into action with speed and efficiency, shooting down several of their attackers. Damage-control parties worked manfully to minimise the consequences of flooded compartments, counter-flooding to keep the foundering ships on an even keel, restoring electric and water power and communications, fighting the fires. One battleship, *Nevada,* even succeeded in getting under way and heading for the harbour entrance.

Meanwhile, however, high up above the smoke and confusion, hardly able at first to credit the total absence of any fighter opposition, and little inconvenienced by the sparse gunfire directed at them, Fuchida's high-level bombers were selecting heir targets and aiming with cool precision. An armour-piercing bomb sliced through the ve inches of armour of a turret in the *Tennessee* to burst inside it; another plunged own through the several decks to explode n the forward magazine of the *Arizona*, vhich blew up. Both the *Maryland* and the *California* were hit with devastating effect.

When a lull occurred at 0825 hours, as the rst wave of Japanese aircraft retired, lmost every US aircraft at the air bases was amaged or destroyed, the *West Virginia* vas sinking and on fire, the *Arizona* had ettled on the bottom with more than a housand of her crew fatally trapped below. he *Oklahoma* had capsized and settled on he bottom with her keel above water; the *Tennessee*, with a turret destroyed by an rmour-piercing bomb, was badly on fire; nd the *California* had received damage that vas eventually to sink her, in spite of all fforts of her crew. Elsewhere, all that was risible of the *Utah* was her upturned keel. he *Raleigh*, deep in the water from flooding nd counter-flooding, was being kept upight only by her mooring wires.

While all this had been taking place, at east one Japanese midget submarine—esides that sunk by the *Ward*—had succeeded in penetrating the harbour, passing hrough the gate in the boom defences which ad been carelessly left open after the entry f two minesweepers at 0458 hours. During a ull in the air attacks this submarine was ighted just as it was firing a torpedo at the eaplane tender *Curtiss*. The torpedo missed nd exploded harmlessly against the shore, s did a second one. The submarine was ttacked by the destroyer *Monaghan* and unk by depth charges. Of the other three nidgets launched from their parent submarines, two were lost without trace; the hird, after running on a reef and being fired t by the destroyer *Helm*, was finally eached and her crew taken prisoner. The arent submarines and the 11 other large oats of the Advanced Expeditionary Force chieved nothing.

The second wave of Japanese aircraft—54 bombers, 80 dive-bombers, and 36 fighters, led by Lieutenant Commander Shimazaki of the aircraft-carrier *Zuikaku*—had taken off an hour after the first wave. They were met by a more effective defence and thus achieved much less. In the breathing space between the two attacks, ammunition supply for the US anti-aircraft guns had been replenished, gun crews reorganised, and reinforced; and a number of the Japanese dive-bombers were shot down. Nevertheless they succeeded in damaging the *Pennsylvania*, wrecking two destroyers which were sharing the dry-dock with her, blowing up another destroyer in the floating dock, and forcing the *Nevada*—feeling her way towards the harbour entrance through the billowing clouds of black smoke from burning ships—to beach herself. Meanwhile the high-level bombers were able to make undisturbed practice and wreak further damage on the already shattered ships.

At 1000 hours it was suddenly all over. The rumble of retreating aircraft engines died away leaving a strange silence except for the crackle of burning ships, the hissing of water hoses and the desperate shouts of men fighting the fires. For the loss of only nine fighters, 15 dive-bombers, and five torpedo-bombers out of the 384 planes engaged, the Japanese navy had succeeded in putting out of action the entire battleship force of the US Pacific Fleet.

To the anxious Nagumo the success seemed so miraculously complete, and the price paid so small, that when Fuchida and other air squadron commanders urged him to mount a second attack, he felt it would be tempting fate to comply. Against their advice, he gave orders for his force to steer away to the north-west to rendezvous with his replenishment aircraft-carriers, and thence set a course for Japan.

This was a bad mistake—but Nagumo, who was no airman, was not alone at that time in a lack of appreciation of the fact that the massive gun armaments of majestic battleships were no longer the most effective means of exercising sea power. In the vast spaces of the Pacific, only the aircraft-carrier had the long arms with which to feel for and strike at an enemy fleet—and a rich reward would have awaited a second sortie by his exultant airmen. Not only was the *Enterprise* approaching Pearl Harbor from her mission to Wake, and could hardly have survived a massed aerial attack, but the repair facilities of Pearl Harbor and the huge oil-tank farm, its tanks brimming with fuel, still lay intact and now virtually defenceless. Without them the naval base would have been useless for many months to come, forcing what remained of the US Pacific Fleet to retire to its nearest base on the American west coast, out of range of the coming area of operations in the south-east Pacific.

Thus Yamamoto's daring and well-planned attack failed to reap the fullest possible harvest—though undoubtedly the blow it delivered to the United States navy was heavy indeed. But it had one effect even more decisive than that on sea power, for it brought the American people, united, into the war.

Perhaps only such a shock as that delivered at Pearl Harbor could have achieved such a result.

CAPTAIN DONALD MAC-INTYRE retired from the Royal Navy in 1954 after a career spent partly in the Fleet Air Arm and later, for many years, in command of small ships and destroyers. During the Second World War he was a successful Escort Force commander in the Battle of the Atlantic, gaining the DSO and two bars and the DSC. His experience was described in his book *U-boat Killer,* and in *Jutland* he gave a new account of one of the greatest naval battles of all time. In *Narvik* he told in detail the story of some desperate battles at sea. He has done *The Battle of the Atlantic*, *The Struggle for the Mediterranean*, and *The Battle for the Pacific* for the Batsford Battles series. Other publications include *Rodney* and *Wings of Neptune* (Peter Davies). Captain Macintyre assisted in the naval television series *Sea War*, was naval adviser to *Mutiny on the Bounty.*

Pearl Harbor A POSTSCRIPT

David Elstein and Richard Humble

Only the formalities remained. It was an ironic situation: Churchill, who had promised to come to America's aid 'within the hour' if the US were attacked, actually declared war on Japan before Roosevelt did—while the President was debating whether or not to include Germany and Italy in his declaration. He eventually decided to ask Congress to name Japan alone; for even now the American conscience baulked at declaring war without dramatic and direct provocation.

Hitler finally rescued Roosevelt from his predicament by declaring war on the United States on December 11, because of repeated US 'provocations' in the Atlantic. Obviously it was the Japanese attack and not the American 'provocation' which induced Hitler to declare war, for otherwise he would have done so a month before. Possibly Hitler had expected an American declaration of war and wanted to strike the first blow; possibly he felt himself under an obligation to support Japan—though Japan had felt herself under no obligation to come to his aid in Russia.

The 'Grand Alliance' was now complete: Britain, the USSR, and the United States of America were ranged against Germany, Italy, and Japan. Such an alliance amounted to a declaration of war to the death against the feverish aggression of the Axis 'geo-politicians'. The Free World had pledged itself to destroy Germany's hopes of a 'New Order in Europe' and a new 'Greater German Empire' in Russia and central Europe, Italy's hopes of a 'Second Roman Empire', and Japan's 'Greater East-Asian Co-Prosperity Sphere'.

Yet the future looked black for the Allies in December 1941. German armies stood at the gates of Moscow and Leningrad. The Japanese were supreme in the Pacific. Only in the Western Desert had the Allies scored a definite success; and Auchinleck's recovery of Cyrenaica was to have as little permanence as the victories of Wavell and Rommel before him. There seemed no possible immediate counterstroke to halt the run of Axis successes on the land, at sea, or in the air.

In such a gloomy hour, it needed more than unreasoning courage to see a way through to Allied final victory, and the reaction of Churchill to Pearl Harbor was typical of the stature of the man. He recalls that:

'I thought of a remark which Edward Grey had made to me more than thirty years before —that the United States is like "a gigantic boiler. Once the fire is lighted under it, there is no limit to the power it can generate". Being saturated and satiated with emotion and sensation, I went to bed and slept the sleep of the saved and thankful.'

AMERICA'S AIR ARM

When the war in the Pacific opened, the American and Allied air forces were tactically and numerically inferior. Their standard fighter aircraft (F-2A Buffalo and the P-40) were totally outclassed by the Japanese Zero. The B-17 Flying Fortress bomber proved a formidable weapon, but for all its toughness and hitting power its value was jeopardised by the lack of Allied fighter protection — and this only time could remedy

◁ **Lockheed P-38 Lightning**
Known to the Germans as the *Gabel schwanzteufel* ('Two-tailed devil'), the Lightning first saw service in the Mediterranean theatre in late 1942, during Operation Torch. *Max speed:* 414 mph. *Max range* 450 miles. *Armament:* one 20-mm cannon four ·50-inch machine-guns; various combinations of bombs and rockets

Curtiss P-40 was the first mass-produced US monoplane fighter, and constituted more than half the US fighter strength at the beginning of the war. It was supplied to the RAF, where it was known as the Tomahawk. **Max speed:** 357 mph. **Max range:** 1,400 miles. **Armament:** two ·30, two ·50 machine-guns ▽

Brewster F-2A Buffalo was the US Navy's first monoplane fighter. Official vacillation resulted in its near obsolescence by the beginning of the Pacific war. **Max speed:** 321 mph. **Max range:** 965 miles. **Armament:** four ·50 machine-guns △

Boeing B-17 Flying Fortress served with the US Army Air Force throughout the war, also serving with the RAF. Japanese pilots respected its bristling armament. **Max Speed:** 300 mph. **Range:** 1,850 miles. **Armament:** up to 13·50 machine-guns; up to 8,000 lb of bombs

△ **North American P-51B Mustang**
The Mustang was to the US air force what the Spitfire was to the RAF—but the American fighter had a far greater versatility: it served as long-range fighter, as fighter-bomber, dive-bomber, for close support, and for photo reconnaissance. *Max speed:* 441 mph. *Max range:* 1,300 miles. *Armament:* four wing-mounted ·50-inch machine-guns; two 500-lb bombs (or extra fuel tanks)

▽▽ **Bell P-39 Airacobra**
The Airacobra was no match for the new fighter designs; but nevertheless it served in large numbers in Russia and with the Free French air forces. *Max speed:* 360 mph. *Max range:* 1,100 miles. *Armament:* one 37-mm, two ·50-inch machine-guns in nose; four ·30-inch machine-guns in wings

▽ **Republic P-47 Thunderbolt**
One of the most welcome surprises to the Allied fighter pilots was the ability of the bulky Thunderbolt (nearly twice as heavy as the Spitfire) to 'mix it' in combat with the more graceful Axis designs. *Max speed:* 426 mph. *Max range:* (clean) 637 miles. *Armament:* six or eight wing-mounted ·50-inch machine-guns; one 500-lb bomb

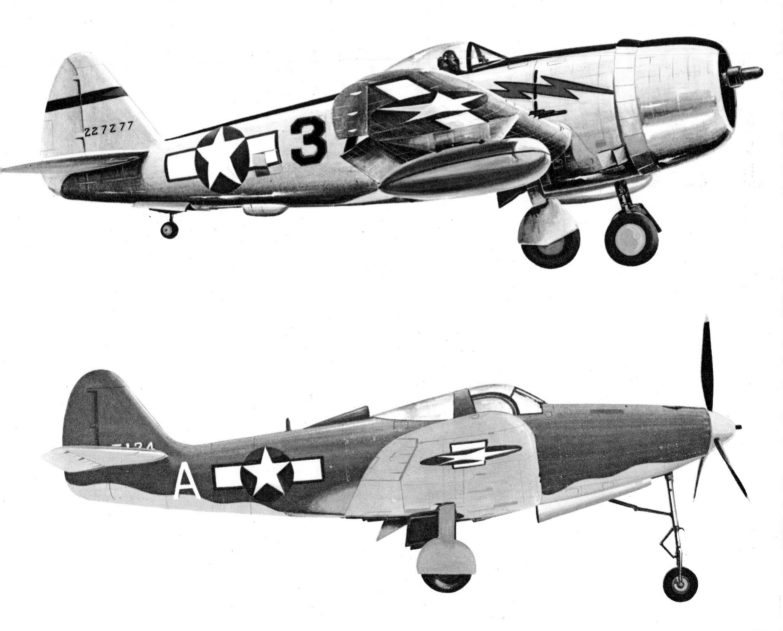

A blazing B-17 bomber after a Japanese air raid on Bandung airfield in Java

Pacific Theatre, December 1941/June 1942

AIR WAR IN THE FAR EAST

During the early months of 1942 the Japanese had achieved almost complete control of the air in the Far East. Allied pilots were unable to cope with the Zero fighter, and Japanese bombers were able to attack land targets and shipping with almost complete safety. Raids on Darwin and Broome led the Australians to believe that a landing on their own soil was imminent – but by June the tide had turned, and Allied fighters and bombers were gaining superiority both in quantity and quality. *John Vader*

Within a few short weeks of the attack on Pearl Harbor the Japanese were masters of the skies over a vast area of the Pacific. In the hands of highly proficient pilots, their Zero fighters had swiftly accounted for most of the American, British, and Dutch aircraft in the area, and had provided safe passage for the Japanese bombers in their attacks on land targets and shipping.

The versatile Zero could fly at a speed of over 300 mph, had a range of 1,500 miles, was armed with two 7·7-mm machine-guns and two 20-mm cannon, and could carry two 132-pound bombs. Although fighter tactics had been developed by the American Volunteer Group pilots in China to overcome successfully the superior qualities of the Zero, their experience had not been passed on to the Allied pilots in the Pacific area. The inability to cope with the Japanese fighter was a major factor in the

conduct of the war in the air during the first few months.

Also, the Japanese bomber crews had achieved a remarkable degree of accuracy in high-level bombing, dive-bombing, and torpedo-dropping during their intense training and war experience in China.

The rapid military successes of the Japanese had given them control of captured territory that extended down the peninsula and chain of islands of the western rim of the Pacific to the Bismarck and Arafura Seas. To provide their area of control with a deep defence, their plan required operational points across the islands north of Australia to the Solomon Islands, up through the centre of the ocean, and past the Gilbert and Midway Islands to the outlying islands of the Aleutian Group near Alaska.

For this ambitious scheme, the Japanese air forces were given the gigantic task of

maintaining superiority in the air, while still supporting assault troops and naval units. The Japanese army air force had the primary mission of offensive operations in Burma and China, and of the defence of the Netherlands East Indies; their naval air force was responsible for most of the air operations around the Pacific.

The Pacific war in the air began on December 8 (west of the International Date Line; December 7 east of the Line) with lethal and accurate Japanese bombing of naval and air units at Pearl Harbor, and aircraft at Luzon in the Philippines. At Wake Island their attacks provided an early indication that the war in the Pacific would be decided primarily in the air, for the first attempt to land troops on the island without air support failed, and even high-level bombing had little effect on the American military installations. The Japanese were forced to send Rear-Admiral Yamaguchi's II Carrier Division – a two-carrier force with Kate bombers, Val dive-bombers, and Zero fighters – to pound the defending artillery and destroy the Wildcat fighters, before Japanese troops could land to overrun the defenders.

Early in January 1942, Rabaul and Balikpapan were bombed in the prelude to invasion of New Britain and Borneo. By the end of the month Japanese troops had landed at Lae, the capital of New Guinea, and at several points on Borneo and at Rabaul, where air bases were established in preparation for the eastward expansion of the Japanese southern defence perimeter.

In Malaya, the RAF and RAAF aircraft were swiftly decimated by the superior Japanese air force; the British lacked modern fighters and they were ignorant of the qualities of the Zero. One spectacular RAF success occurred on January 1 when a single Hurricane shot down eight unescorted bombers, but on the following day five Hurricanes were shot down when they attacked bombers escorted by Zeros.

One major Japanese objective was Port Moresby – which they planned to capture by invading across the sea from Rabaul – and the port's first air raid was on February 3, 1942. It caused little damage but a raid two days later knocked out three Catalinas and damaged a fourth, and the fall of the port seemed to be a foregone conclusion when, on February 27, the Japanese sank five cruisers and six destroyers of a combined American, Australian, and Dutch force without loss to themselves. Nevertheless the Australians continued to extend the fortifications of the base while the Japanese kept it under observation from reconnaissance aircraft and continued their bombing raids.

The next key target – Darwin

On February 19, 1942, the port of Darwin in northern Australia was attacked by 135 carrier- and land-based aircraft flown by Japan's most experienced and highly trained pilots. The aircraft-carriers *Akagi, Hiryu, Kaga,* and *Soryu,* under the command of Admiral Nagumo (who led the assault on Pearl Harbor) moved down from the Celebes to a point east of Timor Island to fly off their aircraft.

The Japanese had a double purpose in this raid on Darwin: first to neutralise the Allied air and naval forces there while Japanese paratroops and their assault convoy moved in to Dili and Koepang; second to destroy shipping, aircraft, and ground installations.

△ A wrecked hangar at Darwin after the Japanese raid of February 19, during which some 240 people were killed and 150 were injured. The raid opened a series of attacks on Australian territory which convinced the defenders that invasion was imminent. But the Japanese saw the attacks as tactical interventions to cover their moves against Port Moresby
◁ The Japanese bomber crews who flew these raids were the air force's élite

The raid was thus tactically defensive, although it led the Australians to believe that a landing on their own soil was imminent.

Flying at 14,000 feet, 27 Kate single-engined bombers opened the attack, followed by a formation of 27 Val dive-bombers escorted by 27 Zero fighters with orders to concentrate on shipping in the harbour; the Kates were to pattern-bomb in runs across the harbour, and the Vals and Zeros to follow with low-level dive-bombing and strafing of individual ships, flying boats, and land installations.

The meagre Allied air force at Darwin on February 19 included 17 Hudson bombers (six without crews), 14 Wirraway single-engine trainers that were being used for short-range reconnaissance, and 10 USAAF Kittyhawk fighters which were to take off that morning for Koepang, on the way to Java. In the harbour there were 47 naval and merchant vessels (including the US destroyer *Peary* and the US seaplane tender *William B. Preston,* two sloops and five corvettes of the RAN, two Catalina flying-boats of the USN, and the Qantas Empire flying-boat, *Camilla*). It all made a tempting and important target for a Japanese strike. Intensive air activity over Timor during the previous few days had caused several air raid alerts to be sounded in Darwin, and a raid was expected—although not quite so soon.

By 0940 hours, Major Pell, USAAF, had returned with his ten Kittyhawks, after abandoning the flight to Koepang, and he sent up a flight of five to patrol over the harbour while his other aircraft refuelled. A few minutes later the patrolling Kittyhawks were attacked by Zeros, and four Kittyhawks were shot down—but their leader, Lieutenant R. G. Oesteicher, had broken away quickly enough to escape the diving Zeros, and even managed to shoot one down before he found the safety of a cloud.

Meanwhile, the Bathurst Island mission station radio operator had sent a message that a large number of aircraft had been seen flying south towards Darwin—yet, despite this report, the sirens were not sounded until the minesweeper HMAS *Gunbar* was attacked by nine Zeros as she was passing the harbour boom gate, at 0957. Two minutes later the bombs were falling from the high, circling bombers.

The first pattern of bombs was dropped over the shipping, the next extended across the shore and into the town itself, and after the bombs came the dive-bombers and the strafing fighters. Expecting action, the commanders of the *Peary* and   ▷

Japan's Aerial Élite—Her Long-Range Strike Force

The Japanese Navy and Army Air Forces had a numerous fleet of medium bombers with remarkable ranges, needed to deal with the vast distances of the Pacific theatre. Japanese bombers all suffered to some extent from weak defensive armament—none of them had as many machine-guns as the US B-25 Mitchell, for example. But in the first Japanese sweep through the Pacific—when the Zeros ruled the skies—Japanese bombing-strikes were never effectively challenged; and their weaker army fighters were able to hold their own

Mitsubishi G4M01 *(Betty)* was the Japanese navy's principle wartime bomber; but the needs of its strike and support role demanded range, which had to be purchased at the expense of defensive armament. This inevitably meant high losses for the *Betty* crews. It served as transport, level- and torpedo-bomber, and reconnaissance aircraft. **Max speed:** 276 mph. **Range:** 2,620 miles. **Armament:** up to five 7·7-mm machine-guns. **Bomb load:** 1,765 lbs

Mitsubishi Ki-21 *(Sally)* was the standard bomber type at the time of Pearl Harbor, and played an important role throughout the war, although it had become obsolescent long before 1945. **Max speed:** 248 mph. **Range:** 1,180 miles. **Armament:** up to five 7·7-mm machine-guns. **Bomb load:** 2,100 lbs

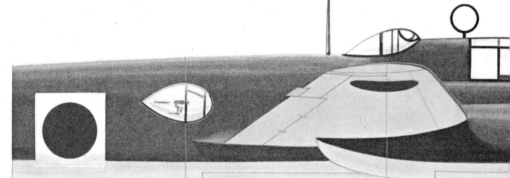

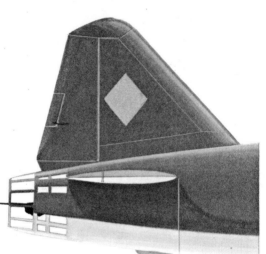

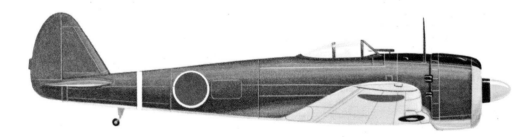

Nakajima Ki-43 *(Oscar)* had the highest production of any of the Japanese army's fighters. It served in all theatres of the Pacific war, although it was far outclassed by later Japanese fighter designs; and it had the typical manoeuvrability of Japanese fighters. **Max speed:** 308 mph. **Range:** 745 miles. **Armament:** two 7·7-mm machine-guns

John Batchelor

America's Challenge—Her Carrier-borne Aircraft

In the first year of the Pacific war, the US carrier-borne aircraft had no fighter which could match the Japanese Zero in manoeuvrability and hitting-power. But both the Dauntless and Devastator strike aircraft—although obsolescent at the time of Pearl Harbor—served with great distinction, and inflicted heavy damage on the ships of the Japanese navy

Douglas SBD-III Dauntless became the backbone of the US carrier light-bomber force. Not only could it absorb considerable punishment, but it also had the lowest loss figures of any US carrier aircraft. **Max speed:** 275 mph. **Max range:** 875 miles. **Crew:** 2. **Armament:** twin ·50 machine-guns; one 500-lb bomb

Douglas TBD-1 Devastator suffered heavy losses because of its inadequate defensive armament, but it formed the mainstay of the US navy's carrier torpedo-bomber force in the early stages of the Pacific war. **Max speed:** 225 mph. **Max range:** 985 miles. **Crew:** 3. **Armament:** one ·30, one ·50 machine-gun; one 1,000-lb torpedo

Grumman F4F Wildcat was the standard US navy fighter in 1941 and the first five months of 1942. It earned undying battle-honours in its defence of Wake Atoll, and also served with the RAF as the 'Martlet'. **Max speed:** 331 mph. **Max range:** 860 miles. **Armament:** four ·50 machine-guns

Doolittle's Raid on Tokyo—great dividends from a small investment

Some of Col Doolittle's B-25 bombers on the *Hornet*'s flight-deck before the attack on Tokyo. ▽ A B-25 takes off: flying off these big bombers from a carrier was a considerable feat. **Inset:** Doolittle (front row, third from right) in China with his crew after the raid

Preston had maintained steam since arrival in Port Darwin, so they managed to get their ships under way; but the *Peary* was holed by a direct hit as she manoeuvred in the harbour, and she slowly sank by the stern, her forward guns still firing as she went down. One of the corvettes, HMAS *Katoomba*, was propped up in dry dock yet managed to put up a strong barrage of anti-aircraft fire.

Dive-bombing caused most of the havoc on the harbour: a 12,000-ton transport, the *Meigs*, and four other merchant ships were sunk and three were beached; the hospital ship, *Manunda*, was damaged; the RAN lost a 14-ton lugger and a supply hulk; the two Catalinas were destroyed but the Empire flying-boat luckily survived under a screen of smoke from a burning ship. The shore end of the wharf was hit by a heavy bomb which killed 21 waterside workers and blew a railway engine into the sea, while at the wrecked wharf the *Neptuna*, carrying 200 depth-charges, was set on fire.

Ashore, the Administrator's office, police barracks and station, the post office, and the postmaster's house were demolished, Government House and the civil hospital were severely damaged, and an army hospital, 9 miles out of town, was strafed. At the RAAF airfields, Vals and Zeros destroyed buildings and equipment.

Major Pell had 'scrambled' his refuelled

group of Kittyhawks, and they were thus in that most vulnerable position of taking off when they were attacked. Four were shot down and the fifth destroyed before it was airborne; Major Pell baled out below 100 feet, and might have survived had he not been caught on the ground in a burst of cannon fire from a Japanese fighter. The three other pilots survived.

The raiders departed, and during the respite which now followed troops and civilians fought fires and collected the dead and wounded, while in the harbour a tug pulled an oil-lighter away from a burning ship just as the *Neptuna* was blasted to pieces at the wharf by its cargo of depth-charges.

Then, two hours later, sinister droning heralded the approach of more raiding aircraft. Two formations of Japanese high-level bombers flew in from opposite directions, at a height of 18,000 feet, to drop their bombs in a tight pattern over one concentrated area – the RAAF airfield. This attack further increased the destruction so that in the end the two main hangars, the central store, and the transport section were left in ruins, together with other badly damaged huts and sheds on the station.

The Japanese air crews flying on these raids were the élite of Japan's air forces, and with such a lightly defended target laid out before them as Darwin harbour the destruction could have been very much greater. Over the target area the Japanese bomber pilots had the advantage of a fine, sunny morning to pick their targets and make their bombing runs. Although there was some evidence of Allied fighter opposition, the presence of the ubiquitous Zero inspired confidence in the bomber crews and contributed to the accuracy of their operations. However, the Japanese losses amounted to 15 aircraft, most of which were accounted for by fire from the Allied guns on ship and shore.

With 240 people killed and 150 wounded in this one raid at Darwin, there was a severe drop in the morale of the civilians, and even a few of the ground personnel at the RAAF station decided to move south, without orders; most of the airmen, however, anticipated an invasion and were ready to fight alongside the army units to repel the landings.

The activities in the Dutch East Indies had brought the harbour and airfield at Broome, Australia, into constant use as a refuelling depot for the air shuttle service between Java and Perth. On the afternoon of March 3 a Japanese reconnaissance aircraft flew over the harbour in which three flying boats were moored. These would be target enough, but during the night another 13 flying boats alighted and were still there when on March 4 the expected Zeros swept in at low level through the harbour entrance. On the airfield there were two Flying Fortresses and two Liberators as well as three other aircraft.

One Liberator had taken off as the raiders arrived and was shot down in flames into the sea. The rest of the aircraft at the airfield and all the Catalina, Dornier, and Empire flying boats in the harbour were destroyed in the attack, which lasted only 15 minutes, and the only gun that fired as the Japanese was an aircraft machine-gun held by a Dutch gunner as he fired over one blistering arm; but there were no reports of enemy losses.

On their way back to the Timor base the Zero pilots sighted, some 60 miles from Darwin, a Dutch DC-3 – one of the last aircraft to leave Java and carrying a very valuable consignment of diamonds – and shot it down into the sea. There were no survivors.

On the same day, Wyndham – a small town on the coast between Darwin and Broome – was raided by eight Zeros which destroyed a light aircraft and a fuel dump at the airfield, and a near-miss opened the plates of the SS *Koolama,* which sank where she was tied up at the wharf. Also, on March 4, Darwin was raided again, this time by eight Zeros which found a Hudson on the RAAF airfield and quickly gunned it to destruction. Zeros continued to reconnoitre the coast between Darwin and Broome, and as far inland as Katherine and Daly Waters.

Before the Allies could rush fighters up to meet the intruders, there were two more major raids on Darwin – one on the RAAF station, and the other on the naval headquarters and part of the town's residential section.

Then, on March 17, led by Lieutenant-Colonel Paul B. Wurtsmith, the first of three American fighter squadrons from No. 49 Fighter Group arrived at Darwin and immediately the position changed. Although the Japanese raids continued they became little more than armed reconnaissances except for more determined efforts on April 25, and four consecutive days, 13-16, in June. By the end of June the combination of the early warning by the RAAF radar units, and the skill of the American Kittyhawk pilots caused the loss of 24 Japanese aircraft for only nine Kittyhawks.

Wurtsmith's men quickly learned the tactics that the American Volunteer Group in China had used to shoot down the highly manoeuvrable Zero. The Kittyhawk was dived to pick up a higher speed than the Zero, the target was chosen and fired at, and then the Kittyhawk was pulled away and down, picking up enough speed to avoid the Zero and possibly climb again without interception to another high position for attack.

Along the Pacific coast of the United States there were far better targets for the Japanese than Darwin or Broome. Vulnerable aircraft plants – such as Boeing in Seattle, Douglas and Lockheed in Los Angeles, and Consolidated in San Diego – were sitting ducks for a carrier-borne air attack – yet they were overlooked or considered too risky in the immediate Japanese war plan. In December 1941 these hundreds of miles of coastline had only 45 modern fighters, ten heavy bombers, and 78 medium bombers for protection, and even as late as February the seaboard defences were inadequate and not properly organised.

But the only drama of war along this coast happened in Los Angeles. On the night of February 24/25 radar tracked an unidentified object approaching from over the sea, and an air raid alert was sounded. At 0300 hours a red flare was seen over Santa Monica; four batteries of anti-aircraft guns opened fire, and much of the ensuing confusion probably arose from the fact that the shell bursts, caught in the glare of the searchlights, were themselves taken for enemy aircraft and fired at, causing more shell bursts to be illuminated in the criss-crossing beams. There were thus many eye-witnesses of numerous 'enemy aircraft' in the night sky, but in fact no Japanese aircraft was

sighted in the vicinity, and the only damage to property was caused by falling shell splinters.

The Panama Canal was also neglected in the Japanese navy bombing operations. There were several weak points that were quite vulnerable, and the canal would have been closed to shipping for many months had they been bombed.

The surprise attack on Tokyo
When a plan to make a bombing raid against Tokyo was submitted by General H. H. Arnold to President Roosevelt, the President gave it his whole-hearted support: an avenging blow against the Japanese would help stimulate the morale of the Americans and, indeed, all Allies in the Pacific who had suffered Japanese aggression, although such a small force would not be expected to effect much material damage.

Because there were no Allied airfields within a 'bomb and return' range of Tokyo the US Air Force planned to fly land-based bombers from an aircraft-carrier – a feat never before achieved in modern aircraft use – in a tactical move which would doubly confuse the Japanese: they would not expect an attack from any Chinese air units, and they would not expect the American navy to risk carriers close enough to Japan to fly off short-range naval aircraft. It was a brilliant plan which was not too hazardous; it only required the right aircraft and a special skill from the pilots.

Lieutenant-Colonel James H. Doolittle, a foremost Air Force bomber expert, was chosen to lead the raid. He picked 24 crews from the 17th Bombardment Group who were sent to Eglin Field, Florida, to be coached in the difficult techniques of taking off a large, heavily-laden bomber from the short runway that a carrier would provide.

The twin-engined B-25 Mitchell bomber was chosen as the most suitable aircraft. Three auxiliary fuel tanks, ten 5-gallon tins, and a 360-gallon-capacity collapsible rubber bag were added to the normal fuel load to give the B-25 an 'attack-and-escape' range. The bomb load was small, but the three 500-pound bombs and single incendiary cluster could do a lot of damage on the right target. For security reasons the Norden bombsight was removed and a very effective substitute, called the 'Mark Twain', was especially designed by Captain C. R. Greening, USAAF, for low-altitude bombing. For 'protection' from astern, two fake wooden ·50 machine-guns were installed at the tip of the stingless tail.

After attacking their targets, the raiders were to fly 1,200 miles across the East China Sea to various points in China where they were to remain as a valuable bomber-group supporting the Chinese armies. Unfortunately, because of the close secrecy surrounding the operation, full information could not be given to Chiang Kai-shek, and he was reluctant to give consent to the use of facilities at Kweilin, Kian, Yushan, Chuchow, and Lishui; at the last minute he even refused the use of Chuchow airfield, as he wanted an extension of time to prevent the Japanese occupation of the Chuchow area.

On April 1, 16 B-25s were lifted on board the aircraft-carrier USS *Hornet* and lashed to the flight deck. North of Midway the carrier and its escort were joined by Vice-Admiral Halsey's carrier, USS *Enterprise,* and, accompanied by four cruisers, eight destroyers, and two oil tankers, the task force headed towards Japan. Doolittle hoped to reach a point 450 miles from Japan for the take-off, to allow a successful flight to China – 650 miles would be the absolute limit – but a Japanese patrol boat, sighted early in the morning of April 18, drastically changed the plan. Rather than risk the invaluable carriers, the bombers were ordered off some ten hours before the original time for the night attack, 823 miles from Tokyo.

As they made ready for the take-off, the *Hornet* was plunging through a 40-knot gale that sent green water spraying over the bows, and a man was detailed to signal each aircraft to begin its run so that it would coincide with the rising of the forward end of the pitching deck. Doolittle's lead aircraft had a run of only 467 feet, but it was enough, and in due course he was joined in the air by the remainder of the squadron. The task force turned and escaped without interference, and the bombers flew on at low level towards Japan, where the patrol vessel's warning had alerted the defence to expect a raid the following day.

In Tokyo, an air raid drill was actually in progress when the B-25s roared overhead at 1,000 feet, unopposed by fighters and hardly troubled by the small amount of anti-aircraft fire. The surprise was complete: oil storage tanks, factory areas, and military installations were bombed in Tokyo, Kobe, Yokohama, and Nagoya, and one bomb from Lieutenant McElroy's aircraft hit the aircraft-carrier *Ryuho*, which was in dry dock at the Yokosuka naval base. Lieutenant-Colonel Doolittle was able to report: 'Damage far exceeded the most optimistic expectations.'

Only one Mitchell bomber was slightly damaged by anti-aircraft fire, and they all escaped the Japanese home islands, but the crews knew that they would not reach the Chinese airfields as the range was impossible. A strong tail wind helped them across the East China Sea towards Chuchow, flying through darkness, rain, and cloud to eventual crash-landing or baling out when the fuel tanks emptied. Of the 50 aircrew who parachuted over China, only one was killed; 49 were led to safety by Chinese. From the aircraft that crash-landed along the coast the Chinese rescued ten more, but the Japanese captured eight men, three of whom were executed after a trial at which they were accused of deliberately bombing civilians; the others were imprisoned, one to die a prisoner of war.

There were other results from this raid, apart from the bomb damage – the heartening news it provided for the Allies and the psychological shock felt in Japan. Some 16 American bombers were lost and China suffered the loss of Chihkiang Province, which the Japanese quickly captured to deny to their enemy future use of the airfields. The Allies did, however, eventually benefit more from the raid: extra Japanese troops were sent to China, and four army fighter groups were kept in Japan during 1942-43, when they were badly needed elsewhere.

During February 1942, the Allies began to strike back with their growing force of bombers. At Darwin the RAAF used Hudsons, which did not have a very high performance – a Hudson could only manage to get a 1,000-pound warload to Ambon and 500 pounds to Timor, whereas a Betty or a Kate of the Japanese air force could carry a bomb load of 2,000 pounds from Timor to Darwin. Apart from a few raids made by US Fortresses brought up from the south, the Hudsons were used for bombing and recon-

naissance as well as dropping food and equipment to the RAAF rear party and the 2/2nd Independent Company, AIF (Australian Imperial Force), which had not been evacuated and had continued to fight the Japanese in Portuguese Timor. Much success was achieved by the Hudsons against shipping and flying boats in Koepang Harbour, and against aircraft and installations on the nearby airfield, Penfui.

From their bases in Queensland, the Americans carried bombs in Fortresses, Mitchells, and Marauders to be dropped with greater frequency on Rabaul. The first strike was made by six Fortresses on February 23, and the number of raids increased when B-25 Mitchells and A-24 Martin Marauders were made available for use in the attacks. Some Japanese shipping and grounded aircraft were destroyed in the raids, which usually started from Townsville and routed via Port Moresby. The main effect appeared to be that the Japanese were reluctant to risk many aircraft at Rabaul – but the fighters they did keep were effectively used against the Americans: in one attack, on May 24, eight unescorted Mitchells were attacked, five being shot down while one crashed on landing at Port Moresby.

During this period the vital staging post at Port Moresby was defended by Kittyhawk fighters from 75 Squadron, RAAF, commanded by Squadron-Leader J. F. Jackson. The pilots soon demonstrated that by using the right tactics the Zero could be shot down: within 44 days they had shot down or destroyed on the ground 35 aircraft, probably destroyed four, and damaged 47. Their own losses were 22 aircraft destroyed, and 12 pilots killed or missing. Jackson was shot down at the end of April, and his place as commanding officer of the squadron was taken by his brother, Squadron-Leader L. B. Jackson.

The encouraging sight of friendly fighters patrolling the skies and attacking intruders had a lot to do with building up morale in Darwin and Port Moresby. Once the Allies established their fighter and bomber bases they were gradually able to increase their strength. When 75 Squadron was relieved – by which time it was down to three serviceable aircraft – the Allies could provide two squadrons, 35 and 36 of the US 8th Pursuit Group, to replace it on the Port Moresby fighter airfields. The Americans, under the command of Lieutenant-Colonel Boyd D. Wagner, maintained the protective cover over the base, although in a two-day raid on June 16/17 the Japanese managed to hit and set alight the vessel *Macdui* – which was abandoned, and drifted until grounded in the shallows of the harbour.

On May 29 the slow, long-range Catalina flying boats of 11 and 20 Squadrons, RAAF, made their first raid against the Solomon Islands base of Tulagi, which had already been heavily attacked by aircraft from US aircraft-carriers on May 4 and 5. Further Catalina raids on June 1, 25, and 26 were highly effective, and hundreds of Japanese troops were killed by bombs and the machine-gunning that followed at low level. The squadrons also flew in raids against Lae, Salamaua, and Rabaul. The report of the operations of the night of June 27 describes how two Catalinas involved in the mission were over the Lae-Salamaua area continuously for four hours, and had dropped 'eight 500-lb bombs, 20 20-pound fragmentation bombs, and four dozen empty beer bottles'. Beer bottles falling through the air

made a screeching sound which helped to terrorise the enemy and spoil his sleep.

Sometimes the Allies' aircraft recognition was not up to standard – even the RAAF roundels and Japanese red circles looked alike to a few over-excited pilots and gunners. Returning from a raid on June 26, an 11 Squadron Catalina was making its approach to alight on Havannah Harbour at Efate when a USN Wildcat fighter attacked, firing its ·5-inch machine-guns at the flying boat. The pilot of the Wildcat had been alerted to look for an unidentified aircraft, and the red centres of the RAAF roundels, he explained later, were so prominent he mistook them for Japanese markings. Fortunately the Catalina was not badly damaged in the attack and alighted safely, but this incident led to the replacement of red with white centres in all RAAF roundels.

An important event, concerning Australia's rapid development of an aircraft industry, took place on the night of June 25 when Australian-built twin-engined Beaufort bombers made their first attack. From their base at Mareeba, inland from Cairns, several Beauforts moved to Port Moresby from where they set out to strike at a Japanese ship which had been reported approaching Lae. While two Beauforts bombed and strafed the Salamaua isthmus area, three others scored hits on the reported ship, which was disabled and left sinking. One Beaufort was lost on the return from Salamaua, and another was forced to make a belly landing when it returned to Port Moresby.

By the end of June 1942, the Allied fighters and bombers around the Pacific were increasing in numbers every week: their qualitative and quantitative factors were obviously becoming superior to the enemy's, and Japan's ring of airfields – cradling its defensive bombers and fighters – was under constant surveillance. Australia had become an immense staging ground for hundreds of aircraft on their way to attacking positions in the south Pacific. Engineers were preparing huge bulldozers and earth-moving equipment to be transported to thick tropical forests and plantations, where many new airstrips would be scraped in the soil and coral.

The end of June 1942 saw the Japanese at the limit of their expansion – and the holocausts they had brought in their bombing raids were being returned, in an ever-increasing volume, against their bases and their shipping. Their future activity in the air would be primarily defensive. Any hope the Japanese may have had of diplomatic negotiations for a peace at this stage – the only possible way they could have consolidated their conquests in a permanent way – would be forlorn.

 JOHN LANDERS VADER was a jackeroo, in the outback of New South Wales, who travelled several hundreds of miles to join the colours of the AIF at the outbreak of war. After serving with the 6th Division in Libya, Greece, and Syria he returned with the 19th Brigade to Darwin in 1942. Transferring to the RAAF he piloted Spitfires of 79 Squadron in the South-West Pacific. A sometime sheep farmer, small magazine publisher, and bird fancier, he is now working as a freelance journalist in London, and is in the middle of writing a comic-travel book and a slapstick-murder mystery – both of which will appear under a pseudonym. He does not know who won the war but every now and then he celebrates its end.

PACIFIC AIR WAR
The Japanese View

Sado-Opera Mundi

In this unique account, a Japanese fighter pilot gives his reasons for Japan's aerial superiority in the early days of the war — and in the process explodes the old Allied myth that Japanese pilots (above) were forbidden to wear parachutes   *Saburo Sakai*   **New Guinea, April/August 1942**

From mid-April to mid-August 1942, the days seemed to blur into one another. Life became an endless repetition of fighter sweeps, of escorting our bombers over Moresby, of racing for our fighters to scramble against the incoming enemy raiders. The Allies seemed to have an inexhaustible supply of aircraft. A week never went by without the enemy suffering losses, and yet his planes came, by twos and threes and by dozens.

In 1942 none of our planes carried pilot armour, nor did the Zeros have self-sealing tanks, as did the American planes. As the enemy soon discovered, a burst of their ·50-calibre bullets into the fuel tanks of a Zero caused it to explode violently in flames. Despite this, in those days not one of our pilots flew with parachutes. This has been misinterpreted in the West as proof that our leaders were disdainful of our lives, that all Japanese pilots were expendable and regarded as pawns instead of human beings. This was far from the truth. Every man was assigned a parachute: the decision to fly without them was our own, and not the result of orders from any higher headquarters. Actually, we were urged, although not ordered, to wear the parachutes in combat. At some fields the base commander insisted that 'chutes be worn, and those men had no choice but to place the bulky packs in their planes. Often, however, they never fastened the straps, and used the 'chutes only as seat cushions.

We had little use for these parachutes, for the only purpose they served for us was to hamstring our cockpit movements in a battle. It was difficult to move our arms and legs when encumbered by 'chute straps. There was another, and equally compelling, reason for not carrying the 'chutes into combat. The majority of our battles were fought with enemy fighters over their own fields. It was out of the question to bale out over enemy-held territory, for such a move meant a willingness to be captured — and nowhere in the Japanese military code or in the traditional *Bushido* (Samurai code) could one find the distasteful words 'Prisoner of War'. *There were no prisoners.* A man who did not return from a fight was dead. No fighter pilot of any courage would ever permit himself to be captured by the enemy. It was completely unthinkable.

During the month of June, we encountered an ever-increasing number of enemy fighters and bombers. We were told that the enemy was staging a major build-up of air power in the area, and that from now on we would carry out stronger fighter sweeps. It was clear to all that we would need every Zero we could lay our hands on. The enemy was hacking more airstrips out of the jungle growth in the general area of Moresby.

We entered a new phase of fighter operations on July 21 when a Japanese army division landed at Buna, 110 miles south of Lae. The troops at once worked their way inland on a frantic march through wild jungle towards Port Moresby. On a map the proposed manoeuvre appeared simple to execute. Buna seemed but a stone's throw away from Moresby, across the neck of the Papuan peninsula.

But the maps of the jungle islands are altogether different from the fierce conditions below in the dense foliage. The Japanese High Command made a terrible and fatal error in committing our troops to the Moresby attack. Before the battle was ended, Japan had suffered one of her most tragic and humiliating disasters.

The overland attack was a move of desperation. Originally our high command had scheduled a massive amphibious assault against Moresby, but this move had been eliminated on May 7 and 8, during the Coral Sea battle, when two enemy carriers had encountered two Japanese carriers in the first sea duel in which no surface ship fired at an opponent. Each force used its aircraft to pound the other with constant aerial attacks. We had won the battle, but the enemy had achieved his objective: the amphibious assault was cancelled.

With our troops ashore at Buna, Rabaul headquarters ordered our attacks against Moresby to be discontinued, and called for constant air support of the beach-head. The Buna landings were only a part of a larger operation, which was doomed to defeat even as it got under way. Not only did the jungle pose a threat of enormous magnitude, but our men were hobbled by a thorough lack of understanding of the problems of logistics on the part of their leaders.

During the daytime, Lae juggled its 20 to 30 operational fighters to keep six to nine Zeros always in the air over Buna, as well as a standby force to protect the field. The air cover at Buna was far below our needs, but the fighters managed to prevent any large-scale attacks from destroying the beach-head facilities.

Buna was a shock to me on my first patrol. I had seen many landing operations before from the air, but never had I witnessed such a pathetic attempt to supply a full infantry division. Soldiers milled around on the beach, carrying cases of supplies into the jungle by hand. Only *two* small transports, with a single sub-chaser as escort, stood off the beach unloading new supplies!

The next few weeks were spent in maintaining cover over the Buna beach area, but the latter half of July meant a new and strange phase of the war for us. No longer did we fly without parachutes. Orders had come down from higher headquarters and Captain Saito directed every pilot to wear his 'chute into combat. Equally disturbing to us were further orders which carried unspoken but ominous implications. We were taken off the offensive. Captain Saito issued orders that from now on no fighters would cross the Owen Stanley Range, no matter how compelling the reason.

[From 'Samurai' by Saburo Sakai, published by William Kimber & Co., Ltd.]

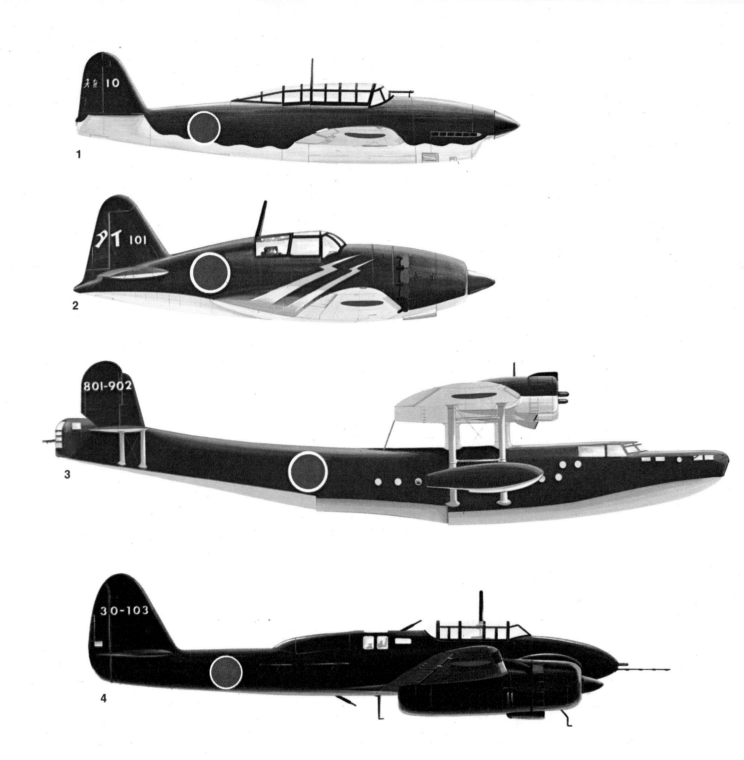

Japan's later warplanes

Japan's air forces went to war largely relying on the navy's Zero fighter, Kate torpedo-bomber, and Nell and Betty long-range bombers, and on the army's Oscar fighter and Sally bomber. Production of these machines was kept up to speed the 'Runaway Victory', and the newer designs were shelved. But after 18 months of the Pacific War the back of Japan's carrier fleet had been broken at Midway and her outermost conquests had already fallen to Allied 'island-hopping' offensives. Now the Japanese needed aircraft capable of operating more from shore bases than from aircraft-carriers, and the new aircraft were rushed ahead. The Zero was supplemented by the Jack, the Kate by the Jill and the Judy. For the army, the new single-engined Tony and the twin-engined Nick began to replace the ageing Oscar. A new long-range bomber – the Helen – was intended to replace the Sally, Nell, and Betty, but never did. Yet none of these aircraft, old or new, could halt the swelling flood of Lightnings, Thunderbolts, and Fortresses

1. JUDY: Yokosuka D4Y-2 *Susei*
A navy carrier bomber, the Judy first sav service as a reconnaissance plane at Mic way, was later used extensively, an finally – like most Japanese types – sa service as a Kamikaze. *Max speed:* 33 mph. *Range:* 1,320 miles. *Crew:* two *Armament:* three 7·7-mm machine-gun 1,100 lb of bombs

2. JACK: Mitsubishi J2M-3 *Raiden*
Designed as a single-seat shore-base interceptor fighter at the same time as th Zero, the Jack had so many teething trouble that it only entered service in small nun bers. *Max speed:* 371 mph. *Range:* 65 miles. *Armament:* two 20-mm cannon, an two 7·1-mm machine-guns

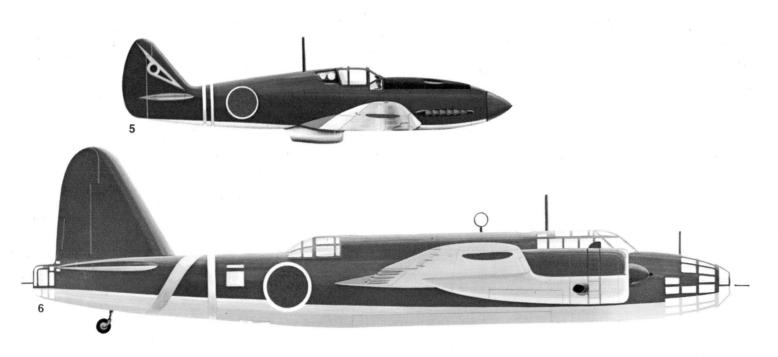

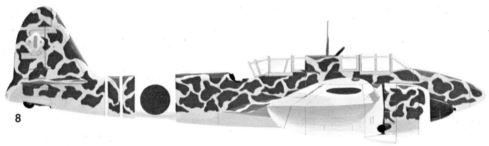

3. MAVIS: Kawanishi H6K4-L Flying-boat
This was one of the more elderly Japanese long-range navy patrol bombers; it was an unarmed type, and the lessons learned from it resulted in the 'Emily', which was given five cannon and four MGs. Mavis was then relegated to transport duties. *Max speed:* 237 mph. *Range:* 4,000 miles. *Crew:* nine (plus 18 passengers)

4. IRVING: Nakajima JINI-S *Gekko*
Designed first as a fighter, then used by the navy in reconnaissance, then converted to a night fighter. It had a unique armament of two pairs of 20-mm cannon above and below the fuselage at an angle of 30°. *Max speed:* 315 mph. *Range:* 1,360 miles. *Crew:* two. *Armament:* four 20-mm cannon

5. TONY: Kawasaki Ki-61 *Hien*
When Allied pilots first met Tony in action in 1943, it was thought to be a version of the German Me-109. Well armed and well protected, Tony was a formidable opponent; but its engine gave considerable trouble in service. *Max speed:* 348 mph. *Range:* 1,185 miles. *Armament:* two 20-mm cannon, and two 12·7-mm machine-guns

6. HELEN: Nakajima Ki-49 *Donryu*
Helen was an army heavy bomber, designed for use in the event of Japan going to war with Russia, but was first used in action in a raid on Darwin in 1943. It was never produced in great numbers. *Max speed:* 306 mph. *Range:* 1,490 miles. *Crew:* eight. *Armament:* one 20-mm cannon, five 7·7-mm machine-guns

7. JILL: Nakajima B6N-2 *Tenzan*
The Jill was the direct replacement for the Kate torpedo-bomber, and its first major action was the Battle of the Philippine Sea in June 1944. *Max speed:* 299 mph. *Range:* 1,600 miles. *Armament:* one 13-mm, one 7·9-mm machine-gun; one 1,764-lb torpedo OR six 220-lb bombs

8. NICK: Kawasaki Ki-45 *Toryu*
The Nick was the first twin-engined fighter to enter service with the Japanese army air force; the Allies first met it in action over New Guinea in 1943, and it was also used in home defence duties. *Max speed:* 340 mph. *Range:* 932 miles. *Crew:* two. *Armament:* varied, but a typical combination was: one 37-mm, two 20-mm cannon, and one 7·7-mm machine-gun

The Greatest Air Battle of the War

The primary object of the Royal Air Force during the Dieppe raid was not only to provide close support, but to lure the Luftwaffe in the west into the air and destroy it. The bait was the presence of 252 ships close offshore in a confined space. In this object the Royal Air Force accepted the disadvantage of fighting 'Away' in the enemy air while at the same time supporting the assaults on the beaches and protecting the shipping.

It seemed at first that the Luftwaffe would refuse the challenge. At 0730 hours there were no more than 30 enemy fighters, mostly FW-190s, in the air, and it was 1000 hours before the enemy appeared in strength. Typhoons flew diversionary feints to draw off enemy bombers flying south from Holland and Beauvais, while Spitfires intercepted large bomber forces. At this hour withdrawal operations from the beaches were under way, and it was vital for the air force to give close support over the Dieppe beaches and Pourville. In the half-hour from 1010 hours to 1040 hours, while fully engaged against enemy fighters and bombers, Bostons and Hurricanes assaulted the Bismarck headland with unrelenting fury. Over Dieppe and Pourville Spitfires broke up the enemy bomber formations, fighting in and out of the thickening cloud cover, while Blenheims, Bostons, and Hurricanes went in again and again in support of the ground troops. Many pilots by this time were flying their third and fourth sorties since dawn against fresh enemy pilots, yet by 1300 hours the RAF had gained a clear advantage: in the crucial phases of the withdrawal not one enemy bomber succeeded in attacking the landing-craft or the mass of shipping offshore.

In the final analysis the RAF flew 2,617 sorties for the loss of 106 aircraft, including 88 Spitfires. The enemy admitted to 170 losses in what was the greatest air battle in a single day of the whole war. The margin was narrow, but in the air that day it was a victory.

Throughout the battle air-sea rescue launches weaved on their rescue missions in the midst of the maze of assault craft and shipping, adding their page or paragraph to the deeds of the day. Some 13 pilots and one wounded observer were rescued at a cost of 11 officers and 26 men, killed, wounded, and missing.

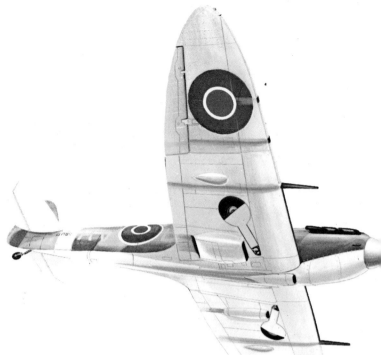

SPITFIRE VB: Single-seat fighter. This mark suffered in its first encounters with the FW-190. **Speed:** 369 mph at 19,750 ft. **Max range:** 1,135 miles. **Armament:** Four ·303-inch machine-guns. Two 20-mm cannon

FOCKE-WULF FW-190 A-4: Single-seat fighter. One of the outstanding aircraft of the war. **Speed:** 404 mph at 20,500 ft. **Operational range:** 592 miles. **Armament:** Two 7·92-mm machine-guns. Four 20-mm cannon

△ A crippled Blenheim flies low over German troops on the Dieppe beach

Ullstein

HAWKER TYPHOON IB: Single-seat fighter and ground-attack aircraft. **Speed:** 404 mph at 10,000 ft. **Operational range:** 374 miles. **Armament:** Four 20-mm cannon. (Later, eight rocket projectiles or two 500-lb bombs)

BRISTOL BLENHEIM Mk V: Twin-engined medium bomber. **Speed:** 303 mph at 15,000 ft. **Operational range:** 1,900 miles. **Armament:** One remote control ·303-inch machine-gun in a blister beneath the nose, two ·303-inch machine-guns in turret, and 1,000 lb of bombs

DOUGLAS BOSTON Mk III: Twin-engined attack bomber. **Speed:** 350 mph at 12,000 ft. **Operational range:** 1,050 miles. **Crew:** Five. **Armament:** Four fixed machine-guns in the nose (two ·30, two ·50), two ·30 machine-guns in turret, and one ·30 machine-gun in belly. 1,000 lb of bombs

John Batchelor

'One of our planes is missing' . . . and here, reconstructed from the meticulous records of the Luftwaffe, is the minute-by-minute story of the fate of RAF Stirling BK-712

Flight-Lieutenant Alfred Price

1. The men and their mission

The town of Krefeld lies just inside Germany, near the frontier with Holland, on the western fringe of the great Ruhr industrial complex. Since the 17th century it has been famous for the manufacture of silks, an industry started by French Huguenots fleeing religious persecution in their own land. In addition to the silk factories, the town's boundaries enclose light engineering, soap, and chemical works. With a population exceeding 150,000, Krefeld compares in size and importance with Bolton, England. And on the night of June 21/22, 1943, it was the subject of a 705-aircraft attack by RAF Bomber Command.

In many respects the attack was typical. The raid was to be opened at 0127 hours by a single high-flying Mosquito of the Pathfinder Force. This aircraft was to use the 'Oboe' bombing technique, an extremely accurate method whereby it was controlled during its bombing run from special ground radar stations back in England. The Mosquito was to carry just four of the new target marker bombs, highly effective devices which had been introduced into action only a week earlier. These markers fell like ordinary bombs, but when 1,000 feet above the ground they explosively ejected 60 brilliant red pyrotechnic candles. The candles then scattered in the air and fell, to form an inextinguishable red circle of fire, 100 yards in diameter, on the ground. The candles burned for only about three minutes, so during the planned 53 minutes of the Krefeld attack relays of Pathfinder aircraft were to reinforce this marking. A total of 85 aircraft were to be involved in the business of marking the target, though many of these aircraft would be four-engined heavy bombers, carrying high-explosive bombs as well as markers.

At 0132 hours, precisely five minutes after the first target markers went down, the first wave of bombing aircraft — 104 Lancasters flown by selected crews — were to release their bombs on the vivid red pools of fire on the ground. The remaining 516 bombers were to follow them, in four distinct waves.

In order to saturate the German fighter defences along the route of the attack, the bomber crews were ordered to make every endeavour to keep together in a concentrated 'stream'. The passage of 705 aircraft in 53 minutes would result in an average of 14 aircraft flying over the target every minute. Since each German radar-controlled fighter interception took about ten minutes, and a ground radar station could direct only one fighter at a time, the tactic of concentration served the British well.

The period from 0149 to 0157 hours at the target was allocated to the 98 Stirling bombers of No. 3 Group, which comprised the third wave. With this in mind Pilot Officer W. Skillinglaw of No. 218 Squadron took off in Stirling BK-712 from the airfield at Downham Market, near King's Lynn, at 0015 hours. His aircraft carried its maximum bomb load, more than 6 tons of high-explosive and incendiary bombs. Since the round trip to Krefeld and back amounted to a distance of less than 500 miles, there was no requirement to reduce the bomb load to enable extra fuel to be carried.

While the heavily laden Stirling clawed its way to height the navigator, Sergeant McArdle, busied himself with his route. The assembly point for the third wave was Aldeburgh, on the Suffolk coast south of Lowestoft. From there the bombers were to fly east south-east, on a heading of one-zero-five degrees, straight to Krefeld.

As Skillinglaw's Stirling left the coast of East Anglia behind it, the gunners — Sergeant Lunn in the nose, Gurney in the mid-upper, and Hart in the rear turret — each fired a short burst to test their guns. Like strings of pearls the bright tracer rounds sailed lazily away from the aircraft. Now both pilots and gunners settled down to the deadly serious business of each scanning his allotted piece of sky for lurking night fighters. The three-quarters full moon gave the crewmen a distinct feeling of nakedness. As the bomber droned on over the sea each minute brought it nearly 4 miles closer to the shores of Occupied Europe . . . and the now alerted German defences.

A Stirling of No. 218 Squadron prepares for take-off. On the night of June 21/22, 1943, some 98 of them set out for Krefeld in the Ruhr. But even as the bombers were crossing the coast of Britain, the German defences were alert and ready

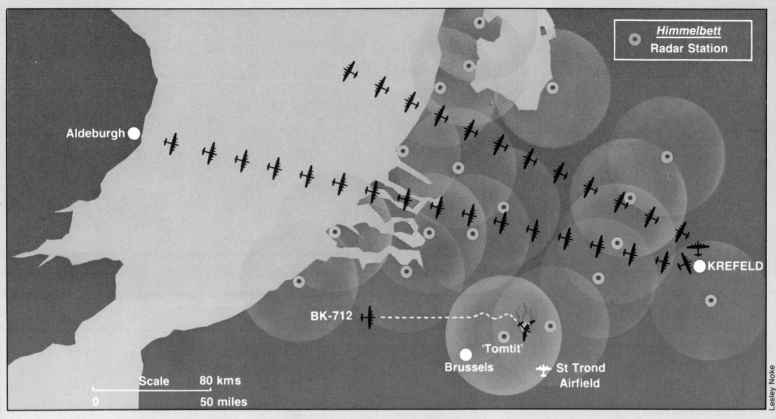

Himmelbett
Radar Station

Aldeburgh

BK-712

'Tomtit'
Brussels
St Trond
Airfield

KREFELD

Scale   80 kms
0   50 miles

Lesley Noke

2. The chase and the kill

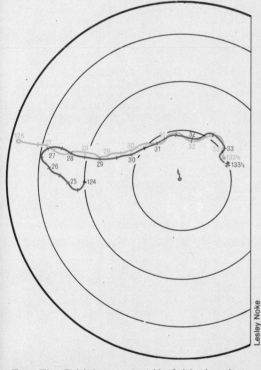

Lesley Noke

Top: The British target at Krefeld, showing the intended flight-track from the English coast. Stirling BK-712 was fatally off course as it entered the zone of the *Himmelbett* radar station 'Tomtit'. *Above:* The track chart—painstakingly traced off a radar plotting table by an unknown Luftwaffe airman—showed the last seven minutes in the life of Stirling BK-712. The bomber enters the radar zone at left—at point 126—and within minutes Schnaufer's night fighter (red line) has homed on to its target, intent on hunting it to its doom

For Leutnant Kühnel and the men of XIII Company, 211th Luftwaffe Signals Regiment, this night seemed to be something of a disappointment. The radar station they manned, code-named 'Tomtit' and situated 15 miles to the north-east of Brussels, was fully alerted. But tonight the stream of British bombers was passing more than 40 miles to the north of the station, out of range of its Giant Würzburg precision radar sets. By 0110 hours the radar stations to the north, Hamster, Butterfly, and Wasp, Gorilla, Beaver, and Robin, were all busily directing their fighters on to incoming bombers. But for Tomtit there seemed nothing.

Then the crew of Tomtit's long-range Freya radar observed a lone aircraft which, if it held its present course, would run right into the range of their precision radars. All this was unknown to the men on board Stirling BK-712. For some reason Skillinglaw and his crew had strayed over Belgium and now, at 0115 hours, they were moving eastwards on Krefeld. But between them and their target was radar station Tomtit.

Orbiting overhead Tomtit in a Messerschmitt 110 was Leutnant Heinz-Wolfgang Schnaufer, a 20-year-old pilot belonging to II Gruppe of Night Fighter Geschwader I. Schnaufer had been scrambled from St Trond airfield near Brussels at 0054 hours. Now, at 0120, he received Kühnel's radioed warning of a 'courier' (target) approaching from the west.

One of the Tomtit station's Giant Würzburg radar sets was already tracking Schnaufer as he flew west to intercept. Meanwhile, in the cabin of the second Giant Würzburg set, Unteroffizier Deller and his six-man crew endeavoured to pick up the intruder on their screens. At 0126 hours they made contact with the inflying Stirling: 'Courier range 34 kilometres, height 4,300 metres, bearing 285 degrees.' On the frosted-glass screen that comprised Tomtit's plotting table, the red light representing the bomber's position moved steadily eastwards. The blue light representing Schnaufer's position closed upon it, slowly but purposefully. A half minute before the two aircraft, flying on their almost opposite headings, crossed, Kühnel directed Schnaufer to turn starboard through almost a half circle. The Messerschmitt pilot followed these instructions precisely, and slid in neatly behind the Stirling and its unsuspecting crew.

In the rear of the Messerschmitt Leutnant Baro, Schnaufer's radar operator, huddled over the screens in front of him. Then he saw what he was looking for: a small hump of light, hardly perceptible at first, then becoming larger and larger, rose from the flickering base line on his tube: contact to starboard, range 2,500 metres. Baro now passed Schnaufer a running commentary on the bomber's movements until 0130 hours when, 500 yards away to the right and above, the young German pilot caught sight of the flames from the Stirling's engine exhausts. As Schnaufer closed in underneath the bomber he was seen by one of the Stirling's gunners, and Skillinglaw hurled his aircraft into a violent corkscrew in an effort to shake off the pursuer. But in vain. The German pilot closed in to 50 yards, firing his powerful battery of cannon and machine-guns whenever he managed to get the twisting bomber in his sights. The Stirling crumpled under the impact of exploding shells, then the fuselage and wings burst into flames. Mortally wounded, the bomber flew on for a short time, then plunged earthwards.

From the balcony of Tomtit's headquarters Unteroffizier Schellenburg, duty watch-keeper of the XIII Company, had observed the one-sided battle taking place 2½ miles above. Unteroffizier Deffer also watched it, on his radar screens. As the stricken bomber plummetted down, the position where its 'blip' disappeared off the radar tube was carefully noted: that was where the search for the wreck would begin at first light that morning.

3. The end: a terse telegram

As dawn broke Leutnant Kühnel duly set out to look for the wreck, to enable him to verify Schnaufer's claim. It was not difficult. On returning to his headquarters Kühnel reported to his superiors:

The wreck is 3 kilometres north-east of Aarschot, in map reference NK 31B. There are seven enemy crewmen, all of whom are lying dead in the wreckage . . . The Short Stirling was completely wrecked in the crash and subsequent fire. The rudder and rear turret are about 1,500 metres from the rest of the wreckage.

Kühnel had a guard placed on the wreckage to discourage souvenir hunters. Later it would be examined by technical experts. The bodies of the dead British airmen were removed, for identification and subsequent burial. A terse telegram would bear the news of their death to Britain, via the Red Cross in Switzerland.

Skillinglaw's Stirling was Schnaufer's thirteenth 'kill'. In the Krefeld attack Bomber Command lost 41 other aircraft, nearly 6% of the force committed. The next night would see 40 or so new crews making their first attacks. However Krefeld had suffered heavily too, on that summer night in 1943. Skillinglaw and his crew did not reach the target but some 3,000 of their comrades did, and in an extremely concentrated attack they reduced nearly half of the town to rubble. More than 1,000 civilians were killed. Both for RAF Bomber Command, and for the German people, it was a long hard war.

△ Leutnant Heinz-Wolfgang Schnaufer; BK-712 was his thirteenth kill

▷ One of the many documents in the Luftwaffe file of BK-712's last mission is Leutnant Kühnel's report on the work of his radar station. The translation is given above right, in text

Kühnel, Lt.
Jägerleitoffizier

O.U., den 22.6.1943

Meldung

zum Dunkelnachtjagdabschuss Lt. Schnaufer - Lt.Baro
am 22.6.43 um 01.33 1/2 Uhr.

Ich melde der Gruppe, dass ich am 22.6.1943 um 06.00 Uhr am Aufschlagort der von Lt. Schnaufer am 22.6.43 um 01.33 1/2 Uhr abgeschossenen Short Stirling I war.
Der Bruch liegt 3 km nordostwärts Aarschot, Planquadrat NK 31 b.
Die Anzahl der feindlichen Besatzungsmitglieder beträgt 7, die sämtlich tot in den Trümmern der Maschine, zum Teil völlig verbrannt, lagen.
Durch den Aufschlagbrand ist die Short Stirling weitgehendst zerstört, das Höhenleitwerk mit Heckstand liegt ca. 1500 m vom übrigen Bruch entfernt.

▷ The wreckage of Stirling BK-712: none of its seven-man crew survived

THE DUEL OVER GERMANY

RAF Bombing Offensive, July 1943/March 1944

Flight-Lieutenant Alfred Price

On July 28, 1943, horror struck the city of Hamburg: a savage RAF raid kindled the first 'firestorm' and more than 50,000 people died in the holocaust. The German fighter defences, which had previously been holding their own against the RAF attacks, had been thrown into chaos by the new 'Window' radar countermeasure and desperate solutions had to be found. Found they were – and within nine months the RAF itself faced disaster over Nuremburg

It was still light at 2155 hours on the evening of July 24, 1943, when the first of the 'Pathfinder' aircraft – Lancaster G-George of No. 7 Squadron – roared down the runway at Oakington airfield near Cambridge. Regular as clockwork, at half minute intervals, the remaining bombers at Oakington followed it into the air. Soon this scene was being repeated at more than a score of bomber airfields spread throughout East Anglia, Lincolnshire, and Yorkshire.

In the half light the bombers clawed for altitude, moving eastwards in an untidy mass like a swarm of bees. By midnight the force had assembled over the North Sea, a mighty phalanx of 791 aircraft – 347 Lancasters, 246 Halifaxes, 125 Stirlings, and 73 Wellingtons – sprawled out over an area 200 miles long and 20 miles wide. This airborne armada moved eastwards at 225 miles per hour – $3\frac{3}{4}$ miles per minute. And as the aircraft formed up, attentive German eyes followed their progress.

Shortly before 2300 hours, an early warning radar site near Ostend reported: 'Approximately 80 aircraft at Gustav Caesar 5, course east, altitude 23,000 feet.' At the headquarters of the Luftwaffe III Fighter Division, at Arnhem-Deelen in Holland, a small spot of light moved swiftly across the darkened situation map. It came to rest at position GC-5 on the German fighter grid, just to the north of Ipswich. Soon the spot of light was joined by others as more and more bombers appeared over the radar horizon. The attack was obviously going to be a big one. Where this time?

As yet the Germans could only speculate on the raiders' goal, whose mere name had dried the throat of many an experienced bomber crewman at the briefing earlier: Hamburg. Hamburg was well known to the men of the RAF. By the third week in July 1943, the port had been raided on 98 occasions. Her defences were formidable: she was ringed by no less than 54 heavy flak and 22 searchlight batteries, and six major night fighter airfields were within easy flying distance. Previous operations had, in consequence, cost the RAF heavily.

If it was the flak that caused damage and forced bomber crews to jink their aircraft, thus making accurate bombing difficult, it was the venomously efficient night fighters that were the real killers. Their tactics had been evolved by General Josef Kammhuber, the commander of the Luftwaffe night fighter force, and tested and improved during a hundred battles. His system, codenamed 'Himmelbett' (four-poster bed), depended for its success on a lavishly equipped chain of ground radar stations. Each station had a maximum effective interception range of 30 miles, and to form a defensive barrier through which the raiders would have to pass, Kammhuber erected a line with Himmelbett stations at 20-mile intervals. This line extended down occupied Europe, shaped like a giant inverted sickle: the 'handle' ran through Denmark, from north to south, the 'blade' curved through northern Germany, Holland, Belgium, and eastern France to the Swiss frontier. Each station was equipped with one 'Freya' and two Giant 'Würzburg' radar sets.

At the approach of the raiders the fighters were scrambled, and told to orbit radio beacons positioned next to the radar stations. Once there, a short-range, narrow-beam Giant Würzburg radar would swing round and hold the fighter in its gaze. Meanwhile the long-range, wide-beam Freya radar directed the second Giant Würzburg on to the approaching bomber. With precise information relayed from the operators of the two Giant Würzburg sets, the German ground controller radioed his orders to the fighter pilot, to bring the latter on to the quarry's tail. In the rear of the cockpit the fighter's own radar operator would be watching the flickering tubes of his lightweight 'Lichtenstein' radar for the first glimpse of the enemy. Once in contact with the bomber the German crew would radio a brief 'Pauke' call. 'Pauke', literally 'beat the kettledrum', was the Luftwaffe equivalent to the RAF 'Tally Ho!': it meant the target was in sight, and about to be engaged. The fighter radar operator now passed his pilot a running commentary of instructions until the latter caught sight of the exhaust flames from the bomber's motors. The hunter closed on his victim, endeavouring to get into a firing position without being seen. Like that of the infantry sniper, the task of the night fighter crew – of either side – amounted to little short of cold-blooded murder. If it was possible to get to within 50 yards behind and astern of a still unsuspecting victim, a favourite German tactic was to pull the fighter up on to its tail, at the same time opening fire. The battery of cannon pumped out a stream of explosive shells, to rake the raider from stem to stern. All too often the first thing the hapless bomber crew knew of the attack was the shudder as their aircraft buckled under the impact of exploding shells. The German fighter crews were fighting to defend their homes and loved ones; they did so with the same determination that had characterised the RAF during the Battle of Britain. Men charged with such a mission give no quarter.

By July 1943 the German defences were knocking down an average of more than five out of every 100 bombers attacking their homeland, and this rate was rising steadily. Three quarters of those lost fell to fighters, the rest to flak and accidents.

Clearly, it was vital to the continued success of the British bomber offensive that some means of neutralising the devastatingly efficient Himmelbett system should be found. Technically the answer was to be amazingly simple: little strips of aluminium foil. Known by the cover-name 'Window', the strips measured 30 centimetres long and 1·5 centimetres wide and came in bundles of 2,000, held together by an elastic band. When released from an aircraft, the bundle broke up, to form a 'cloud' of strips which gave a 'blip' on a radar screen the same size as that from the bomber itself. By releasing one such bundle per minute from each aircraft in a concentrated bomber stream, it was possible to saturate the area with 'blips', thus making radar-controlled interceptions impossible.

During 1942 British scientists had conducted a series of trials with the 'Window' strips, under the greatest secrecy. Quite independently, and under equal secrecy, their German counterparts had been doing exactly the same thing. In both countries the men reached the same conclusion: the new countermeasure was dynamite. If used properly it could wreck the radar-dependent air defences of either nation. Neither side had then felt that its bomber arm had a margin of strength over its opponent's sufficient to justify the risk of introducing such an innovation. But by the summer of 1943 the striking power of RAF Bomber Command had expanded out of all recognition, while the demands of the war of attrition on the Eastern Front had reduced the German bomber force to comparative impotence.

The bombing was costly in life to both sides. *Below:* A Liberator bursts into flames after being hit by flak. Over Schweinfurt the Americans lost 60 aircraft in one raid alone. And the RAF lost 95 aircraft (of 795) over Nuremberg in one night. *Bottom:* Bomb damage in Hannover. In one raid on October 19, 1943, 2½ square miles of this city were destroyed

Germany's shield: and Britain's bizarre response

By 1943, the Germans had perfected a defence system against the British night attacks. (1) From a series of radar stations strung across northern Europe at 20-mile intervals a long-range, early-warning radar, 'Freya' (far right) would pick up the bomber (red beam). (2) As it closed, one short-range narrow-beam Giant 'Würzburg' set (right) would fix on to the bomber (blue beam), while another would fix on to the night fighter orbiting the station. This would then be guided to the bomber until (3) the fighter's 'Lichtenstein' radar (orange beam) had made contact with its quarry. (4) The British countermeasure 'Window' was extremely simple: on normal 'Würzburg' screens (A,B,C) bearing and elevation tubes (centre and right) showed the target on both sides of a base line. When the target was dead central on both screens, the radar was fixed on target. But by dropping clouds of aluminium foil strips the British could produce an effect (a,b,c) which made precise measurement impossible

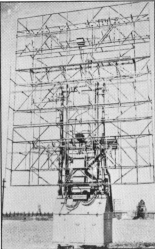

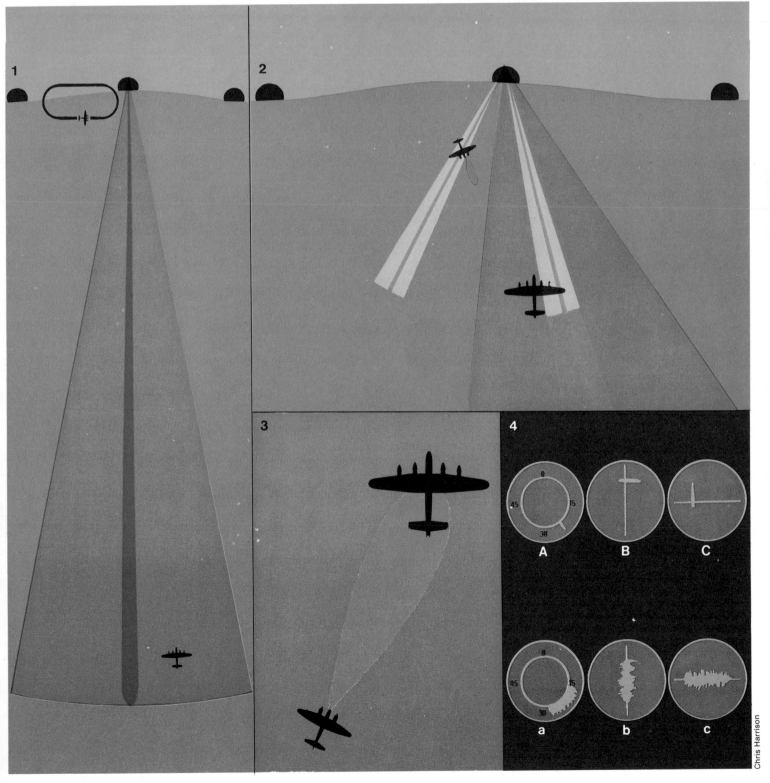

Chris Harrison

89

Messerschmitt Bf-110G: Although unsuccessful as a long-range fighter and fighter-bomber, the Me-110 was used widely and successfully as a night fighter. **Span:** 53 feet 4⅞ inches. **Length:** 41 feet 6¾ inches. **Speed:** 342 mph at 22,000 feet. **Ceiling:** 26,005 feet. **Range:** 1,305 miles. **Armament:** Two 30-mm and two 20-mm cannon, and two 7·9-mm MG. **Crew:** Three

Junkers Ju-88G6: This variant of the famous medium bomber was one of the most widely-used night fighters. It could carry 'Schräge Musik' – upward-firing cannon mounted in the central fuselage. **Span:** 65 feet 10½ inches. **Length:** 47 feet 1½ inches. **Speed:** 311 mph at 20,000 feet. **Ceiling:** 32,500 feet. **Range:** 1,950 miles. **Armament:** Three 20-mm cannon, three 7·9-mm MG, and two 20-mm Schräge Musik cannon. **Crew:** Three

The first use of 'Window'

On July 15, 1943 a meeting of the War Cabinet, presided over by Winston Churchill, finally permitted the use of the new counter-measure.

Now, at 0025 hours on the morning of July 25, 1943, as the leading bombers in the stream passed the island fortress of Heligoland on their way to Hamburg, the first 'Window' bundles were dropped into the black air beneath each bomber.

The first report of anything out of the ordinary came from radar station 'Hummer', on Heligoland itself. By 0040 hours the incoming bombers could be seen on the radar screens, together with the 'Window': since each cloud of foil remained effective for 15 minutes before the strips dispersed, the British force appeared to have a strength of 11,000 bombers! The Germans could not believe their eyes. The Hummer station reported back that it was 'disturbed by many apparent point-targets looking like aircraft, either stationary or slow moving. The picking-up of genuine aircraft is made extremely difficult. Once they have been picked up it is possible to follow them, but only with difficulty.' Station 'Auster', on the southern tip of Sylt, reported similar trouble. So, in turn, did the rest of the radar stations sited around Hamburg proper.

Circling over their appointed radio beacons, the German night fighter crews waited with growing impatience for instructions from their ground controllers.

But below them all was chaos.

Soon the ether was thick with confused appeals and exclamations: 'The enemy are reproducing themselves.' 'It is impossible – too many hostiles.' 'Wait a while. There are many more hostiles.' 'I cannot control you.' 'Try without your ground control.'

When the first wave of bombers – 110 Lancasters from No. 1 and 5 Groups – arrived over Hamburg at 0103 hours their crews were struck by the air of unreality: instead of the precise control which had always been the case in the past, the searchlights now seemed to be groping blindly. Where beams did cross, others would quickly join them, and as many as 30 or 40 beams would build up to form a cone – on nothing.

The radar sets controlling the searchlights were now useless, as were those which controlled the guns. The gunners were forced to abandon predicted fire, and now they loosed off round after unaimed round ineffectively into the sky.

Saved from the accustomed harassments of fighters on the approaches to the target, and searchlights and shell bursts over it, the British crews now made their bombing runs on the almost defenceless Hamburg. The Pathfinders' radar-aimed yellow markers had fallen accurately round the aiming point, and had been followed almost immediately by reds from the Visual Marker Force.

The leaders of the Luftwaffe had never expected that they would be called upon to meet a concentrated bomber attack. But as the British and American air forces began the raids which were to develop into 'round the clock' attacks, the Germans were forced to improvise: a number of fighter-bombers and medium bombers were adapted to carry heavy gun armament plus the Lichtenstein radar, while development of specialised aircraft was accelerated

John Batchelor

Dornier Do-217N: Another medium bomber which was developed for use as a night fighter. **Span:** 62 feet 4 inches. **Length:** 58 feet 9 inches. **Speed:** 320 mph at 18,700 feet. **Ceiling:** 31,170 feet. **Range:** 1,550 miles. **Armament:** Four 20-mm cannon, four 7·9-mm MG, one 13-mm MG in a remote-control dorsal turret, and one 13-mm MG in a dorsal turret. **Crew:** Three

Heinkel He-219A Uhu (Owl): Although the prototype of this formidable specialised night fighter first flew in 1942 it never achieved widespread operation. Only 268 were built. **Span:** 60 feet 8⅓ inches. **Length:** 50 feet 11¾ inches. **Speed:** 416 mph at 22,965 feet. **Ceiling:** 41,660 feet. **Range:** 960 miles. **Armament:** Two 30-mm and two 20-mm cannon, and two 30-mm Schräge Musik cannon

It was upon these, and the green markers dropped at intervals by 'Backers-up' of the Pathfinder force, that the first and succeeding waves of bombers aimed their loads: scores of the huge 8,000- and 4,000-pound 'blockbusters', thousands of the smaller 1,000-pound bombs, and a veritable rain of the nasty little 4-pound incendiaries. In general the crews far above the target were able to make out only the flashes as their high-explosive bombs burst, and a few shimmering fires started by the incendiaries. But at 0110 hours there was an explosion which lit up the sky for miles around.

After bombing, the RAF crews flew straight on for six minutes to get well clear of the target. Then the pilots swung their machines round on to a north-westerly heading parallel to the one that had brought them in. To the men now returning from battle there was no doubt that this new-fangled 'Window' stuff really did work. In fact Bomber Command lost only 12 aircraft (1·5%) out of the large attacking force. The new 'Window' tactic had clearly been a great success. Had the raid cost the 6% losses normal for a raid on Hamburg, the RAF would have lost about 50 bombers. So about 35 or more had been saved, by the dropping of 40 tons of 'Window' —92,000,000 strips of aluminium foil.

But Sir Arthur Harris had already warned that the 'Battle of Hamburg' was not going to be won in a single night: 'It was estimated that at least 10,000 tons of bombs will have to be dropped to complete the process of elimination. To achieve the maximum effect of air bombardment this city should be subjected to sustained attack.'

So it came about that RAF Bomber Command launched a further attack on Hamburg at 0057 hours on the morning of July 28. The 722 bombers involved flew across the city from north-west to south-east this time, and by 0112 hours crews running in to bomb saw beneath them a vast carpet of fire, covering almost the whole of the north-east quarter of the city. Into this inferno succeeding aircraft were dropping thousands of incendiary and high-explosive bombs.

During the whole of July, less than 1·7 inches of rain had fallen on the city, and the previous day had been very hot: the kindling was everywhere. Under the torrent of well-placed incendiary bombs the fires soon took hold. With the city's water supplies disrupted and the civil defence headquarters already blitzed in the previous raid, the blaze was able to rage unchecked.

The firestorm
In principle, a firestorm is horrifyingly simple, and from the comfort of an armchair is an interesting exercise in applied physics. A multitude of fires heat the air above them, and as the hot air rises more air rushes in to take its place; this inrushing air fans the

A running battle over Germany

After 'Window' had enabled the RAF to burn Hamburg almost undisturbed, the Germans introduced several new tactics. In 'Wild Boar' the night fighters waited over the target to intercept the bombers by visual sighting alone; for 'Tame Boar' radar guided the fighters into the areas where the 'Window' was thickest so that they could close with the bomber streams and then search for their targets independently. On March 30, 1944, 'Tame Boar' proved its value in a battle against bombers attacking Nuremburg *(below)*. The night was clear so that visual sighting was easy, while strong winds made the bomber streams lose cohesion. As the bombers came over Beacon 'Ida', the first fighters were zeroed in by the ground controllers *(right),* and all along the route to Nuremburg new groups were being fed in, until more than 200 night fighters from all over Germany were engaged in the running battle. The British lost over 94 aircraft in that one raid

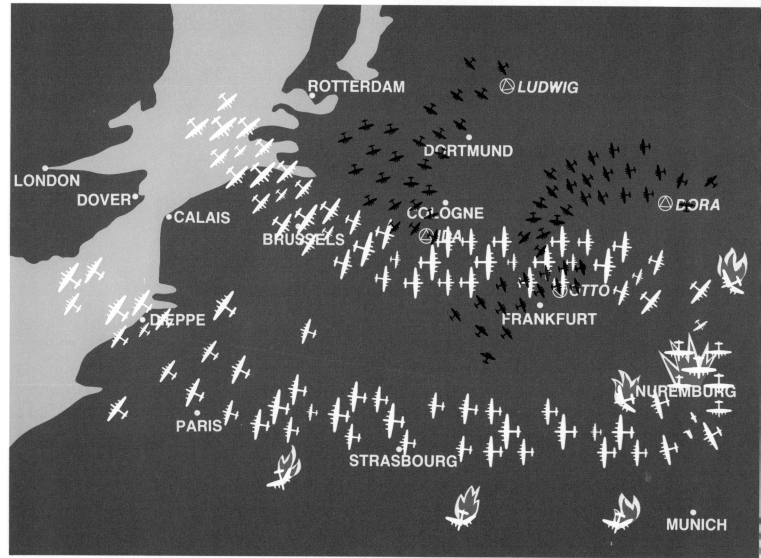

flames, before itself becoming heated and rising, and the process repeats itself continuously while the flames blaze hotter and hotter. This was what now happened in Hamburg. Soon, in places, the temperature exceeded 1,000° Centigrade, the mighty convection currents causing winds of up to 150 mph—twice hurricane force. As the air sucked in to the larger fires fanned the small ones, these too grew in size; quickly the fires linked with each other, until a built-up area 3½ miles long and 2½ miles wide was burning itself to death: 9 square miles of fire. It was a highly populated area that was going up in flames and Major-General Kehrl, the Hamburg civil defence chief, later reported:

The scenes of terror which took place in the firestorm area are indescribable. Children were torn away from their parents' hands by the force of the hurricane and whirled into the fire. People who thought they had escaped fell down, overcome by the devouring heat, and died in an instant. Refugees had to make their way over

the dead and dying. The sick and the infirm had to be left behind by the rescuers as they themselves were in danger of burning . . .

On the following morning, July 29, Gauleiter Kaufmann appealed to all non-essential civilian personnel to leave Hamburg. They needed no second bidding. Between dawn and dusk nearly 1,000,000 civilians, many of them swathed in bandages, streamed out of the city limits.

Bomber Command visited Hamburg again on July 30, and yet again on August 2, to add to the earlier holocaust. The number of people killed has never been established, but informed sources put the total at about 50,000. As the number of British civilians killed in German attacks on Britain up to this time was some 51,000, in one week the slate had been wiped almost clean.

Following the Hamburg fiasco the German night fighter tactics underwent a sweeping reorganisation. The system of close ground control, which General Kammhuber had pioneered, was largely

Hamburg: a wave of terror

The first raid on Hamburg on the night of July 24/25 had caused widespread damage, but the city continued to function. 'At least 10,000 tons of bombs will have to be dropped to complete the process of elimination. To achieve the maximum effect of air bombardment this city should be subjected to sustained attack' announced Air Chief-Marshal Harris, and so the RAF visited Hamburg again on the night of July 28 *(below),* and a new horror was added to the practice of aerial warfare. Colonel Adolf Galland describes the effect of the first firestorm on German morale: 'A wave of terror radiated from the suffering city and spread throughout Germany. Appalling details of the great fires were recounted, and their glow could be seen for days from a distance of 120 miles. A stream of haggard, terrified refugees flowed into the neighbouring provinces. In spite of the strictest reticence in the official communiqués, the Terror of Hamburg spread rapidly to the remotest villages of the Reich. Berlin was evacuated with signs of panic.' *Right:* Major Hajo Herrmann (centre, with Göring, left), one of the leading 'Wild Boar' pilots, personally led his fighters into action

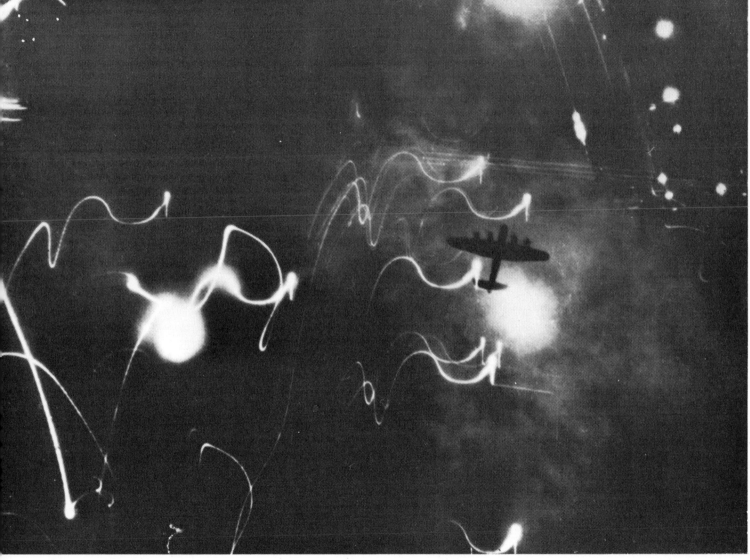

Imperial War Museum

abandoned and in its place the Luftwaffe introduced two new night fighting methods: 'Wild Boar' *(Wilde Sau)* and 'Tame Boar' *(Zahme Sau).* Kammhuber himself was quietly shunted out of his position as commander, and replaced by General Josef Schmid.

The Wild Boar tactic called for the concentration of night-fighting units over the target itself. There the massed searchlights, the vast conflagrations and the British Pathfinders' own marker fires lit up the sky for miles around, silhouetting the bombers for the German fighters. Thus the latter could now attack visually, and there was no need for the previously essential and comparatively expensive radar-equipped two-seater fighters. And significantly, for this same reason, Window could not degrade the system in any way. Under the command of Major Hajo Herrmann, the originator of the system, a number of specialist Wild Boar units were formed and equipped with single-seater Messerschmitt Me-109 and Focke-Wulf FW-190 day fighters.

The twin-seater radar-equipped specialist night fighters could also engage in Wild Boar-type tactics at the target, but to use their potential to the full, Colonel von Lossberg, a night fighting expert, devised the Tame Boar method. His idea was for the now jammed ground control stations to direct the fighters into the area where the Window concentration was densest, and once there the German pilots were to search visually for targets. When they were in the concentrated bomber stream, and aligned on the same heading, Lossberg hoped it would be possible to set up long running battles which would last the whole of the time the bombers were over occupied Europe.

Obviously, both the new German tactics demanded accurate and up-to-date information on the position of the bomber streams, but, while the radar network was dense and efficient enough for this purpose along the old Himmelbett line, elsewhere in Germany sets were comparatively few and far between. Luftwaffe signals

Firestorm: a German Hausfrau remembers . . .

'A great flame was shooting straight towards us. A flame as high as the houses and nearly as wide as the whole street. As I stared in fascination, the giant flame jerked back and then shot forward towards us again. "My God, what is it?" I said. "It's a firestorm," the old man answered. . . .'

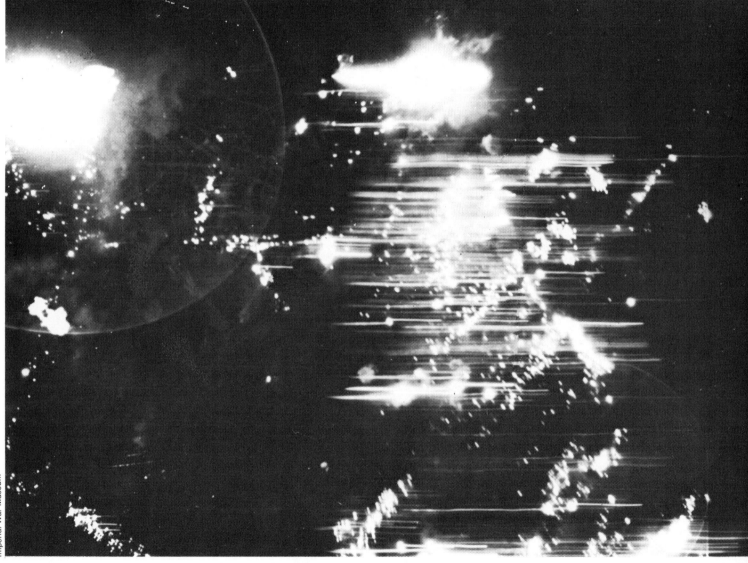

Imperial War Museum

personnel struggled to reposition radar sets in the new enlarged fighting area, but while they did so, some means had to be found of keeping tabs on the continually moving bomber streams. Fortunately for the Germans, the solution was presented by the raiders themselves.

To find their targets, the RAF Pathfinder crews used H2S — for those days an extremely advanced radar device which scanned the ground over which the aircraft flew. The German signals service exploited this factor by setting up a chain of 'Naxburg' and 'Korfu' ground direction-finding stations, which were able to follow precisely the sources of the distinctive H2S signals. Since the Pathfinders were invariably at the van of the bomber streams, this clever ploy meant that the raiding forces could be tracked with a high degree of accuracy almost from take-off to landing.

In the late summer of 1943, as the German fighter force gradually became more familiar with the new tactics, British losses

started to rise again. Both the Wild Boar and Tame Boar methods relied heavily on a running commentary broadcast from powerful ground transmitters, which passed details of the position, height, course, and estimated strength of the bomber streams. As British Intelligence officers listened in to the broadcasts one thing became clear: if this information could be denied to the German pilots, the new tactics might be set to nought.

So, once again, it was necessary to step up the radio counter-measures offensive. This time the target was the German fighter control channels, which now became a cacophony of wails, shrieks and groans. To this the Luftwaffe replied by transmitting orders simultaneously on a large number of separate frequencies, and introducing transmitters radiating even higher powers.

One interesting little piece of chicanery tried at this time rejoiced under the cover-name 'Corona'. If the German aircrews depended on orders radioed from the ground to find the bombers,

After the holocaust

When Hamburg's week of terror ended, more than 50,000 people had died *(left)*, and 9 square miles in the centre of the city had been burned out *(below)*. The most terrible description of the effect of the firestorm comes from this secret report, sent to the top leaders of Germany: 'Trees three feet thick were broken off or uprooted, human beings were thrown to the ground or flung alive into the flames by winds which exceeded a hundred and fifty miles an hour. The panic-stricken citizens did not know where to turn. Flames drove them from the shelters, but high-explosive bombs sent them scurrying back again. Once inside, they were suffocated by carbon-monoxide poisoning and their bodies reduced to ashes as though they had been placed in a crematorium, which was indeed what each shelter proved to be. The fortunate were those who jumped into the canals and water-ways and remained swimming or standing up to their necks in water for hours until the heat should die down.'
Below left: Birth of the first firestorm: a photograph taken during the raid of July 28, showing the widespread fires shortly before they linked up

would not false orders from a station in Britain lead them astray? The idea was first tried on the night of October 22, during a 569-aircraft attack on Kassel. The furious German fighter controller warned his crews not to be tricked by the enemy, and shouted 'In the name of General Schmid I *order* all aircraft to Kassel.' During the rumpus that followed the German swore into his microphone, at which the German-speaking 'ghost' controller in Britain re-marked: 'Now the Englishman is swearing!' Beside himself with rage the German shouted back: 'It isn't the Englishman who is swearing, it's me!'

But in spite of this hilarious interlude, Bomber Command was to lose 42 aircraft (6·2%) of the force dispatched. The German orders went out on many frequencies, and for technical reasons it was impossible for the British to carry on separate arguments on each. After a few evenings the 'Corona' operators ceased trying to imitate the German controllers, and instead took to reading bits of Goethe,

turgid pieces of German philosophy, and even playing records of Hitler's speeches on the German fighter control channels.

As the summer of 1943 turned to autumn, the first German night fighters arrived at the front fitted with a new radar device, code-named 'SN-2', in place of the Window-vulnerable 'Lichtenstein'. Because it worked on a much lower frequency than the earlier radar, SN-2 was able to see through the Window with little diffi-culty. The introduction of the new set, in combination with the Tame Boar tactics, was to have an important bearing on events during the winter to come.

On November 3, 1943, Air Chief-Marshal Sir Arthur Harris minuted to Churchill: 'We can wreck Berlin from end to end if the USAAF will come in on it. It may cost us 400-500 aircraft. It will cost Ger-many the war.'

This was the kind of promise that Churchill could not resist, and Harris was authorised to launch the 'Battle of Berlin'. The

American bomber force, however, was still licking its wounds following the attempt to push unescorted bomber formations through the German defences in daylight. It had suffered swingeing losses in the process, and could not now 'come in on it'. Harris decided to go it alone.

The first attack on the German capital of the new series was launched on November 18, 1943, and only nine of the 444 heavy bombers engaged failed to return. Bombers returned to Berlin three more times during November, and four times during the following month, and on each occasion losses were surprisingly low in view of the target's importance—possibly in consequence of the bad weather over Germany at the time.

This was an auspicious start, but as the new year opened Bomber Command's losses began to rise alarmingly. The first of a series of great and costly battles occurred on the night of January 21, when 55 bombers were lost out of 648 which set out for Magdeburg.

The bomber crews had fought back hard, but the German losses for the evening amounted to only seven aircraft—though one of the German fighters shot down that evening was a Junkers 88 piloted by the famous ace Major Prince zu Sayn Wittgenstein, the top-scorer with 83 'kills' to his credit. Wittgenstein's radar operator, Sergeant Ostheimer, later described how, after taking off at 2100 hours on a Tame Boar operation:

At about 2200 hours I picked up the first contact on my [SN-2] radar. I gave the pilot directions and a little later our target was seen: it was a Lancaster. We moved into position and opened fire, and the aircraft immediately caught fire in the left wing. It went down at a steep angle and started to spin. Between 2200 and 2205 hours the bomber crashed and went off with a violent explosion. I watched the crash.

Again we searched. At times I could see as many as six aircraft on my radar. After some further direction, the next target was in sight—another Lancaster. After the first burst from us there was a small fire, and the machine dropped back its left wing and went down in a vertical dive. Shortly afterwards I saw it crash. It was some time between 2210 and 2215 hours. When it crashed there were heavy detonations; most probably it was the bomb load.

After a short interval we again saw a Lancaster. After a long burst of fire the bomber caught fire and went down. I saw it crash some time between 2225 and 2230 hours. Immediately afterwards we saw yet another four-engined bomber: we were in the middle of the bomber stream. After one firing pass, this bomber went down in flames, at about 2240 hours. I saw the crash.

Such a personal score of four raiders in less than 40 minutes was by no means unique in the German night fighter force. Once within the tight mass of heavily laden bombers, the cannon-armed fighters were able to wreak havoc—and with the bitter memory of Hamburg still fresh in their minds, Wittgenstein and his colleagues fought like tigers.

Within a few minutes of the fourth 'kill' Ostheimer had directed the Prince into a firing position yet again, and the first burst set the bomber on fire. But then the fire went out—and as Wittgenstein moved in for a further attack, his own aircraft rocked under the impact of an accurate burst of machine-gun fire. Ostheimer managed to bail out and land safely, but the Prince was killed. Almost certainly the attack had come from one of the other bombers in the stream, thus avenging its fallen comrades.

As the new year progressed the German defences took an increasingly heavy toll of the attacking bomber force. On January 28, 43 bombers failed to return of 683 attacking Berlin, and the month that followed was even worse. On February 15, 42 were lost out of 891 attacking Berlin, and four days later the command lost 78 out of 823 attacking Leipzig; in March, 72 bombers out of 811 dispatched were lost during the Berlin attack on the 24th. Even a successful attack on Essen two days later, when only nine failed to return out of 705, was overshadowed by the appalling total cost.

During this period the German exploitation of the bombers' own radiations reached a high pitch of efficiency. That Sir Arthur Harris continued to send out H2S-equipped aircraft, even though he had a shrewd idea of the dangers involved, was not due to any pious belief that the Germans might fail to grasp their opportunity. In truth a fine balance had to be struck between, on the one hand, the effectiveness of the bombers in finding and destroying targets, and on the other hand the degree of risk involved in so doing. By removing H2S from its aircraft Bomber Command could undoubtedly have cut losses. But to have done so would have deprived the force of the only radar bombing aid that could be used over Berlin, and the striking power of the force would have been reduced considerably. If, as Harris sincerely believed, Bomber Command could repeat the Hamburg pattern on five or six important cities and thus bomb Germany out of the war, then the stakes were high enough to justify the greatest risks.

Bomber Command did not visit Germany again until March 30. This was to be Harris's final attempt to smash a major German city before the operational control of his force passed to General Eisenhower, in preparation for the forthcoming invasion of Europe. The target for the 781-aircraft force was Nuremberg.

Even before the leading aircraft had crossed the coast of Britain the ever-watchful German listening service had correctly deduced the direction of approach from the H2S bearings. As a result the Chief Operations Officer to the Luftwaffe III Fighter Division was able to order his crews to assembly over radio beacon 'Ida', in the path of the bomber stream, in good time.

Because of unexpectedly strong winds, the bomber stream began to lose cohesion very early on, and even before the first turning point the aircraft were advancing on a front 40 miles wide. And due to the night's unusual meteorological conditions, worse was to follow. Each minute, the petrol burned in one aero engine produced one gallon of water as steam; normally the steam dispersed, but in this very cold night it condensed and the long white condensation trails of vapour suspended in the sky, chased remorselessly behind each bomber as it crossed the Rhine moving eastwards. It was a clear night, and the glow from the half moon gave the vapour trails a phosphorescent quality.

The British radio-jamming barrage was as powerful as ever, and the German fighter corps diarist noted: 'Corps VHF [radios] jammed by bell sounds. R/T traffic hardly possible. Jamming of corps HF [Radios] by quotations from Hitler's speeches. Corps alternative frequency and divisional frequencies all strongly jammed . . .'

But as the mass of bombers passed almost exactly over the Ida beacon, where the fighters were already waiting, the jamming availed them little.

It was over Ida itself that the Luftwaffe III Fighter Division joined battle, and within minutes the horrified British crews were being treated to the spectacle of bomber after bomber going down in flames. This was the beginning of a running fight that was to last for 250 miles and, even as the first shots were being fired, other fighter divisions were converging on the bomber stream from all over Germany. The II, from northern Germany, joined via radio beacons Ludwig and Ida; the 1st from bases in the Berlin area moved westwards on a collision course with the bombers, and joined the stream via beacon Dora; the VII Fighter Division, coming up from southern Germany, was fed in via radio beacon Otto. In all, 21 squadrons of night fighters, some 200 aircraft, went into action: it was an ideal night for the Tame Boar tactics, and they wrought fearful execution on the bomber force.

At the bombers' altitude there was a 50-mph tail-wind which took many of the bombers far to the east of their intended track, particularly during the final south-eastern leg of the approach to the target. The Germans consequently had some difficulty in making out which target the bombers were making for, but if there was doubt where the British were going, there could be no doubting where they had been: the bombers' track from Ida on was clearly marked by the trail of wrecked aircraft burning on the ground. Not until 0152 hours, two minutes before the bombing was due to start, was Nuremburg first mentioned in the German 'running commentary'.

Because of the scattering effect of the strong winds, and the persistent harassing from the night fighters, the actual attack on Nuremburg was diffuse and ineffective. Indeed, so widely scattered was the bomber stream as it withdrew, that the German night fighters lost it almost completely and the surviving bombers were at least allowed to make their return flights virtually unmolested.

For Bomber Command the cost of the Nuremburg raid had been very high indeed: 94 Lancasters and Halifaxes failed to return, and thus Sir Arthur Harris's daring attempt to end the war by strategic bombing ended in failure. The failure came close to crippling Bomber Command: during the 35 major attacks between November 18, 1943, and March 31, 1944, it had lost 1,047 aircraft; a further 1,682 machines had limped back damaged—and although it had been hit hard, Germany was still very much in the war.

In the night skies on the routes to Berlin, Magdeburg, Leipzig, and Nuremburg the men of the German night fighter force had avenged their humiliation over Hamburg in the summer of 1943. Now, in the spring of 1944, they stood at the pinnacle of their success, blooded and confident in the new Tame Boar tactics.

FLIGHT-LIEUTENANT ALFRED PRICE was born in 1936 and educated at Glynn Grammar School, Ewell. He is a regular officer in the Royal Air Force, where he has specialised in electronic warfare, and lectures to present-day Bomber Command crews on target penetration tactics. His book *Instruments of Darkness*, published in 1967, described the struggle for technical and tactical supremacy in radar during the Second World War, as seen from both sides.

THE RESCUE OF MUSSOLINI

When the news reached Hitler that Mussolini had been thrown from power, he determined that his fellow dictator should at least not suffer the indignity of long imprisonment at the hands of his own countrymen. But Mussolini had been spirited away to an isolated hotel on a mountain plateau, so Hitler entrusted the rescue to a force of picked paratroops, commanded by the daring Otto Skorzeny. This epic raid revealed to the British that they were not the only ones capable of small-scale but spectacular actions

Italy, July/September 1943   *Christopher Hibbert*

Mussolini steps on to German soil after his dramatic rescue by German Commandos

SNATCHED FROM THE SKY

Mussolini's rescue was shouted to the world: for the Axis, the operation was a welcome change from a growing tale of defeat. Germany, too, had her Commandos—just as efficient and as daring as the British. **Right:** Mussolini walks to the Fieseler Storch after Skorzeny's brilliant—and bloodless—occupation of the Gran' Sasso plateau. **Below:** The aircraft used in the rescue. The target area was so small and uneven that General Student, the German paratroop chief who planned the raid, ordered Skorzeny not to take any risks—but Skorzeny gambled on a crash landing, which put his men on the doorstep of Mussolini's hotel. It was a superb feat of precision landing, for there was no margin for error—but it was nothing compared to the way in which Captain Gerlach (General Student's personal pilot) landed his tiny Storch on the rock-studded plateau, and then took off again, overloaded with the weights of both Mussolini and Skorzeny. The Storch was possibly the only aircraft which could have been used to deal with a spot-landing and a high-altitude take-off —and with such a horrifying travesty of a landing-ground

Bapty & Co Ltd

DFS Troop-Carrying Glider
Operational towing speed behind Ju-52: 100 mph at 1,000 feet. *Troop capacity:* ten. *Sinking speed with airbrakes:* 240 feet per minute. Three emergency braking rockets in nose; brake parachute in tail

Fieseler Fi-156 Storch ('Stork')
The Wehrmacht's lightweight maid-of-all-work, ferrying generals and staff officers about the battlefield and controlling the movements of front-line troops from the air. *Max speed:* 109 mph. *Landing speed:* 31 mph. *Minimum landing:* 27 yards. *Minimum take-off:* 71 yards.

John Batchelor

With Mussolini's fall, Fascism collapsed without a struggle; and not a single man died in Rome that night in an effort to defend it. The precautionary measures taken against a possible Fascist counterrevolution by General Ambrosio, the Chief-of-Staff, Duke D'Acquarone, Minister of the Royal Household, and their fellow-conspirators were scarcely necessary. The Secretary of the Fascist Party went into hiding; the Chief-of-Staff of the Fascist Militia asked to be relieved of his post.

There was much spontaneous rejoicing in the streets, but little violence. Indeed, most Romans stayed at home in sad disillusionment. The announcement that Marshal Badoglio was to succeed Mussolini as head of the government was followed by the news that the war was to continue, and that Italy would remain true to her allies. After all, the Germans were still in Rome and still in firm control—now an even firmer, more restrictive control—of north Italy. It might have been Mussolini's war, but it could not be ended yet.

Hitler, for his part, was determined to ensure that for Italy the war did not end yet. And on the day after Mussolini's arrest, Captain Otto Skorzeny of the *Friedenthal* (special formation of the Waffen-SS) was summoned to his headquarters in East Prussia. There Hitler told Skorzeny that he could not and would not 'fail Italy's greatest son in his hour of need'. Italy, under Badoglio's government, would eventually desert Germany. But Germany would not desert the Duce. He must be rescued promptly.

The difficulties involved in such an operation were prodigious. In the first place, no one in Germany knew where Mussolini was.

On the evening of his arrest he had, in fact, been removed from the barracks in Via Quintino Sella to another *Carabinieri* barracks in Via Legnano. There he was handed a message from Marshal Badoglio which informed him that the new head of the government would give orders for him to be escorted 'safely, with all due consideration', to any place he indicated.

In a reply which indicated his total capitulation, Mussolini said that the only house at his disposal was Rocca delle Caminate, a feudal, battlemented castle in the Romagna, which had been presented to him years before.

For the whole of the next day Mussolini waited to be taken away, lying for most of the time on a camp-bed in the commandant's office, occasionally getting up to look out of the window at the *Carabinieri* cadets marching up and down in front of a wall on which, in huge white letters, were painted the words: *'Credere! Obbedire! Combattere!'* ('Believe! Obey! Strive!'), the omnipresent slogan of his regime.

He looked tired and ill, his captors thought, but 'resigned and tranquil . . . he ate little and did not smoke'.

At 8 pm on July 27, an officer came into the room and said to him: 'The order to leave has come.'

Mussolini went downstairs to a car waiting in the courtyard and climbed into the back, followed by a man who introduced himself as Brigadier-General Polito of the Military Police. The car drove quickly out of the barracks led by a dispatch-rider who raced on ahead to warn the *Carabinieri* at the road blocks to let it through without question. The blinds of the car were drawn down, but through a crack Mussolini caught sight of the Santo Spirito Hospital and realised that he was being taken not towards Rocca delle Caminate along Via Flamini, but south towards Via Appia. When the car reached Albano his fears were confirmed. The new government had decided that in the interests of public order it would be better if Mussolini did not return to the Romagna.

About 2 am the following morning Rear-Admiral Franco Maugeri, Chief of Naval Intelligence, who was standing on the quay of the Costanzo Ciano Wharf at Gaeta, saw the headlights of three cars approaching rapidly down the road from Formia. Maugeri had been given orders by the Ministry of the Navy the previous afternoon to go to Gaeta where he would find the corvette *Persefone* tied up at the Ciano Wharf. He was to give instructions to her master, Captain Tazzari, to sail for Ventotene, an island 30 miles to the south, having taken on board an 'important personage implicated in a serious charge of espionage'. No one but Maugeri himself was to know until the *Persefone* was at sea who this 'important personage' was.

The three cars drew to a halt on the quay. A squat, black figure got out of the second one, and Maugeri saluted as he met Mussolini's 'enormous eyes shining in the surrounding darkness'. He escorted him aboard the *Persefone,* which weighed anchor and left Gaeta astern.

They reached Ventotene at dawn; but the island was found to contain a German garrison; and so the *Persefone* sailed away to Ponza, an island 25 miles to the north-west, where she anchored in the roadstead at noon.

Mussolini climbed down the ship's ladder into a launch with his hat—as he was usually to wear it now—pulled down well over his eyes, so that the people standing and staring in the harbour and along the mole should not recognise him.

He was taken to a sad-looking, three-storeyed house overlooking the beach of Santa Maria. Shown into a bare, white-washed bedroom, containing nothing but an iron bedstead, a dirty wooden table, and a chair with the stuffing bursting out of its seat, Mussolini gave way to an outburst of despair. 'I have had enough of this,' he cried, clenching his fist as he turned towards the window to pick up the chair, which he placed in the middle of the floor. He sat down on the floor and buried his face in his hands.

Mussolini remained on Ponza for several days, reading, writing, looking out of the window, talking to the *Carabinieri* guards, bored, frustrated, full of self-pity yet accepting his fate with complacent resignation. And then, abruptly, he was woken up one night and transported to the island of La Maddalena, a naval base off the coast of Sardinia from which nearly all the civilian population had been evacuated.

He was kept on La Maddalena until August 28 in a villa which had formerly belonged to an Englishman. He found the atmosphere there 'menacing and hostile'. The days at Ponza, he had complained, were long and lonely; here they seemed even longer, and the 'solitude still more vigorous'.

That August was particularly hot, the sea was calm and there was no wind. 'Everything,' Mussolini afterwards complained, 'seemed to be nailed down under the sun.' He was relieved, therefore, when, almost as suddenly as he had been taken off Ponza, he was flown in a Red Cross seaplane to Lake Bracciano on the mainland north of Rome. From there he was driven high up into the Albrizzi. In an isolated hotel—the Albergo-Rifugio—6,500 feet up on a plateau which stretches for 10 miles beneath the towering Monte Corno (the highest peak in the Apennines), Mussolini learned from a wireless announcement of the Italian surrender and the armistice. One of the conditions of the armistice was that he was to be handed over to the Allies.

On the afternoon of September 12, 12 gliders approached the Albergo-Rifugio carrying a force of German shock-troops with orders to prevent this condition being fulfilled.

Otto Skorzeny had soon discovered Mussolini's whereabouts in the Abruzzi, probably from an intercepted code message intended for the Ministry of the Interior; and he had had nearly a fortnight in which to prepare his plans. He had been faced with three alternatives: a ground attack, a landing by parachute, or a landing by glider. A ground attack was ruled out because of the number of troops that would be needed; the idea of a parachute assault was also discarded because of the danger of dropping through thin air at such high altitudes and the difficulty of getting the paratroops to land on the plateau in a compact and manoeuvrable mass. A landing by glider, therefore, seemed the only solution. This was also dangerous and difficult because the single possible landing-ground was what seemed to be, from aerial photographs, a small triangular flat strip of land just behind the hotel.

As the gliders dropped down towards this strip of land, however, Skorzeny saw that it was not flat at all but a very steep hillside. He realised immediately that they would have to crash land on the rough ground in front of the hotel.

Mussolini watched the gliders swoop down towards the rock, heard the crash of tearing canvas and splintering wood, and then saw several men running towards him. At first he could not see who they were; but then he saw that one of them was an Italian officer, who was shouting at the top of his voice to the stupefied *Carabinieri*: 'Don't shoot! Don't shoot!'

This was General Spoleti, who had been asked to take part in the operation to prevent unnecessary suffering. And the *Carabinieri* did not shoot. Indeed, when Skorzeny burst into Mussolini's room, having kicked the chair from beneath a wireless operator on the ground floor and smashed his set, not a single shot had been fired by either side.

'Duce!' Skorzeny announced, standing stiffly to attention. 'The Führer has sent me! You are free!'

But it was not long before Mussolini was made to realise that he was not free at all.

After being flown off the plateau in a small and overladen Fieseler Storch spotter plane, which dived down dizzily into the valley before its pilot could pull it into level flight, Mussolini was transferred, on the Practica di Mare airfield, into a Heinkel that took him on to Vienna. From there he was taken to Munich and then on to Hitler's headquarters. And there he understood the full irony of Skorzeny's words. He had been released from one sort of captivity merely to be placed in another: a more ignominious captivity, from which he was never to escape.

Early in the planning for the invasion of Sicily, it had been realised that complete local air supremacy must be achieved before any attempt to land could be made. Thus for the Allied air forces, the end of the North African campaign meant only the beginning of a massive new interdiction campaign designed to destroy the Luftwaffe and Regia Aeronautica on the ground. They were aided by the fact that not only were relations between the Luftwaffe and the Regia Aeronautica so bad that they made no attempt to co-operate against the onslaught, but Axis equipment was generally far inferior to that which the Allies used against them. This had been a depressing feature for the Regia Aeronautica all through the war, but it is ironic that only when their country was on the brink of collapse did Italian manufacturers at last begin to deliver a few aircraft which could have held their own against the Allies

Savoia-Marchetti SM 84: A development of the SM 79 torpedo-bomber, and very similar in appearance. It was not produced in very great numbers. **Span:** 69 feet 3 inches. **Length:** 58 feet 9 inches. **Maximum speed:** 260 mph at 11,500 feet. **Range:** 1,000 miles at 225 mph. **Armament:** Three 12·7-mm and two 7·7-mm MG, 2,200 lb of bombs or two torpedoes. **Crew:** Four or five

Macchi C-202 Folgore: Another of the Italian designs which benefited from the new German engines. The Folgore was not only fast but tough and highly manoeuvrable. **Span:** 34 feet 9 inches. **Length:** 29 feet. **Maximum speed:** 373 mph at 18,370 feet. **Armament:** Two 12·7-mm and two 7·7-mm MG

Piaggio P-108 B: The first Italian heavy bomber, which began entering service in 1942. It was notable for the installation of a remote-controlled gun in each of the outer engine nacelles. **Span:** 108 feet 3 inches. **Length:** 81 feet 6 inches. **Maximum speed:** 290 mph at 11,480 feet. **Range:** 2,500 miles. **Armament:** Eight 12·7-mm MG, up to 7,716 lb of bombs. **Crew:** Six or seven

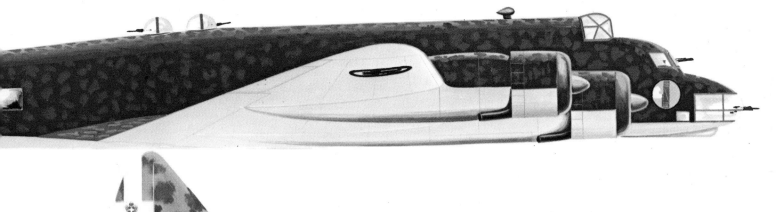

Fiat RS-14: Italy's last operational float-plane, designed originally as a land-based bomber, but adapted first for coast patrol and then for torpedo bombing. **Span:** 64 feet. **Length:** 44 feet 11 inches. **Maximum speed:** 242 mph at 13,210 feet. **Range:** 1,553 miles. **Armament:** One 12·7-mm and two 7·7-mm MG, 880 lb of bombs or two 335-lb depth-charges. **Crew:** Four or five

Reggiane RE-2001 Falco: One of the several useful Italian designs which followed the importation of liquid-cooled, low-drag engines from Germany. Only 252 had been completed by the surrender. **Span:** 36 feet 9 inches. **Length:** 29 feet 2 inches. **Maximum speed:** 360 mph at 17,876 feet. **Armament:** Two 12·7-mm MG

Build-Up for D-Day
ALLIED AIR POWER

R. W. Thompson

The importance of air power in particular relation to the success or failure of Overlord was fully realised in the summer of 1943. The combined bomber offensive, authorised at Casablanca in January, designed to destroy the enemy economy and to undermine the morale of the German people, had not, at first sight, brought satisfactory results. In July, General Morgan—now known as COSSAC—revealed his disquiet:

The most significant feature of the German Air Force in Western Europe is the steady increase in its fighter strength which, unless checked and reduced, may reach such formidable proportions as to render an amphibious assault out of the question. Above all, therefore, an overall reduction in the strength of the German fighter force between now and the time for surface assault is essential. . . . This condition, above all others, will dictate whether amphibious assault can or cannot be successfully launched on any given date.

A month earlier it had been noted on a higher level that unless the fighter strength of the enemy could be broken 'it may become literally impossible to carry out the destruction planned'. A new plan was drafted, Operation 'Pointblank', raising the reduction of the German fighter strength to the first priority while retaining the ultimate object of the bomber offensive.

These conclusions, with their notes of pessimism, were not shared by the bomber commanders, and were echoes of a new problem of immense significance. Air power, and particularly the bomber, had introduced a new dimension into warfare. Despite results, which were at best inconclusive, and the continued growth of enemy fighter strength, the commanders of the Allied strategic air forces had reached the conclusion that they controlled the decisive instrument; that they could achieve victory alone. General Spaatz, commanding the US Strategic Air Force Europe (USSAFE), believed simply that Overlord was unnecessary. Air Chief-Marshal Harris, his British opposite number, agreed with him. General Arnold, the representative of the US air arm on the Joint Chiefs-of-Staff, had reached a similar conclusion. None of these commanders 'objected' to Overlord, or resented its demands upon their forces. They believed simply that if they continued with their bombing strategy the demands would be met.

In the early days of 1943, the Americans had refused to profit by British experience and had sustained heavy losses in daylight raids, particularly over Stuttgart and Schweinfurt. By the end of the year these growing pains had been overcome, and the strategic air forces of the two nations were well integrated in an almost continuous all-round-the-clock bombing programme. The continued growth of the German fighter force, despite the priorities of Pointblank, was not necessarily a guide to its real strength, and the confidence of the bomber commanders remained unshaken. They 'knew'—they 'felt'—that they were winning, even if the statistics failed to prove it.

All this was highly unsatisfactory to the military commanders and planners, and Air Marshal Tedder wrote later: 'I could not help feeling a certain sympathy for my soldier and sailor colleagues in the earlier days who could not understand why, before their operations began, I could only say that I "thought" and "felt" the air situation would be all right . . .'

Clash over choice of targets

Even if the claims of the Air Marshals were not yet wholly true —and they would never be true while war held its historic meaning —the signs were sufficiently ominous. Nazi Germany was being dissected, and destroyed behind its armies. The vast concentrations of heavy industry in the Ruhr and Saar valleys, coal, oil, synthetic fuels, ball bearings, roads, railways, cities, and hamlets were all being steadily reduced to rubble at the whim of this man or that. The bomber chiefs were agreed on their mission, but not on their choices of targets. Oil, General Spaatz believed, was the essential upon which a modern nation at war must depend. Ball bearings, said another. Communications and morale, yet others.

These beliefs made the commanders of the strategic bomber forces careless of the tactical demands of armies. Strategically, they declared, the bomber is winning the war. To divert the bomber from its strategic mission was old fashioned and short-sighted. The German armies in the field, immensely powerful as they were,

were nevertheless powerless to prevent the utter destruction of the homeland and people it was their rôle and purpose to defend.

Military thinkers, prominent among them Captain B. H. Liddell Hart, discerned the new pattern and portent of 'war' with which we now uneasily co-exist. Liddell Hart's warning that 'You cannot surrender to a bomber in the sky' went unheeded. Meanwhile, on the very highest levels there were forebodings of a very grave nature. Early in 1943, air photography and espionage, aided by the daring of Polish allies, had produced physical evidence of the enemy progress in the development and manufacture of rockets and pilotless aircraft capable of carrying warheads of high explosive distances of 150 miles plus. Such weapons might prove devastating in a high degree, and posed new problems of defence. In addition, the terrible secret of atomic progress engendered fears of enemy achievement in that field. The world had begun to fill with dark shadows, altering all accepted values, forewarning that the days of courage, ethics, morality, 'right or wrong', and those attributes of humanity known as 'virtues', were drawing to a close. The implications must undermine the faith in a just cause, in the virtues of steadfastness which, hitherto, had stimulated and sustained peoples to defend themselves successfully against odds.

Politics, and its age-old weapon of war, was giving way fast to blackmail, and its weapon of the 'push button'. The odds were new and had to be considered urgently in the context of survival in a fight to the finish against an enemy who, it could be predicted, would stop at nothing. Never was the calm light of reason more necessary to mankind; seldom has it been less in evidence.

The bomber commanders, confident in their power, accepted an urgent mission to add the destruction of rocket and 'flying bomb' sites and bases to their commitments, and on August 17 Air Chief-Marshal Harris opened the attack with 571 heavy bombers on the enemy rocket base at Peenemünde. Finally, bombed out of Peenemünde, the German rocket experts under General Dornberger moved into 'factories' deep in the Harz mountains, and continued their production on a reduced scale; while the 'ski-sites' for launching their pilotless aircraft grew in numbers, demanding constant vigilance and hammering from the air.

Attacking the V-weapons

The main burden of the attacks against rocket bases and ski-sites was borne by the tactical air forces. By the end of 1943, 93 sites for launching the pilotless aircraft known as the V-1, and to Air Intelligence as FZG-76, were pin-pointed within a 150-mile radius of London, and most of them in the Pas de Calais region. Nine thousand sorties were flown against these sites in the ensuing three months, and the enemy was forced to find alternative means of launching. Meanwhile the attacks by heavy bombers had severely hindered German development of the A-4, presently to be known as the V-2, and the major fear of the Overlord command was confined to the lesser, more recognisable—and defensible—danger of the V-1.

Despite successes it seemed that the Allies were faced with a grim race against time, even up to the end of March 1944. It was by then known that the enemy had improvised some form of modified launching site, very easily hidden from view. Many of these were suspected to exist in the Pas de Calais and the Cherbourg Peninsula, but the heavy and varied demands on the entire Allied air strength as Overlord approached its hour, made it difficult to press consistent attacks.

The army commanders were at no time inclined to underestimate the gravity of the threat, and in early December COSSAC had made an assessment. The immediate decision was to 'leave things as they were', but it was not until March 28 that Eisenhower, emerging from 'a sea of troubles', reported that the 'secret weapon' attack 'would not preclude the launching of the assault from the south coast ports as now planned, and that the probable incidence of casualties does not make it necessary to attempt to move the assault forces west of Southampton'.

The task would have been monumental. From the Wash southward and westward to the Severn Estuary, Britain was girdled with a belt 10 miles deep, a maze of assembly points, dumps, vehicle parks, camps, training grounds, embarkation 'hards', barbed wire, airfields, anti-aircraft and searchlight sites and all   ▷

Allied air power, it had long been realised, would be the key to Overlord's success: only with the Luftwaffe neutralised could the men and landing vessels hope to reach the beaches of Normandy. More-over, Germany's war potential had to be weakened and her supply lines to the future front destroyed. The task was enormous—and so were the arguments over how it was to be carried out

From the outset, the US contribution to the strategic bombing of Germany was based on different concepts to the British: there was never any attempt to smash German resistance by indiscriminate bombing of her cities; instead, the Americans concentrated on pinpoint daylight attacks on economically vital targets. To a great extent, these American bombing tactics were designed to employ the heavily-armed B-17 Flying Fortresses (below) with their highly accurate Norden bomb sights to full advantage. But the unescorted bombers suffered such heavy losses during their first year of operations that the US attacks had to be suspended from August 1943 to May 1944, when long-range fighter escorts — such as the North American Mustang with the bombers below — could be provided

'In the weeks before D-Day, German troops lay almost helpless under the Allied bombs'

The heavy bombers of the 8th Air Force and Bomber Command provided the punch to destroy the large targets, but much of the detailed work in the Transportation Plan—the destruction of smaller targets such as trains or vehicle convoys—was undertaken by the ubiquitous medium bombers and ground-attack aircraft of the tactical air forces under Air Chief-Marshal Leigh-Mallory

Martin B-26 Marauder: At first known as the 'Widow maker' due to a large number of early accidents. *Span:* 71 feet. *Length:* 58 feet 3 inches. *Maximum speed:* 282 mph at 15,000 feet. *Range:* 1,150 miles at 214 mph. *Armament:* Up to 12 .50-inch MG, 4,000 lb of bombs. *Crew:* Up to seven

North American B-25 Mitchell: The most widely used US bomber of the war; some versions were adapted to carry a 75-mm cannon. *Span:* 67 feet 6.7 inches. *Length:* 52 feet 10 inches. *Maximum speed:* 284 mph at 15,000 feet. *Range:* 1,525 miles at 233 mph. *Armament:* Up to 14 .50-inch MG, up to 4,000 lb of bombs. *Crew:* Six

De Havilland Mosquito Mk XVIII: A fighter-bomber version of the aircraft which was used by the RAF in almost every role from long-range bomber to night-fighter and high-speed transport. *Span:* 54 feet 2 inches. *Length:* 40 feet 10¾ inches. *Maximum speed:* 380 mph at 13,000 feet. *Range:* 1,270 miles. *Armament:* One 57-mm Molins gun, four .303-inch MG, two 500-lb bombs or eight rockets under the wing

he massing paraphernalia of war, while every port, large or small, on the island's coasts bristled with shipping. Wherever Britain, from the extremities of Scotland and Wales to Cornwall and the Kent coast, was less than a camp, a dump, a training ground, or any other of the multitude of activities relevant to the cross-Channel assault, it was a munitions works.

The problem of attempting to move all this was a greater hazard than the threat of the V-1s and V-2s on London and the south coast ports. The chance of massive enemy interference had to be taken.

The attitude of the 'Bomber Barons', who, in General Morgan's words 'remained obstinately aloof', manifesting many of the characteristics of a 'new élite', made it inevitable that a serious command crisis would follow upon the appointment of a supreme commander for Overlord. General Eisenhower was not slow to point out that: 'The strategic air arm is almost the only weapon at the disposal of the supreme commander for influencing the general course of action, particularly during the assault phase.'

This is a simple statement of fact, and no supreme commander worth his salt could have accepted the attitude of the strategic air force commanders, and abrogated his right to command. The command of the ground forces was in the hands of General Montgomery, and with General Bradley commanding the US 1st Army, Commander Designate of the US 12th Army Group. The great invasion fleet was under Admiral Ramsay, and it was not until April that the obstructive and obstinate Admiral King authorised the full complement of US naval resources. Without the command of the air forces in his hands the Supreme Commander would be reduced to a cipher, a mere pusher of the button, afterwards to sit back, certainly for days, possibly for weeks, with no real prospect of influencing the battle. In this context Eisenhower's statement to Churchill on March 3 that he would 'simply have to go home', and his subsequent memo to Washington, dated March 22, 'unless the matter is settled at once I will request relief from this command', lose all trace of petulance.

The fact was (and is) that the Supreme Commander in his fight with the strategic air force commanders in 1944, and to a great extent with the British Prime Minister and the Chiefs-of-Staff, emphasised the obvious truth that air, sea, and land forces had become the three prongs of a single weapon. The proud and jealous distinctions, worse than 'nationalism', between the services, were already becoming blurred. A supreme commander must command them all, and in submitting each service must lose some part of its separate identity.

Welding the air/sea/land forces

In a small way Combined Operations Headquarters had functioned as an embryo of this trend. It had welded land and sea forces into a potent combined weapon, and had often 'used' the air weapon effectively in close support, at first under Lord Louis Mountbatten, and then equally well under General Laycock.

But the stand of the strategic air force commanders, and their supporters, was not aimed solely at the Supreme Commander. Apart from the fact that they believed they knew best how to use the strategic air arm, they objected also to relinquishing some of their command power into the hands of Air Chief-Marshal Sir Trafford Leigh-Mallory, Air Commander-in-Chief, Allied Expeditionary Air Force, on the grounds that his experience in Fighter Command, which had been mainly exercised in the defence of Britain, had not fitted him for an aggressive rôle with the strategic air weapon. But primarily they feared that he – and the Supreme Commander – would use strategic air power tactically.

In fact the demands of Overlord and Pointblank, the combined bomber offensive, were certainly not mutually exclusive or incompatible. The Supreme Commander had made it clear that in seeking command of the air forces he had not the smallest intention of interfering with, for example, Coastal Command. He had no quarrel with the strategic aims pursued by the bomber commanders, as far as they went, but he and his staff must have the right to state and to press their views on the use of air power in direct relation to Overlord, and to control it, at least, in the assault stages, and now, urgently, in the last 90 days.

Coincidentally, therefore, with the rather confused command arguments, an argument raged on the best way to serve Overlord from the air. The Deputy Supreme Commander, Air Chief-Marshal Sir Arthur Tedder, became the champion and chief exponent of what was known as 'The Transportation Plan' against General Spaatz, the champion and chief spokesman of 'The Oil Plan'. The argument, at times bitter, carried also grave political implications, and was pursued in an atmosphere of 'tense anxiety' until April.

All these difficulties were resolved by the middle of April largely by the efforts of two of the most experienced airmen in the world, both of whom happened to be men of outstanding character and ability, Air Chief-Marshal Sir Charles Portal, a member of the Chiefs-of-Staff, and Tedder, Eisenhower's Deputy Commander.

Briefly, the Transportation Plan aimed at the disruption of the enemy communications, the destruction of railways, locomotives, marshalling yards, repair and maintenance facilities, roads and bridges, and the prevention of enemy reserves reaching the battlefield. This, in General Eisenhower's view, was 'the greatest contribution he could imagine' to the success of Overlord, and Tedder was his worthy champion.

Some idea of the feeling generated by this argument may be gathered from a remark made by General Spaatz to General Arnold, that he hoped 'the AEAF plan (the Transportation Plan) will be repudiated by Tedder of his own accord, thus avoiding hard feelings'.

But Tedder stuck to his guns, which were also the Supreme Commander's guns. Early in March he set about the dual tasks of reconciling the bomber commanders to the minimum command needs of the Supreme Commander, while at the same time fighting for the Transportation Plan, not only against Spaatz and Harris, but against 'the facts' produced by Air Intelligence, the doubts of 21st Army Group, and the grave misgivings of the British Prime Minister and the War Cabinet. It was one of the very few matters in regard to strategy upon which the British War Cabinet was consulted. This does not indicate that the War Cabinet was a rubber stamp, but that it had plenty of work to do without commenting on command problems, unless called upon to do so.

In the final resolution of these two important matters, the command problem, and the air targets to be adopted in support of Overlord, Sir Charles Portal acted in the rôle of 'umpire', 'chairman', 'interpreter' to the Prime Minister and the Chiefs-of-Staff, holding the balance of the arguments with great skill while retaining a powerful personal judgement and opinion. On March 9 Tedder drafted a scheme of command acceptable to Eisenhower, and on March 27, with Portal's aid, he 'supervised' the Strategic Air Command for Overlord, co-ordinating the combined air effort with Leigh-Mallory's tactical air forces. On that day, also, having won agreement for the Transportation Plan, he relieved Leigh-Mallory of responsibility in the running of it. Thus the Deputy Supreme Commander became Eisenhower's direct channel of air command for Overlord, while the Combined Chiefs-of-Staff retained the last word in strategic matters.

Eisenhower wins use of air power

This arrangement did not suit everyone, but it was the best possible in the difficult circumstances. The US Joint Chiefs-of-Staff objected to the word 'supervised', and wanted the stronger word 'directed'. The vital point was that the Supreme Commander had won the use of the air power he needed for Overlord and would retain essential control over it in the relevant period.

The target argument, waged by the main protagonists, Tedder and Spaatz, was less confused. In early March, General Spaatz produced a reasoned and carefully worked out Oil Plan, while Tedder produced his plan for the disruption of communications. This was not an attack on combined bomber offensive strategy embodied in Operation Pointblank. Eisenhower and Tedder were agreed that the destruction of the Luftwaffe bomber and fighter strength – which had continued to grow in numbers – must remain the first priority. They had no quarrel with Pointblank, as far as it went, but they were resolved to prevent the movement of enemy reserves into the battle area. Spaatz, they felt, might be right in his belief that by depriving the enemy of oil both the Luftwaffe, and almost all ground movement, would cease. They did not object to the Oil Plan, except as an alternative to their own. It was all very well for the commanders of the strategic air forces to state with conviction that the power of the enemy was being sapped at source, that at a given moment the whole 'house' would collapse, but the evidence for such an optimistic view was not conclusive. At best, it would be a nerve-racking wait as zero hour approached.

The real crux of the argument lay probably in the use of air power as an independent air weapon, and its use, as Ehrman put it, 'within the context of other operations'.

While the arguments and counter-arguments were pursued hotly throughout March both plans were virtually in operation. Pointblank, designed as an operation in support of Overlord, had been in action for a full nine months. Tedder's 'Transportation Plan' had been partially in operation since the beginning of the year. Neither plan was, therefore, wholly speculative.

The original Transportation Plan put forward in January by Allied Expeditionary Air Force Headquarters was based on an analysis by Professor Zuckerman. It called for a sustained 90-day attack directed against 72 carefully chosen targets, 39 of them in Germany and 33 in France and Belgium. The plan, constantly shorn of its targets, which were subject to constant pressures and permutations

Overwhelming air power: 'the greatest contribution to D-Day'

from air, civil, and military authorities, operated on a limited basis while the arguments were being hotly debated. The strategic views expressed by General Spaatz, Air Chief-Marshal Harris and their supporters, were that it would be quixotic and totally wrong to divert strength from the main bomber offensive at a time when it was beginning to take powerful effect; and, secondly, that railway and marshalling yards were notoriously difficult targets, and that no effective slow-down of enemy transport would be achieved in time for D-Day.

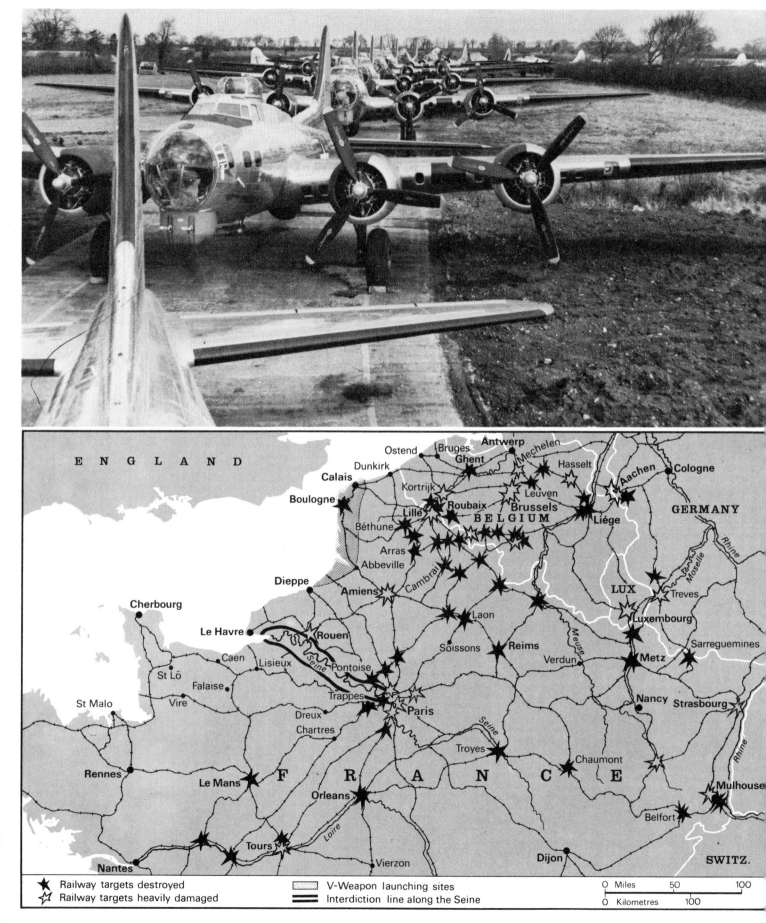

Railway targets destroyed
Railway targets heavily damaged
V-Weapon launching sites
Interdiction line along the Seine

0 Miles 50 100
0 Kilometres 100

The British Chiefs-of-Staff, largely sympathetic to this view, and beset by grave fears of the consequences of heavy bombing in France and Belgium, were reluctant to clear the 'Zuckerman' targets, changed their minds constantly, and forced the AEAF to operate under grave handicaps against limited objectives.

Assessments of early results by Air Intelligence, by SHAEF G-2, and by 21st Army Group HQ, pointed to almost total failure of the effort. As late as May 9, 21st Army Group, more directly concerned in the end results than any other body, referred to the Transporta-

tion Plan, as 'pin-pricking on rail communications'. They were frankly scornful.

Never have assessments been more wide of the mark. The German communications were at the point of almost total collapse, for it was misleading simply to count trains and engines destroyed. Hundreds of engines, physically still 'in existence', were on the verge of breakdown, and the maintenance and repair facilities had sustained such a hammering, that it would prove impossible to get most of the battered trains on the move.

◁ On these two pages are shown the aim and effect of the massive Allied air offensive which General Eisenhower was to describe as: 'the greatest contribution he could imagine' to the success of Overlord. To prepare for the invasion, the Allied air forces undertook a concentrated campaign, which was so planned as to isolate the Normandy area by hitting vital railway junctions in northern France and destroying the bridges across the Seine, while seeming to prepare for an invasion in the Calais area. By D-Day, all the main objectives had been achieved: the amount of supplies reaching the troops in Normandy was minimal, while the Germans were still convinced that the attack would come further north. *(Above)* Flying Fortresses, newly arrived in Britain, await issue to combat units.

▷ The Allied Expeditionary Air Force at work: *(Top left)* The aftermath of an attack on a flying-bomb site. 'A' marks the launching ramp, and 'B', 'C', 'D', and 'E' are V-1s which crashed on launching. *(Top right)* A flying-bomb site under attack. *(Below left)* The damage at Amiens marshalling yard after a visit by Bomber Command. *(Below right)* RAF Typhoons attacking a road and rail junction.

Paul Popper (left and right)

Imperial War Museum (left and right)

Nevertheless, at the height of his argument for the Transportation Plan most of the facts seemed to argue against Tedder. He stood as firm as a rock, convinced of the correctness of his view, and that nothing else would be of direct physical aid to Overlord. But it would have taken arguments of greater potency than those put forward by Harris, Spaatz, and their Intelligence supremo to prevail against the direct and urgent desire of the Supreme Commander. The arguments of greater force concerned the fear that the French and Belgians would suffer heavy civilian casualties, which, it was believed, must inevitably follow upon intensive bombing of marshalling yards. Some authorities put the expectation of civilian casualties as high as between 80-160,000. The possibility gave Churchill, among others, grave misgivings, and Portal was forced to draw the attention of the air planners to the fact that attacks on occupied countries, which might cause heavy civilian casualties and damage, were prohibited under a ruling dated June 3, 1940.

'This is war, and people will be killed'

The War Cabinet was then consulted, and was extremely uneasy. Tedder stood his ground; questioned the estimates, and agreed to avoid routes south of Paris on the 'Grande Ceinture', and danger points like Le Bourget. Nevertheless, the fear of civilian casualties on a high scale remained a source of grave uneasiness to all concerned, but least of all, it seemed, to the French people. Major-General Pierre Koenig, commanding the French forces in Britain, in consultation with Tedder, expressed himself forcibly: 'This is war and it must be expected that people will be killed . . . We would take twice the anticipated loss to be rid of the Germans.'

But there were also difficulties in tying in the French Resistance in support of the operation. A Forced Labour Edict by the Nazis in 1943 had inspired thousands of young Frenchmen and women to 'take to the hills and woods', and from these the Maquis was formed. As saboteurs they had proved remarkably effective, and in the early stages of the air attack on the railways they were credited with the destruction of 808 locomotives against the 347 destroyed from the air. This was used as a further argument against the communications plan.

None of the difficulties had escaped Tedder. Even, he believed, if the enemy rail traffic could be reduced by 10% by D-Day it would be worth while. He and the Supreme Commander were convinced beyond a doubt that only in this way could air power make a direct contribution to Overlord.

The arguments, heart searchings, accompanied by constant changes of targets, and the inclusion of roads and bridges, continued almost up to the eve of D-Day, as also did the derogatory and derisory intelligence estimates of the effects on traffic, and of the 'load of hatred being generated in the hearts of the French people'. They were hopelessly wrong on both counts. The civilian casualties were less than 10% of the worst fears, and were suffered without rancour.

Meanwhile, on March 25, Portal called a meeting with the object of reaching a decision. There was no longer room for delay. The Air Ministry, the War Office, the Ministry of Economic Warfare, the Joint Intelligence Committee, were all represented. The Supreme Commander, his deputy Tedder, together with Leigh-Mallory, Harris, and Spaatz, attended with their staffs. The debate favoured Overlord, and with that, on March 27, the Deputy Supreme Commander co-ordinated air operations in support of Overlord, and assumed responsibility for carrying out the 'Transportation Plan'.

The British Prime Minister, however, continued to urge upon Eisenhower the need to avoid civilian casualties, and remained uneasy until the middle of May, far from sure that military implications should outweigh the possible political implications. In the end he was fully reconciled. The results were significant.

Throughout all the arguments and disagreements, covering command, strategy, and tactics, the Allied air forces met all the great variety of demands upon them, and pursued their offensive with unabated vigour, while planning and training to lift three airborne divisions simultaneously into Normandy. Even General Spaatz continued to hammer away at his oil targets, and one is inclined at times to wonder what all the fuss was about.

In March, a minor command crisis followed Leigh-Mallory's establishment of an advanced headquarters of AEAF under Air Marshal Sir Arthur Coningham to operate in direct support of the ground forces. The objections of the bomber commanders to this appointment may not have been more than a last sop to their prejudices. In spite of everything Operation Pointblank had operated for a full ten months by the eve of D-Day. Up to the end of March, with the combined bomber offensive the aims were:
- The reduction of the Luftwaffe;
- The general reduction of the German war potential;
- The weakening of the will of the German people.

In the last phases the direct demands of Overlord, and of the assault landing, Neptune, took priority with five primary tasks:
- To attain and to maintain an air situation whereby the Luftwaffe was rendered incapable of effective interference with Allied operation;
- To provide continuous reconnaissance of enemy dispositions and movements;
- To disrupt enemy communications and supply channels for reinforcement;
- To deliver offensive strikes against enemy naval forces;
- To provide airlift for airborne forces;
In the assault phase the plan was designed:
- To protect the cross-Channel movement of assault forces against enemy air attack, and to assist the naval forces to protect the assault against enemy naval attacks;
- To prepare the way for assault by neutralising the beaches;
- To protect the landing beaches and shipping concentrations;
- To dislocate enemy communications and movement control during assault.

Plastering Northern France with bombs

In addition to all these tasks a sustained attack was pressed against the flying bomb sites and rocket bases, thus to stave off the threat to the assembly areas, the massed shipping, and all the intricate preparations within range of the new weapons.

To meet these commitments Air Chief-Marshal Leigh-Mallory disposed some 5,677 aircraft of the US 9th Air Force and the 2nd Tactical Air Force of the Royal Air Force. Of these, 3,011 were medium, light, fighter, and fighter-bombers, and the remainder transport aircraft, gliders, reconnaissance, and artillery observation aircraft.

Between February 9 and D-Day these forces, aided by the heavy bombers of combined bomber offensive, attacked 80 rail and road targets with 21,949 aircraft dropping 76,200 tons of bombs. Some 51 targets were destroyed, 25 severely damaged, and slight damage was caused to the remaining four. On March 6 Bomber Command made the first heavy attack on Trappes, some 20 miles to the north of Paris, claiming 190 direct hits. The final effect revealed the inadequacy of the existing Intelligence estimates, and went some way towards justifying the claims of the air marshals that they 'felt' and 'thought' they were achieving their various objects. By D-Day railway traffic within 150 miles of the battlefield was at least 75% unusable, and the whole railway system of north west Europe had been dislocated. Air photography, or even visual observation on the ground, failed to reveal the condition of locomotives and rolling stock still 'in existence', but often held together 'by the last cotter pin'.

Early in May, the tactical air forces opened an all-out assault on trains, railway bridges, and road bridges over the Seine below Paris. Heavy attacks were pressed on Mantes-Gassicourt, Liége, Ghent, Courtrai, Lille, Hasselt, Louvain, Boulogne, Orleans, Metz, Mulhouse, Rheims, Troyes and Charleroi. The pattern of the bombing might as easily have been designed to isolate the Pas de Calais as Normandy, and did not reveal the planned area of the Allied assault. Substantial attacks against road and railway bridges over the Loire waited upon the day. In the event, every bridge serving the battlefield was down.

Attacks on radar installations, wireless telegraphy, and navigational stations paralysed enemy signals, and made air and sea reconnaissance virtually impossible. A total of 49 coastal batteries covering the sea approaches were also attacked with some success, while the long sustained assaults on the German aircraft industry had reduced production by some 60%. It was known that more than 5,000 enemy aircraft had been destroyed in combat between the middle of November and D-Day. These facts, combined with the constant harassing of airfields, and the German losses in trained pilots effectively banished Luftwaffe interference from the battlefield.

Meanwhile the combined bomber offensive pursued by Harris and Spaatz steadily sapped the industrial strength of the German nation, reducing it to a meagre skeleton, yet with astonishing power of endurance.

An important side-issue of the offensive against the railways was that 18,000 men of the Todt Organisation (the German forced labour organisation) were forced off urgent work on the strengthening of the 'Atlantic Wall' to undertake the even more urgent task of railway repair.

In the last weeks before D-Day German troops, many of them of low calibre, lay almost helpless under the Allied bombs by night and day.

Such is a brief glimpse of the overwhelming contribution of air power in direct support of the Normandy landings. It was enough.

STRIKE FROM THE SEA: BRITAIN'S CARRIER AIRCRAFT

Supermarine 'Seafire' Mk IIC
Developed for the carrier arm from the Mk V Spitfire fighter. The Seafire IIC was later replaced by the more sophisticated Mk III, which had fully folding wings and a superior flight performance. *Max speed:* 333 mph. *Max range:* 755 miles with drop tank. *Service ceiling:* 32,000 feet. *Armament:* two 20-mm cannon, four .303-inch machine-guns; one 500-lb bomb OR two 250-lb bombs

Fairey 'Firefly' Mk I
Fighter and reconnaissance aircraft. Most of its service with the Fleet Air Arm was in the Pacific theatre. *Crew:* two. *Max speed:* 316 mph. *Max range:* 1,300 miles. *Service ceiling:* 28,000 feet. *Armament:* four 20-mm cannon; eight 60-lb rockets OR two 1,000-lb bombs

Fairey 'Barracuda' Mk II
Torpedo-bomber and reconnaissance aircraft. The 'Barracuda's' most celebrated battle honour was the Fleet Air Arm strike against the battleship *Tirpitz*
Crew: three. *Max speed:* 228 mph. *Max range:* 686 miles. *Service ceiling:* 20,000 feet. *Armament:* two Vickers 'K' machine-guns; six 250-lb bombs OR four 450-lb depth-charges OR one 1,620-lb torpedo

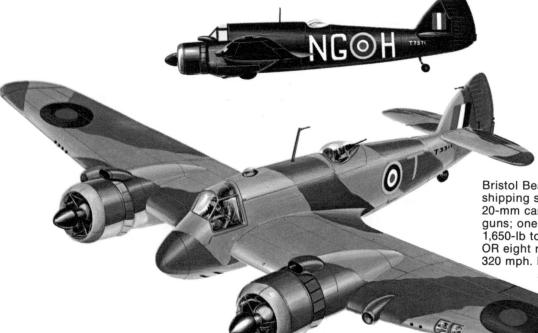

Bristol Beaufighter night-fighter and anti shipping strike aircraft. Armament: four 20-mm cannon, six ·303-inch machine-guns; one 2,127-lb torpedo OR one 1,650-lb torpedo and two 250-lb bombs OR eight rocket projectiles. Max speed: 320 mph. Range: 1,480 miles

The Fairey Swordfish, the veteran Royal Naval strike aircraft of the war, played a key role in the chase of the *Bismarck*.
Crew: two or three.
Normal range: 770 miles. **Armament:** one 1,610-lb torpedo OR one 1,500-lb mine OR eight 110-lb bombs OR six rocket projectiles; two ·303-inch machine-guns.
Max speed: 154 mph

Bristol Beaufort Mk I—the RAF's standard torpedo-bomber for four years of the war. Some 1,120 Beauforts were completed, of which 955 were Mk Is, and Beauforts saw action in almost every theatre of the war. **Max speed:** 265 mph. **Range:** 1,035 miles **Crew:** four. **Armament:** four ·303-inch machine-guns; up to 2,000 lbs of bombs or mines OR one 1,605-lb torpedo, carried semi-externally

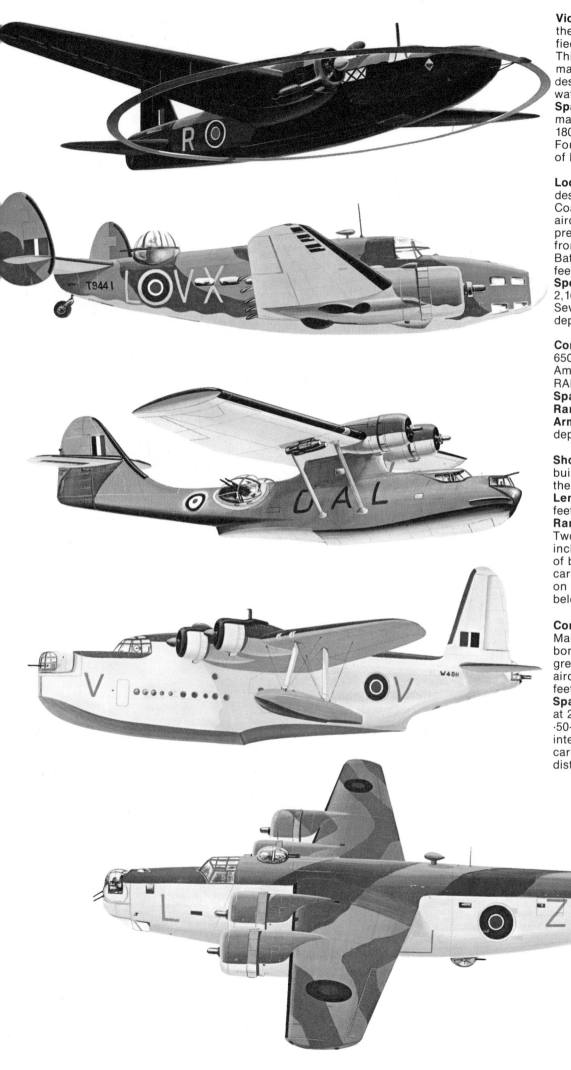

Vickers Wellington Mark I: One of the older designs which was modified for use by Coastal Command. This aircraft is fitted with the magnetic ring which was used to destroy magnetic mines in shallow waters. **Length:** 64 feet 7 inches. **Span:** 86 feet. **Speed:** 265 mph maximum. **Range:** 3,200 miles at 180 mph. **Crew:** Five. **Armament:** Four ·303-inch MG. Up to 6,000 lb of bombs

Lockheed Hudson: An American design which was in service with Coastal Command as a training aircraft before the war, and was pressed—very successfully—into front-line service for much of the Battle of the Atlantic. **Length:** 44 feet 2½ inches: **Span:** 65 feet. **Speed:** 292 mph maximum. **Range:** 2,160 miles at 254 mph. **Armament:** Seven ·303-inch MG. Four 500-lb depth charges. **Crew:** Four

Consolidated PBY Catalina: Over 650 of this tough and dependable American design were used by the RAF. **Length:** 65 feet 1¼ inches. **Span:** 104 feet. **Speed:** 185 mph. **Range:** 3,750 miles at 130 mph. **Armament:** Six ·303-inch MG, four depth charges. **Crew:** Up to eight

Short Sunderland: Over 700 were built of this military development of the pre-war 'C' class flying boats. **Length:** 85 feet 4 inches. **Span:** 112 feet 9½ inches. **Speed:** 212 mph. **Range:** 2,980 miles. **Armament:** Two ·50-inch and up to 12 ·303-inch machine-guns. Up to 2,000 lb of bombs or depth charges were carried internally and wound out on racks through panels just below the wing roots

Consolidated B-24 Liberator: Maritime patrol version of the bomber which was built in far greater numbers than any other US aircraft. **Speed:** 300 mph at 30,000 feet. **Length:** 67 feet 2 inches. **Span:** 110 feet. **Range:** 2,100 miles at 215 mph. **Armament:** Up to 14 ·50-inch MG, 5,000 lb of bombs internally—up to 12,800 lb could be carried on wing racks for short distances. **Crew:** 12

John Batchelor

FIRE RAIDS

Marianas Islands and Japan, December 1944/May 1945
John Vader

By winter 1944, the US bomber pilots in the Far East were carrying the air war to Japanese targets in the biggest bombers of the war: Boeing B-29s, the Superfortresses, intended to unleash a non-stop bombing offensive on the Japanese islands from their new bases in the Marianas. But the B-29 crews soon found that accurate strategic bombing offered far more problems than had been envisaged; and so began the terrible fire raids on Japanese cities, directed by General LeMay, the 'Bomber Harris' of the Pacific War. Never before in the history of warfare had such undiscriminating damage been inflicted with such pitiless regularity—and the raids were steadily built from strength to strength as the summer of 1945 drew on

Top left: A B-29 Superfortress formation unloads its incendiaries over Yokohama. *Top right:* Bombing triumvirate (left to right): Brigadier-General 'Rosie' O'Donnell, who led the first B-29 raid on Japan; Major-General Curtis LeMay, advocate of the mass fire raids; and Lieutenant-General Barney Giles

On November 1, 1944, and for the first time since General Doolittle's intrepid raid in April 1942, an American aircraft flew over Tokyo. Flying too high and too fast to be intercepted on its surprise reconnaissance, the B-29 Superfortress returned safely to its base in the Marianas. The air war had at last reached the Japanese homeland, where those who could see high enough into the sky were able to observe the flight of a new aircraft that was to hasten the end of the conflict.

The B-29 was a most formidable bomber, designed from its inception to carry a 2,000-pound bombload 5,000 miles. Designed for war in the Pacific and the great ocean wilderness to be crossed on the way to far-distant targets, the B-29 also had crew compartments which were pressurised to provide comfort and freedom of movement during long flights at high altitude. Continuing a practice that began in the South-West Pacific where B-24s and B-25s were the star 'heavies', lurid emblems and comic names were painted on the sides of the Superfortresses. Two, *Enola Gay* and *Bockscar*, are ensured of their place in the annals of history, for they were to carry the two ugly containers, 'Little Boy' and 'Fat Boy', to Hiro-

shima and Nagasaki. Some that displayed colourful paintings of near-nude girls possibly spoiled the aim of surprised Zero pilots. 'Supine Sue', 'Horezontal Dream', 'Battlin Betty III', 'Strange Cargo', 'Over Exposed' and 'Lassy Too' were titles of some of the fuselage 'pop art' exhibited over Japanese targets.

This gaily-decorated super-bomber was the most important instrument that the Allies possessed when the war against Japan entered its fourth year.

With the B-29 in existence, the Joint Chiefs-of-Staff decided that large-scale landings in China would be unnecessary and that Japan itself could be invaded: the essential softening-up prelude could be made by the huge bombers based on suitable Pacific islands. Thus the Marianas became an objective for the Central Pacific forces. It was also decided to send B-29s to China despite the difficulties of maintenance and service and the doubtful protection afforded to bases by the Chinese army. After deliveries of the planes to training units in the autumn of 1943, enough crews were ready in early 1944 to form two groups, the 20th and 21st Bomber Commands, both under the direct control of General H. H. Arnold and the Joint Chiefs-of-Staff in Washington.

Hundreds of thousands of labourers were employed in constructing four fields in China, and five were constructed in India to accommodate planes of the 20th Bomber Command which flew from America in April 1944. Supplies of fuel and bombs from India were accumulated in China by using the B-29s as transports to augment the hard-worked Transport Command. The first bombing mission was a raid from India on targets at Bangkok and a few days later, on June 15, Yawata in southern Japan was bombed by B-29s operating from a Chinese field. Flying fuel 'over the Hump' into China was a misuse of the Superfortresses, but it was the only way the Command could build up enough fuel to launch attacks on the Japanese mainland. The raid against the iron and steel works at Yawata registered the beginning of the strategic bombing of Japan, although on this raid the estimated damage of the target amounted to a mere 2%. On July 7, Sasebo on Kyushu was ineffectively attacked. After a night raid with incendiaries against Nagasaki there were no signs of fires. On August 20, Yawata was again attacked by day: anti-aircraft fire and fighters shot down 18 of the 70 bombers and

The Teeth of US Air Power

By 1945 the Americans had gained a decisive air superiority over the Japanese, both in quantity and quality. The old-fashioned Japanese machines were up against the aircraft shown here, for which they were no match: the 'Black Widow', the first designed-for-the-purpose US night fighter; the 'Corsair', a successful attempt to bring carrier craft performance up to the level of shore-based aircraft; the 'Mariner', one of the most wide ranging sea-planes of the war; and the 'Tigercat', the most heavily armed carrier-borne fighter of its time

The P-61B-15 'Black Widow':
Span: 66 feet. *Length:* 49 feet. *Speed:* 366 mph. *Range:* 3,000 miles. *Armament:* 4 .50-inch guns, and 4 20-mm guns. *Crew:* Three

The Martin 'Mariner':
Span: 118 feet. *Length:* 77 feet. *Speed:* 213 mph. *Range:* 3,400 miles. *Crew:* Seven. *Armament:* 8 .50-inch guns, and 4,000-lb bombload OR depth-charges OR 2 21-inch torpedoes

The F7F-1D 'Tigercat':
Span: 51 feet. *Length:* 45 feet. *Speed:* 427 mph. *Armament:* 4 .50-inch guns, 4 20-mm guns, and 2 1,000-lb bombs or 1 torpedo. *Crew:* One. *Range:* 1,170 miles

The DF4U-1 'Corsair'
Span: 41 feet. *Length:* 31 feet. *Speed:* 425 mph. *Armament:* 6 .5-inch guns and two 1,000-lb bombs or eight 5-inch rockets.

the target was only slightly damaged.

The standard of bombing improved after Brigadier-General Curtis LeMay, an experienced leader from the 8th Air Force which had taken part in the strategic bombing of Europe, took over command of the 20th and intensified its training. LeMay firmly believed that strategic bombing would destroy the industrial potential of Japan, that it would destroy its fuel supplies and aircraft factories, its ports and communications. In a land assault on Japan, against a Japanese army of some 2,000,000 front-line troops and swarms of missiles and planes manned by suicide pilots, the cost could be higher than a million American casualties and most of the invasion ships sunk. LeMay was prepared to lay waste all the Japanese cities that contributed to their war effort. And he believed that the huge bombers could do the job, that bombing alone could force Japan into unconditional surrender.

LeMay's bomb-aimers improved with experience but they still required the right weather conditions for success. In clear skies the bombers attacked an aircraft depot at Okayama on Formosa and destroyed the target; the Rangoon marshalling yards were destroyed in one raid; and a raid that took the bombers 3,800 miles during an 18-hour flight wrecked the dock gate and blasted the stern off a ship in the Singapore Dock. In these operations the B-29 crews proved that they could fly long distances and bomb accurately from a great height.

During the decisive first seven months of 1944, the central Pacific islands of Kwajalein, Eniwetok, Guam, Saipan, Tinian, and Peleliu were invaded by the Americans. In the Marianas, Guam, Saipan, and Tinian were developed as bases for B-29s of the 21st Bomber Command, which was formed under the leadership of Brigadier-General H. S. Hansell. The task of constructing bases for the Superfortresses was gigantic, yet five bases were developed in a very short time. On Saipan the airstrips were 200 feet wide and 8,500 feet long, served by 6 miles of taxiways and parking bays. On Tinian the engineers constructed 8,000-feet-long strips in the coral, and at one point a valley was filled across to complete the length; 90 miles of hard-surface roads connected various parts of the island. On Guam the asphalt plant, which looked like an open-air factory, mixed 90,000 tons of crushed rock with 1,200,000 gallons of asphalt oil for the hard-surfacing of the runways and taxiways. Although the fighting for these islands lasted until August, Superfortresses were able to land in October and begin operations against Truk at the end of the month.

The first bombing raid against a target in Tokyo, 1,500 miles from the Marianas, was made on November 24. Brigadier-General Emmett O'Donnell, flying in *Dauntless Dotty,* led 111 Superfortresses in an attack against the Musashina engine factory, but only 24 planes found the target and the bombing from 30,000 feet was inaccurate. Despite intensive training and the excellent Norden bombsight, high-level bombing was to prove unreliable—from results in China and Japan it appeared that it was not going to be of much use faltering about at 30,000 feet, losing bombers to flak and fighters, and missing the target. This was not the fault of pilots or aircraft but a result of weather conditions that existed at high altitudes over Japan. Sometimes there were jet-stream winds of over 100 and 200 mph, there was severe icing, and often fog so covered the target that unreliable radar-bombing was resorted to or alternative targets chosen and concentration dissipated.

In order to bring the full weight of the B-29s against the main industrial areas of eastern and central Japan, the 20th Bomber Command was transferred from India and China to the Marianas.

The big raids begin

In January, General LeMay flew to the islands to take charge of the 21st Bomber Command, and when the 20th arrived he was given command of both groups, combined as the 20th Air Force. Until February the formations consisted of about 100 Superfortresses and as more runways were completed strikes were made by nearly 200 and, in March, by over 300 bombers. The heavy fire-power of the big planes amazed the Japanese fighter pilots. The central sighting systems and remote control turrets of the B-29 proved their effectiveness when on one occasion a lone bomber on a photographic mission was jumped by 90 fighters. The bomber was able to use its great unladen speed at a high altitude, and, after a running fight that lasted half an hour, seven fighters were shot down and the bomber escaped. It was perhaps fortunate that there were few Japanese aces still about.

However, the fire from 12 ·50 machine-guns and a cannon did not stop the fighter attacks, and despite the high losses of Japanese fighter aircraft in the south-west Pacific, in Luzon, and Burma, there were still thousands of aircraft reserves in Japan. Many of their pilots were inexperienced, yet they were fanatically determined and their courageous attacks brought down considerable numbers

of B-29s. The new 'George' and 'Jack' fighters were particularly dangerous as they were fast and mounted four cannon, which were highly destructive even against the heavily armoured bombers. As the strikes increased in size losses rose proportionately and the bombing effect was certainly not worth the casualties and loss of aircraft. Sometimes the opposition over a target was as strong as 200 fighters, all of them determined to bag a B-29 regardless of the withering fire from hundreds of machine-guns and cannon, or the bursting shells of their own anti-aircraft defences.

A vital benefit that resulted from the capture of Iwo Jima in March was the introduction of fighter escorts for the bombers. The most important fighter was the improved P-51 Mustang—a fast, long-range aircraft that could fly rings around anything the Japanese might send up. Radar-equipped P-61 'Black Widows' night fighters used their eight cannon and guns to destroy Japanese planes that raided after dark. On April 7, over 100 Mustangs escorted Superfortresses in a daylight raid on Japan and the defenders lost more aircraft than they shot down—a pattern which was to continue in the Americans' favour.

During the unescorted daylight raids in February the bomber losses rose to 5·7%, badly affecting the morale of air crews. When losses reached these proportions, as the USAAF experienced in Europe, bombing results and general efficiency were inclined to deteriorate rapidly. Losses of over 5% meant that the average expectancy was about 16 raids before a crew 'got the chop'; such statistics and the sight of bombers blowing up in the air or falling in blazing spirals were damaging to the morale of the airmen. The escorting Mustang pilots had often sat cramped in their small cockpits for up to nine hours on the long escort flights to Japan, but fighter presence altered the situation in the air over Japan and the high-level raids were increased in number and strength.

Start of the fire raids

The demolition-bomb effect on Japan's industries, however, was still negligible compared with the quantity of bombs dropped and the effort to get them there. The lesson learned in Europe was that it was possible to destroy individual targets by bombing from the comparative safety of a great height—but that it usually took several raids or a massive one to saturate the target *area.* LeMay had quite a problem on his hands. He possessed a powerful force of bombers designed to fly high over long distances, but the enormous amount of fuel needed for such operations meant that the bombloads were relatively small; when they reached the target it was uncertain if it would be destroyed; at this rate the process of whittling down the Japanese manufacturing capability would be a lengthy one, as many factories would be quickly moved to hidden sites. There were thousands of fighter and bomber aircraft reserved by the Japanese for the day the Allies invaded the country; fighter aircraft were still being manufactured and many parts were turned out in the widespread 'cottage industry' that could not be pin-pointed on the Intelligence maps.

A radical variation in tactics had to be made, and the general's experience of one particular raid on Hankow could have brought about the decisive change in operations which was to alter the course of the war. It was a combined raid by Chennault's 14th Air Force and the 20th Bomber Command, at the end of 1944, when it was decided to send in some of the B-29s at a lower altitude than their customary 30,000 feet and to drop incendiary bombs on Hankow. This raid had been considered very successful, due primarily to the incendiaries, and LeMay decided to see if they could set Japan's major cities alight.

The target for the first big incendiary attack was heavily-defended Tokyo. A night attack was planned and there was a strong possibility that the anti-aircraft gunners would be confused by the height of the bombers' approach—between 5,000 and 8,000 feet. Less fuel was needed for the distance at this height and, since little opposition was expected from night fighters, no guns or ammunition were to be carried and crew numbers reduced. Altogether the saving in weight allowed each plane to carry over 6 tons of bombs. As the objective was the great expanse of urban Tokyo, there was no need for the exacting task of forming up behind the leader, and aircraft could make individual attacks. Chosen for the first series of incendiary experiment as well as Tokyo were Nagoya, Osaka, and Kobe, each one a centre of large and small industries. The destruction of the cottage workshops which served as feeder plants would halt the flow of many vital parts to major assembly plants. Also it was feasible that the big factories would either be hit in the widespread bombing or be caught up in the general conflagration LeMay hoped to generate in each city.

The M-69 fire bombs weighed 6 pounds each and were dropped in a cluster of 38 within a container. A time fuse was set to release the small bombs from the cluster at 5,000 feet and they exploded on

△A B-29 after crash-landing on Iwo Jima. Many bombers would have been lost without this vital staging-post. ▽Looking down on vast burned-out areas created by previous incendiary raids

contact, spreading a jelly-gasoline compound. The B-29s usually carried 37 of the 500-pound clusters, fuse vanes held in place by an arming wire that was withdrawn after take-off. To fan the fires it was necessary to have a good ground wind blowing across the target.

The night of March 10 was chosen for the incendiary raid on Tokyo. Loaded with 1,667 tons of cluster bombs, over 300 Superfortresses took off from the Marianas runways, flying at about 7,000 feet and estimated to arrive over the target just before dawn, when they would have the cover of darkness over Tokyo and daylight for possible ditching on the way home.

The results of the raid were incredible. No one could have estimated the inflammability of the city. A photo-reconnaissance made a few hours after the raid showed that 16½ square miles of the city had burned out. Along with the many 'home industry' workshops 16 targets scheduled for future daylight high-level demolition attacks had also gone up in smoke. The fierce fires started by the incendiaries consumed so much air that strong thermal winds were sucked across the city, spreading the flames and making them burn more fiercely. The fire storm raged until nothing was left to burn.

Such a fire had only burned once before—at Hamburg in 1942—but the death toll in the Tokyo blaze was more than double: over 100,000 people were killed and at least 100,000 injured. The Americans lost 14 Superfortresses over the target.

Two nights later the bombers again took off with their loads of incendiaries, this time headed for Nagoya. Fires were started all over the city but, since they did not join up, the firestorm was averted and only about 1½ square miles were destroyed. Osaka was the next target, attacked on March 13 by over 300 bombers which destroyed 8 square miles of the city. A few nights later 2·4 square miles, including 11,000,000 square feet of dock area, were burned out in Kobe. The last attack in the ten-day period was a return to Nagoya when another force of 300-plus dropped 2,000 tons of incendiaries on a more compact area but again the city refused to ignite and only ·65 of a square mile was destroyed. In these five raids the bombers had dropped 9,365 tons of incendiaries and burned out more than 29 square miles of Japan's main industrial cities.

With the careless bombing of civilians and the callous, cowardly forms of total war already established as their standards early in the war by the Axis, the Allies had few qualms about the coarse approach to destroying military and industrial installations in Europe. There is no evidence that the appalling possibilities of fire raids on Japan might encourage the Joint Chiefs-of-Staff to revert to target-only bombing. There would have been few aircrew too horrified to continue the bombing—they were conditioned by their knowledge of the Allied prisoners who had been bayonetted to death, the hospital ships bombed and shelled, the shot-down pilots who were beheaded, the numerous atrocities that had been committed by their enemy. The general mood was expressed in a simple attitude: 'They've only got themselves to blame—they started it.' The burning of Tokyo probably killed more people, and in a more frightful way, than the two atom bombs that ended the war, yet the fire raid is rarely mentioned in the probing of man's conscience that has gone on ever since.

The morale of the B-29 crews quickly improved when they found that these night raids were much safer than the daylight high-level bombing; only 22 bombers (1·4%) were lost over the target in the ten-day period. There was sanctuary at Iwo Jima and ditching at sea was made safe by the presence of 'Dumbos' (B-17s and PBY Catalinas) and 'Superdumbos' (B-29s) which flew in the vicinity of the target, carrying extra life rafts and emergency kits and monitoring the bombers' frequencies so that if one went down the position would be located and rescue planes, ships, or submarines would be sent to pick up the airmen.

For the Joint Chiefs-of-Staff and for General LeMay fire raids were a successful means of destruction; they became the prime operation in the air war against Japan. For the Japanese military and political leaders the ominous result of the visit by B-29s to four cities within a period of ten days proved that their country was virtually defenceless and that there was little that they could do to improve the state of affairs. Their Axis partner was about to collapse and their Kamikaze ('divine wind') was ineffective against bombers that flew at night.

For the 20th Air Force, the pattern had been established. All that was required now was to choose the cities, build up a large stock of fuel and clusters of jelly-gasoline bombs, and begin the assault. After the ten-day incendiary concentration the force began a new series of daylight attacks. In order to carry a heavier bomb load the B-29s reduced their altitude to between 12,000 and 18,000 feet where weather conditions allowed greater bombing accuracy. The expected fighter attacks continued but were no more effective than they were at 30,000 feet. As with the bombardiers hitting their targets, experience improved the aim of the defensive gunners and Japanese fighters suffered as a result. The long-range P-47 Thunderbolt fighters joined the Mustangs in bomber escort flights to establish a fighter superiority over the heart of Japan. They had been assisted in achieving this by the extensive sweeps made by navy aircraft from Task Force 58. Sailing to within 175 miles of Tokyo, Admirals Spruance and Mitscher provided a short range for their fighters and bombers, which shot dozens of Japanese fighters out of the sky and strafed and bombed many more on the ground. They also contributed their share of bombs to industrial targets, primarily aircraft plants. They made their first attacks on February 16 and 17, returning for more strikes on February 24.

By the end of March the end of the war was in sight. There could only be one result of the conflagration being wrought by LeMay's B-29s—bigger and more frequent incendiary bombing that would completely raze the Japanese factories. Since Japan's fanatical leaders did not capitulate after the awful loss of life in Tokyo's fire, something more dramatic would possibly enable them to save face and bow to surrender.

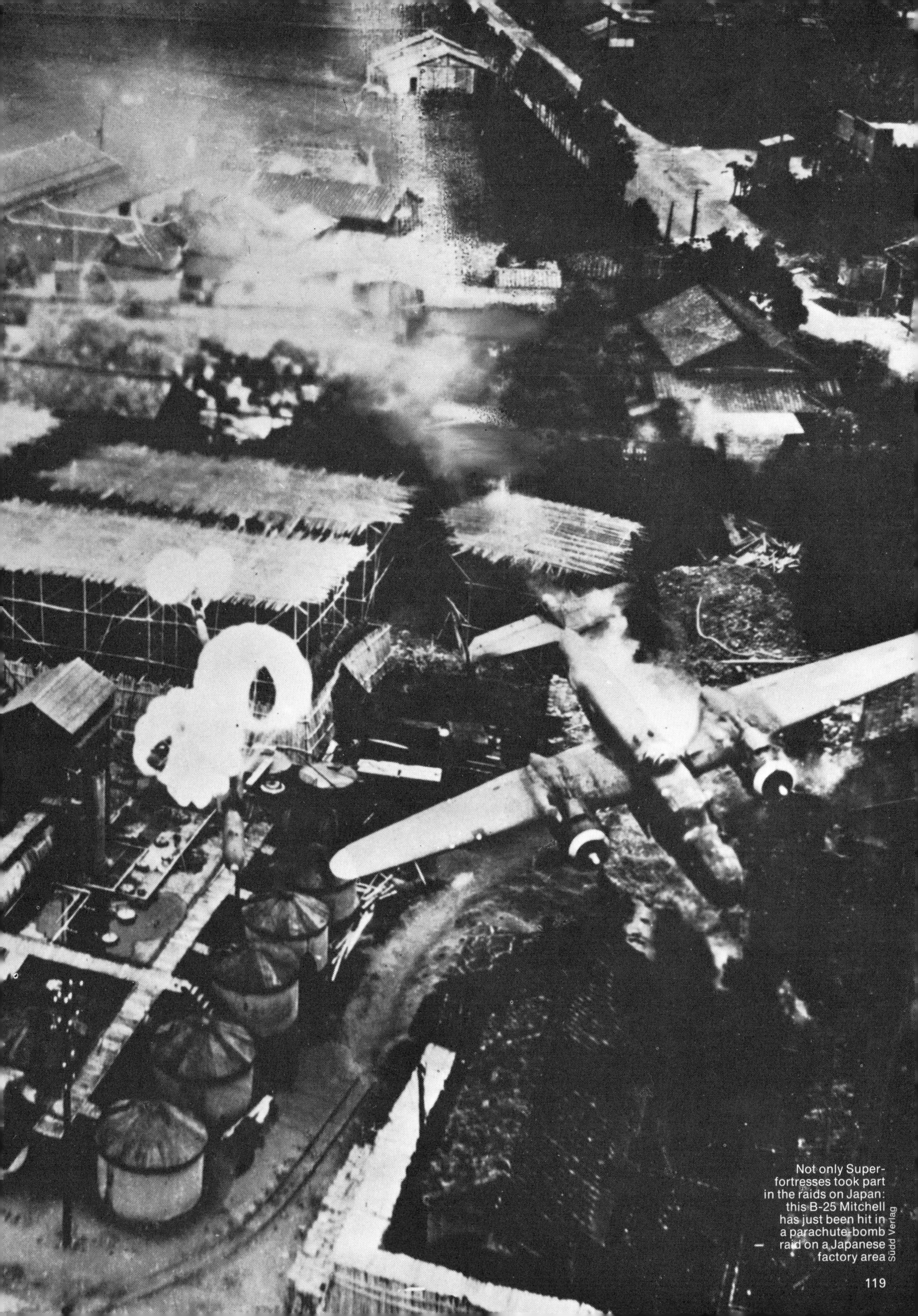

Not only Super-
fortresses took part
in the raids on Japan:
this B-25 Mitchell
has just been hit in
a parachute-bomb
raid on a Japanese
factory area

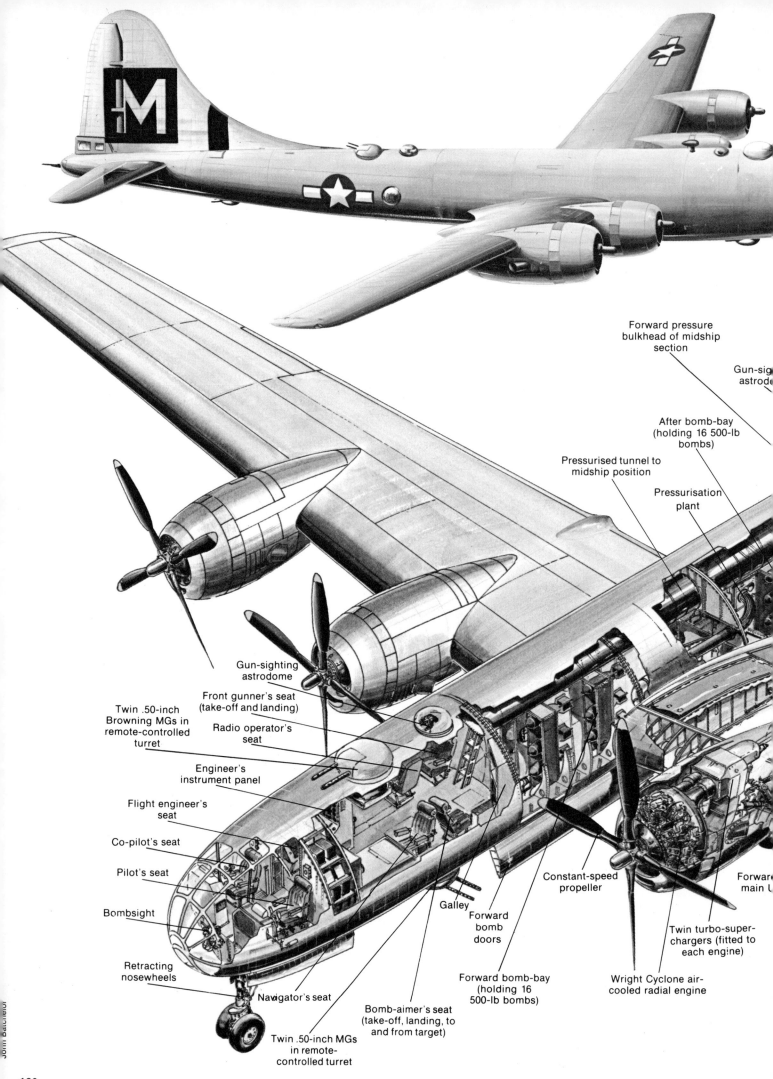

Forward pressure
bulkhead of midship
section

Gun-sig
astrod

After bomb-bay
(holding 16 500-lb
bombs)

Pressurised tunnel to
midship position

Pressurisation
plant

Gun-sighting
astrodome

Front gunner's seat
(take-off and landing)

Radio operator's
seat

Twin .50-inch
Browning MGs in
remote-controlled
turret

Engineer's
instrument panel

Flight engineer's
seat

Co-pilot's seat

Pilot's seat

Bombsight

Constant-speed
propeller

Forwar
main U

Galley

Forward
bomb
doors

Forward bomb-bay
(holding 16
500-lb bombs)

Twin turbo-super-
chargers (fitted to
each engine)

Wright Cyclone air-
cooled radial engine

Retracting
nosewheels

Navigator's seat

Twin .50-inch MGs in
remote-controlled turret

Bomb-aimer's seat
(take-off, landing, to
and from target)

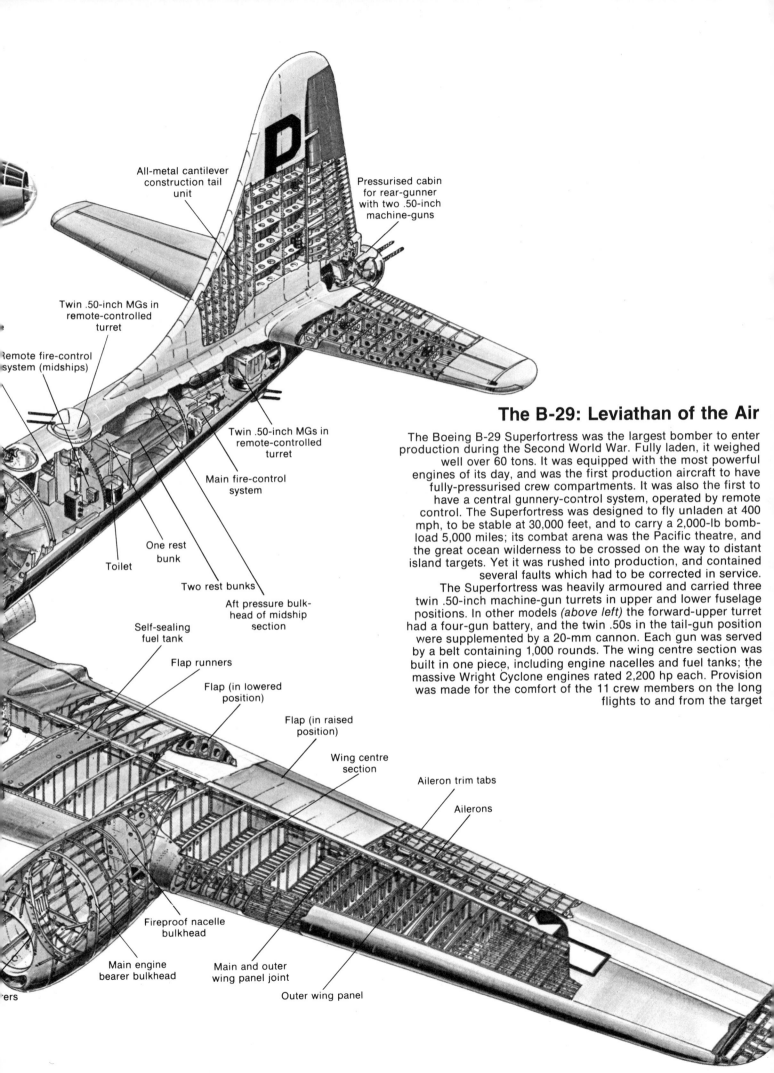

All-metal cantilever construction tail unit

Pressurised cabin for rear-gunner with two .50-inch machine-guns

Twin .50-inch MGs in remote-controlled turret

Remote fire-control system (midships)

Twin .50-inch MGs in remote-controlled turret

Main fire-control system

One rest bunk

Toilet

Two rest bunks

Aft pressure bulk-head of midship section

Self-sealing fuel tank

Flap runners

Flap (in lowered position)

Flap (in raised position)

Wing centre section

Aileron trim tabs

Ailerons

Fireproof nacelle bulkhead

Main engine bearer bulkhead

Main and outer wing panel joint

Outer wing panel

The B-29: Leviathan of the Air

The Boeing B-29 Superfortress was the largest bomber to enter production during the Second World War. Fully laden, it weighed well over 60 tons. It was equipped with the most powerful engines of its day, and was the first production aircraft to have fully-pressurised crew compartments. It was also the first to have a central gunnery-control system, operated by remote control. The Superfortress was designed to fly unladen at 400 mph, to be stable at 30,000 feet, and to carry a 2,000-lb bomb-load 5,000 miles; its combat arena was the Pacific theatre, and the great ocean wilderness to be crossed on the way to distant island targets. Yet it was rushed into production, and contained several faults which had to be corrected in service.

The Superfortress was heavily armoured and carried three twin .50-inch machine-gun turrets in upper and lower fuselage positions. In other models *(above left)* the forward-upper turret had a four-gun battery, and the twin .50s in the tail-gun position were supplemented by a 20-mm cannon. Each gun was served by a belt containing 1,000 rounds. The wing centre section was built in one piece, including engine nacelles and fuel tanks; the massive Wright Cyclone engines rated 2,200 hp each. Provision was made for the comfort of the 11 crew members on the long flights to and from the target

THE KAMIKAZE CREED

'One plane, one warship'

Taking into account the obvious gap in the war potential between the Japanese and the Allied powers toward the end of the Pacific War, it was clear to us Japanese that, unless progress was made in the situation, Japan would eventually face a great crisis. Under such circumstances, it was only natural that Japanese fighting men were determined to sacrifice their lives for Emperor and Nation. Their patriotism was derived from their deep-rooted belief that the entire nation, society, and even cosmos was unified by and into the single Emperor, and for this cause they were willing to die. With regard to the vital question of life and death, we Japanese had based our spiritual foundation on absolute obedience to the sublime authority, the Emperor—even at the sacrifice of our lives.

The cult of the kamikazes was influenced by *Bushido'*, the Japanese warrior's code of conduct based on spiritualism under the influence of Buddhism, which emphasises both bravery and conscience. It was also our ardent desire to be able to die a purposeful death at an appropriate place and time, inviting no public censure about our conduct.

In analysing the attitude of these men it must be borne in mind that they considered their attack mission simply as part of their duty and did not regard the task as something very extraordinary. They were so enthusiastic about how to hit the target ships successfully that they gave little thought to their own destiny. Consciously or subconsciously, they had a firm and profound feeling of 'life through death' and behaved accordingly.

By 'subconscious' I mean that these men were not even aware of the feelings I have just described. They were too deeply involved in the national attitude and psychology which had been nurtured in the long history and tradition of their country.

The kamikaze attack was primarily spiritual, and any pilot with ordinary skills should have been able to carry out his mission adequately. We had no special training method, therefore, other than to point out to the pilots certain factors which had proved important from past experiences in 'special attack'. However, since the pilots chosen for the purpose were short-course trainees with little flying experience, we took pains to give them concentrated technical training so that they could learn the essentials of the kamikaze attack in a short period.

For example, a training programme for those deployed on Formosa went through the following phases: training for new kamikaze pilots lasted seven days, with the first two days spent exclusively in take-off practice. This covered the time from the moment the order for a sortie was given until the aircraft of a unit were assembled in the air. During the next two days, lessons were devoted to formation flying, with continued efforts in take-off practice as well. The last three days were allocated primarily to the study and practice of approaching and attacking the target, including, again, take-off and formation flying practice. Had time permitted, this whole schedule would have been repeated.

For light and speedy aircraft such as the Zero ('Zeke') fighters and the *Suisei* ('Judy') carrier bombers, two methods of approach for special attack were employed and found to be most effective. The approach would be made either at extremely high or extremely low altitudes. Although, from the standpoint of navigational accuracy and range of visibility, a medium altitude was most desirable, this was ruled out in consideration of other factors. An altitude of 18,000 to 21,000 feet was chosen, taking into account two factors:
● The higher the altitude, the greater the difficulties in interception;
● The manoeuvrability of an aircraft with a 500-pound bomb.

In an extremely low-altitude approach, our aircraft would fly close to the sea surface to prevent early detection by enemy radar. In late 1944, enemy radar was estimated to have an effective range of about 100 miles at high altitudes and less than 10 at medium and 20 to 30 miles at low altitudes. When several attack units were available, both the high- and low-approach methods were used in conjunction with varying approach courses.

In a high-altitude approach, caution had to be taken to ensure that the final dive angle was not too steep, as the aircraft would be more difficult to pilot and could go out of control under the increasing force of gravity. It was essential, therefore, to make the dive as shallow as possible, taking careful note of the tailwind and any counter-movement by the target.

In the case of a low-altitude approach, upon the sighting of enemy ships an aircraft would climb sharply to 12,000 or 15,000 feet before going into a steep dive on the target. This method required skill on the part of the pilots since the hit had to be made on the deck of the target ship. This steep dive on the deck, however, was found more effective than hitting the side of the target ship. Hence, the kamikaze pilots were encouraged to employ this steep dive method if their skills were adequate and attack conditions were suitable.

In carrying out a kamikaze mission, it was as crucial as a direct hit on the target ship that a pilot boarded his aircraft, took off, got into formation, and flew along between intensive enemy attacks. Therefore, the kamikaze pilots were given rigorous training for boarding, taking off, formation flying, and assault.

In the case of a heavily loaded take-off, it was important for the pilot to keep the nose of his aircraft from rising too soon, to manipulate the controls slowly, and to hold an altitude of about 150 feet to retract the wheels.

Another important factor at take-off was the joining and keeping formation with a minimum distance possible to avoid making a big circle.

Against carriers, the best point of aim was the central elevator. Next best was either the fore or aft elevator. Against other types of larger ships, the base of the bridge was the most desirable target. Against destroyers, other small warships, and transports, a hit at any place between the bridge and the centre of the ship was usually most effective.

If there had been no shortage of aircraft, it would have been desirable to send four kamikaze aircraft against a large carrier—two to strike the central elevator, and one each the fore and aft elevators. In theory, two or three attackers were considered ideal against an escort carrier. In practice, however, there were too many enemy carriers, and we had too few aircraft available to meet such objectives. Consequently, to ensure a telling direct hit, a single aircraft was usually sent against each carrier: 'one plane, one warship'.

CAPTAIN RIKIHEI INOGUCHI is a graduate of the Japanese Naval Academy and the Naval War College, who served, prior to the Second World War, on cruisers and in the Navy Ministry's Bureau of Personnel. Captain Inoguchi led an air group in the campaigns at Timor, New Guinea, and Peleliu. He was also made senior staff officer under Admiral Ohnishi, the founder of the Kamikaze Special Task Force, and joined the kamikaze operations from the Philippines and Formosa in their early stage. Returning home, he was assigned to the X Air Fleet as staff officer during the Okinawa campaign, with subsequent duty on the staff of the Imperial Japanese Naval Headquarters in Tokyo at the end of the war.

Japan's suicide planes

By 1945 Japanese aircraft were so outnumbered and outclassed by their American counterparts that the Japanese authorities were compelled to fall back on 'Special Attack' (a euphemism for suicide) methods to make any impression at all on the American fleets. Any aircraft that could get off the ground could be adapted for this task, and training aircraft were extensively used. But special aircraft were also produced, designed solely for one 'no return' mission. Below are two of the most effective

The OHKA, a special attack aircraft, was launched from a parent aircraft at 20,000 feet. Powered by three rocket motors it then dived on its target. Max Speed: 620 mph. Max Range: 20 miles. Armament: 4,000 lb of HE in the nose

Nakajima Ki-115 was a cheap, mass produced special attack aircraft. Max. Speed: 343 mph. Range: 750 miles. Armament: One 1,100-lb bomb.

Here are some of the questions asked by the US Bombardment Investigation Mission after the war, along with the answers given by surviving officers of the former 205th Air Group, the kamikaze unit. The questions underline the Allies' reluctance to believe that these attacks were not carried out under compulsion—and the Japanese astonishment that there should be any need of compulsion is reflected in every answer.

So far as the underlying philosophy of the kamikaze unit is concerned, the idea is utterly opposed to the ideas of our country. In the United States nothing is more precious than one's life. For what reason, do you think, could the Japanese forces have involved so many pilots in such a suicide attack mission?
Kamikaze philosophy dates back to a very ancient period in Japanese history. You can find many such examples in our long history. Our nation's basic philosophy is to sacrifice oneself for our country. We are quite familiar with this philosophy. In the course of the Pacific war our critical battle situation inevitably compelled us to employ the idea of the kamikaze attack. Accordingly, the attack was by no means forced from outside.

Admiral Ohnishi simply sensed the feeling of Japanese pilots, particularly the younger ones, which naturally sprang out. As a matter of formality, the admiral initiated the kamikaze attack, but before he took the initiative, we fighting pilots had already discussed the idea of a kamikaze attack at the time of the Saipan battle. The Naval General Staff, however, did not approve of such an idea.

I am firmly convinced that the idea of the kamikaze attack developed quite naturally in the fighting spirit of the younger pilots. In my opinion, the best fighting method is to kill a thousand with one soldier and to sink a battleship with one aircraft.

What do you think about the recruiting of members for the kamikaze units? Was it coercive or voluntary?
It was carried out on a voluntary basis throughout. There were, however, cases in which whole air groups applied for the kamikaze mission due to the tense battle situation on such fronts as the Philippine area.

How were volunteers for the kamikaze units recruited at home?
When I was in charge of recruiting kamikaze pilots for training at home, practically all of the air group members were very eager to join the mission. Some of them even wrote pledges in blood and others would wake me up several times during the night to apply. I sometimes selected volunteers myself, taking their personal and family situations into consideration. A pilot was ruled out if he were an only son. One mother who knew of my decision through her own son's letter sent me a petition begging that her son be accepted. You may easily infer that voluntary atmosphere of recruitment from these episodes.

Judging from the ordinary mentality of our youth who are in their 20s, it is impossible to believe such circumstances. Without the chance of survival, how could you imagine such a suicide attack for the country or the Emperor? Didn't you have any strong educational institution to indoctrinate Japanese youth for the kamikaze units?
There was no such special educational institution at all.

As a volunteer for the kamikaze units, what was your mental state?
Being university graduates, we had only one year of military education. Therefore, we were not so much military men as civilians. However, as civilians, we saw the poor war situation and believed that the Special Attack was the best method. We volunteered and determined to sacrifice ourselves so that our country could win a victory and our juniors could study in a better learning situation.

Don't you think that the kamikaze pilots carried out their missions so that their souls could rest and be celebrated in the Yasukuni national shrine? (The Yasukuni shrine is dedicated to the memory of the war dead.)
It wasn't necessary to carry out the kamikaze mission to be celebrated in the Yasukuni shrine, since any military man killed in action, regardless of rank and place, is celebrated in the shrine. We never had such an idea. The real cause which compelled us to employ such an attack lay in the great discrepancy between the productive power of the two countries and in the lack of alternatives in fighting methods. As a result, we came to the conclusion that the best method was to kill a thousand men with one and to sink a battleship with one aircraft. We were also convinced that so long as we used only ordinary air fighting or bombardment with our inferior and few aircraft, it was impossible to win a victory over the overwhelming American forces.

US Navy

Did you have any form of ceremony at the start of the special sortie? Did you have any instructions from the Admiral? Did you write any letters home or draw up a will?
In the Philippine area, at the beginning, we had a last toast with the Admiral. But it was often impossible, due to tense battle situations, to take time off for any ceremony. Most of us were given short instructions by the Admiral. Some of us wrote letters home and sent wills—but only once, at the time of application, and not before the start of a kamikaze attack.

Life Magazine

Last warplanes of the Rising Sun

On these two pages are illustrated a cross-section of the last of Japan's conventional warplanes. They included some of the best fighters of the war; and the *Shinden* provided an additional example of the far-ranging ideas of Japanese designers. But the final verdict on Japanese aircraft at this stage of the war must be that of Saburo Sakai, Japan's great fighter ace:

'The defensive concepts adopted by the High Command came too late, and were also inadequate. The majority of our fighters were Zeros, well adapted to our offensive tactics earlier in the war, but virtually useless against the B-29s. Most of our bomber pilots still possessed the Mitsubishi Betty, now too old, too slow, and possessed of the unhappy habit of exploding violently into flame under enemy fire . . .

'The loss of Saipan furnished the impetus to discard the cobwebs in our planning. The High Command screamed for the new fighters, designed specially to overcome the Zero's shortcomings. But the production of these new models proved painfully slow. Despite the orders of the High Command, the old Zero remained our fighter mainstay.' *From 'Samurai', by Saburo Sakai, published by William Kimber & Co. Ltd.*

1. RANDY: Kawasaki Ki-102
An army experimental attack fighter, and produced only in small numbers; but it proved to be a useful fighter against the B-29. This was amply demonstrated when a prototype shot an engine off a B-29 on a test flight, with one shot from its 57-mm cannon. *Speed:* 360 mph. *Range:* 1,243 miles. *Crew:* two. *Armament:* one 57-mm, two 20-mm cannon; one 12·7-mm machine-gun

2. FRANK: Nakajima Ki-84 *Hayate*
The most outstanding Japanese army fighter of the Pacific war, the Frank was produced in great numbers and saw extensive service, and was able to out-manoeuvre both the US Mustang and Hellcat. *Speed:* 388 mph. *Range:* 1,815 miles. *Crew:* one. *Armament:* two 20-mm cannon, two 12·7-mm machine-guns; two 500-lb bombs

3. Kyushu J7W1 *Shinden*
The *Shinden* – 'Magnificent Lightning' – was one of the very few 'tail-first' fighters developed during the war. A short-range interceptor ordered 'off the drawing-board', it never achieved production status. *Speed:* 466 mph. *Range:* 528 miles. *Crew:* one. *Armament:* four 30-mm cannon, four 66-lb OR 132-lb bombs

GEORGE: Kawanishi N1K2-J Shiden
eveloped from a float-plane fighter and
sed as a land-based interceptor, George
as very manoeuvrable and possessed a
gh rate of climb. Even in the hands of
n average pilot, it could outfly the
ellcat. *Speed:* 369 mph. *Range:* 1,060
iles. *Crew:* one. *Armament:* four 20-mm
annon, two 7·7-mm MGs

DINAH: Mitsubishi Ki-46III
he fastest Japanese army aircraft of the
acific war, Dinah was used for recon-
aissance of the B-29 bases in the
arianas, using Iwo Jima as a refuelling
ase. *Speed:* 397 mph. *Range:* 2,485 miles.
rew: two

MYRT: Nakajima C6N1 Saiun
fast reconnaissance plane used
xtensively in the closing stages of the
ar to locate enemy shipping for *kamikaze*
ttacks, being able to fly high and fast
nough to escape interception. *Speed:*
79 mph. *Range:* 3,306 miles. *Crew:* three.
rmament: one 7·9-mm MG

PAUL: Aichi E16A1 Zuiun
heavily-armed seaplane which first saw
ervice during the Philippines campaign,
aul was intended as a reconnaissance
pe; but it was often used as a ground-
ttack aircraft and dive-bomber. *Speed:*
80 mph. *Range:* 600 miles. *Crew:* two.
rmament: two 20-mm cannon, one 13.2-
m machine gun, two 7.7-mm machine
uns, and two 550-lb bombs

FRANCES: Yokosuka P1-Y1 Ginga
fast and advanced land-based bomber,
rances first entered service as a *kamikaze*
ype early in 1945. It saw extensive
ervice in the Okinawa campaign, and a
ight-fighter version was also produced.
peed: 345 mph. *Range:* 1,600 miles.
rew: three. *Armament:* one 20-mm
annon, one 12·7-mm machine-gun.
omb load: 1,875 lb

THE LUFTWAFFE'S LAST 'REGULARS'

The sad tale of the Luftwaffe during the last years of the war was similar to that of all Germany's armed forces. Convinced that the war would be short, the Germans failed to develop new designs, and when they did, resources were wasted on experimenting with a large number of promising but untried weapons, and these were then produced in inadequate numbers while the Luftwaffe was starved of the tried aircraft which might have enabled it to stem the vast increase in Allied air power

Below: Dornier Do-335 *Pfeil:* The most unconventional piston-engined fighter developed in Germany during the war, the 'Arrow' had two engines driving 'push-pull' airscrews. Two-seater night-fighter versions were being produced alongside the single-seat fighter-bomber, but neither was encountered in combat. *Length:* 45 feet 5¼ inches. *Span:* 45 feet 3⅓ inches. *Speed:* 413 mph at 26,200 feet. *Range:* 1,280 miles. *Armament:* One 30-mm and two 15-mm cannon, plus a 1,100-lb bomb load

Right: Messerschmitt Bf 109G-6: One of the most important and widely-used production versions of the well-tried 'Gustav'. *Length:* 29 feet 8 inches. *Span:* 32 feet 6½ inches. *Speed:* 387 mph at 22,970 feet. *Range:* 450 miles. *Armament:* One engine-mounted and two wing-mounted 20-mm cannon, two 13-mm MG

John Batchelor

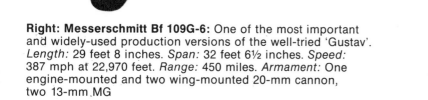

Above: Focke-Wulf Ta-152C: A development of the 'long-nosed' Fw-190D using the Junkers Jumo 213C engine, the Ta-152 series was supervised by Kurt Tank. Few of this very advanced fighter saw action. *Length:* 35 feet 5½ inches. *Span:* 36 feet 1 inch. *Speed:* 463 mph at 34,000 feet. *Range:* 745 miles. *Armament:* One 30-mm and four 20-mm cannon

Below: Junkers Ju-388: A development of the Ju-188 (which it resembled), the Ju-388 was intended as a multi-role aircraft, but only the 'L' reconnaissance model saw action. Other versions included the 'J' night fighter and the 'K' bomber. *Length:* 49 feet. *Span:* 72 feet 2 inches. *Speed:* 378 mph at 38,000 feet. *Range:* 1,100 miles. *Ceiling:* 42,200 feet. *Armament:* 3 13-mm MG

THE DAMS RAID AND AFTER

Special Weapons for the Bomber Most of the bombs used during the Second World War were simple high-explosive or incendiary types. But there were others, and this is the story of the incredible weapons developed by Dr Barnes Wallis: the 'bouncing bombs' that smashed the Möhne and Eder Dams; the 'Tallboys' that sank the *Tirpitz*; and the 'Grand Slams' that wrecked the Bielefeld Viaduct.

Flight-Lieutenant Alfred Price

It was early in 1941 that Mr Barnes Wallis, an employee of the Vickers Aircraft Company, completed his carefully thought out paper 'A Note on a Method of Attacking the Axis Powers'. The treatise ran into 50 pages, with a further 50 pages of appendices, and near the beginning it read:

In view of the large number of objections to a bomb of this size which have been raised by many of the people to whom I have described the idea, it seemed to me essential that I should do enough work on the bomb side of the proposal either:

a) to convince myself that I had been mistaken in my original conception, or

b) to show that the idea had sound foundations.

Wallis's 'original conception' was a very large bomb, weighing 10 tons, for destroying targets previously invulnerable because of their strength or their location underground.

In his paper Wallis concluded that the destruction of massive concrete shelled targets demanded an entirely new bombing technique, a technique which involved two important departures from normal practice. These were, first, the use of bombs far larger than any previously considered; and, second, the use of a jarring pressure set up in the surrounding medium (earth or water) to shake the target to pieces, rather than the surface destruction of a direct hit.

Since the targets Wallis considered were all situated either on or under the earth, or in intimate contact with water, the scientist was able to state: 'To attack these targets successfully it is necessary to inject the largest possible charge to the greatest possible depth in the medium (earth or water) that surrounds or is in contact with the target.'

By careful and reasoned argument Wallis showed that a bomb weighing 10 tons, released from an altitude of 40,000 feet, would produce the effect he was after. Such a weapon would penetrate sandy soil to a calculated depth of 135 feet. If it went off there, no crater at all would be formed on the surface—the entire energy of the detonation would go to produce a shuddering 'earthquake' disturbance.

Wallis's paper was not met with great enthusiasm. It should be remembered that when it appeared in March 1941 the German night bombing blitz was still in full swing, and there seemed a very real possibility that the daylight Battle of Britain would have to be refought again that summer. The British army was still undergoing a hand-to-mouth re-equipment programme, for there was much leeway to make up before its men could meet the confident and aggressive enemy forces on equal terms. Many people understandably felt that Wallis's pie-in-the-sky ideas, involving the use of bombs far heavier than any yet designed, dropped from altitudes beyond the attainment of any bomber in existence or even contemplated, bore no relation to the war then being fought. In any case the perfection of such a weapon system would have demanded a considerable design, development, and production effort, and no such slack existed in Britain at that time.

However there was one facet of Wallis's paper that did seem worth pursuing: the possibility of breaching the massive dams which held back the water so essential for German industry. As a result the Air Attack on Dams Committee was formed early in 1941 under the chairmanship of Dr Pye.

Water roars through the breach in the Möhne Dam, photographed by the Germans the morning after the raid

△Gibson's aircraft bombed-up; 'like a pregnant duck', he commented

Popperfoto

△Barnes Wallis; sceptics said his bombs could not work.
He knew they would—and they did
▷Gibson (centre) with fellow Dambusters

The primary target considered was the Möhne Dam, which encloses the valley of the Möhne and Heve rivers. It was a huge and immensely strong structure 130 feet high and 112 feet thick at its base, tapering to 25 feet at its top. During the subsequent investigation men at the Building Research Station at Watford meticulously constructed an accurate 1/50th scale model of the Möhne Dam. The actual dam was made of masonry blocks laid in cement mortar, so the model was made up of many hundreds of tiny cement blocks, each about half the size of a small sugar lump, held together by courses of very fine mortar.

Wallis's first line of thought had been to destroy the German dams with very large bombs released in the conventional manner. But it very soon became clear that this was not a feasible operation of war. It would have called for a 15-ton weight of explosive to be detonated within 50 feet of the wall. Even if an aircraft could have lifted the necessary weight, it would have been virtually impossible to release such a weapon with the demanded accuracy at night or in the face of defensive fire. In July 1942 the Air Attack on Dams Committee was forced to admit that *'There seems to be no doubt that attack on the Möhne Dam is impracticable with existing weapons . . .'*

The bouncing bomb

But Wallis was not so easily put off. He now concerned himself with the possibility of getting his explosive charge hard against the wall of the dam and setting it off there. If this could be done on the lake side of the dam, the weight of the water would greatly assist the breaking of the structure.

And a far smaller bomb would be able to do the job. A torpedo-like weapon would have been one answer—but the Germans had thought of it too, and had erected strong anti-torpedo nets to protect their dams. To overcome this difficulty of the nets Wallis put forward a childishly simple scheme: a specially developed mine which, released from a low-flying aircraft, would *bounce* its way across the lake until it slammed into the dam. On hitting the massive structure the bomb would rebound off it, then sink. To get the maximum assistance from the weight of the water the weapon had to go off at a depth of 30 feet, and this could be accomplished by means of a hydrostatic fuse similar to those used in depth charges.

For success there was one further prerequisite: when it reached the 30-foot depth the smaller bomb would have to be hard against the dam wall. Here again Wallis came up with an ingenious solution. If the bomb could be arranged to spin *backwards* as it left the aircraft, it would behave exactly as before until it rebounded off the wall of the dam. But after that it would travel *forwards* until it hit the wall again, then wind its way vertically down the wall until it reached the detonation point. Wallis carried out a number of small-scale tests, and on the strength of these he received official permission to proceed with a full-scale weapon.

In its final form the dam-busting weapon, code-named 'Upkeep', was shaped like a large dustbin. It was 50 inches in diameter, 60 inches long, and weighed 9,250 pounds of which 6,600 pounds was powerful RDX explosive. The weapon was mounted *across* the bomb bay of the extensively modified

Lancaster bombers, held between two V-shaped arms which gripped the bomb firmly from either side, while at the same time acting as pivots to allow it to rotate about its axis (see diagram). Power to rotate the bomb up to its release speed of 500 rpm came from a small auxiliary motor mounted in the bomb bay above, via a simple belt drive. When the navigator in the nose of the aircraft pressed his 'tit' to release the weapon the V-shaped supporting arms, pivoted at the tops of each of the arms of the V, sprung outwards sharply to allow the weapon to fall clear.

'Upkeep' was not an easy weapon to use. The crew had to release the bomb while flying at exactly 220 mph, at a height of exactly 60 feet above the water. If a Lancaster went into a tight turn at that altitude, its wing tip would pass within 6 yards of the surface. As if this were not enough, the bouncing mine had to be released at a range of 425 yards from the wall of the dam, with a maximum permissible tolerance of only 25 yards either way. At 220 mph it takes an aircraft one-quarter of a second to cover 25 yards.

Never before nor since had aircrewmen been called upon to handle their machines so precisely in action. Add to this the fact that the attack would have to be carried out at night, and that the Möhne Dam was defended—albeit lightly—and the magnitude of Wallis's demands becomes clear.

To enable the crews to gauge the height of their aircraft as they ran in over the lakes, two spotlights were fitted to each Lancaster, one near the nose and one near the tail. The beams were arranged to shine downwards at such an angle that, when the aircraft was at an altitude of precisely

The Möhne Dam before the raid; note the (useless) torpedo nets

The morning after, with Möhne Lake rapidly emptying

60 feet the spots of light would link to form a figure-of-eight shape on the water. During the bombing run it would be the navigators' task to watch the light pattern, and keep the pilot informed of his altitude.

The even more difficult problem of estimating the aircraft's range from the dam wall, to the accuracy demanded, was solved with an ingenuity which seemed to characterise the entire operation. The bomb aimer in the nose of the aircraft was to use a 'home made' sight comprising a triangular piece of plywood, with a peephole at one corner and a nail at each of the other two. On the Möhne Dam were two towers, 600 feet apart. During the attack run the bomb aimer squinted through the peephole and when the two nails and the two towers lined up—as they did at a range of 425 yards—he released the bomb. During tests this laughably crude method gave release accuracies of the order of 4 yards.

Thus the attack on the dams was to call for the utmost in crew co-operation in each aircraft. With the navigator in charge of the altitude, the engineer the speed, the bomb aimer the range, and the pilot the line, a practised crew could plant the explosives with almost the accuracy achieved by military demolition engineers.

For its attack on the German dams the RAF took the unprecedented step of forming an entirely new squadron, No. 617, in March 1943. Its already distinguished Commander, Wing-Commander Guy Gibson, was allowed the unique privilege of selecting the finest crews from other Bomber Command squadrons for the highly secret operation, code-named 'Chastise'. Sir Arthur Harris himself had ordered that the men should be recruited from among those who had completed, or nearly completed, two tours of bomber operations with ordinary units. Since it was rare for a man to survive the 60 sorties necessary for two tours of operations, this meant that the men collecting for 617 Squadron were among the most skilful, the most experienced, and also the most lucky in Bomber Command. Soon after its formation the new unit began intensive training in low flying in preparation for the attack.

Three waves of Lancasters

On the night of May 16, 1943, nineteen Lancasters took off from Scampton in Lincolnshire to attack the dams. The force was divided into three waves: the first, of nine aircraft, was briefed to attack the Möhne, then the Eder, and finally, if there were any bombs left, the Sorpe Dams; the second wave, with five aircraft, was to attack the Sorpe Dam; the third wave, also with five aircraft, was to act as a mobile reserve. The reserve aircraft were to operate under the control of No. 5 Group HQ back in England, which would order them to reinforce the other two attacks or else attack the secondary targets, the Lister and Eneppe Dams.

Of the first wave, led by Gibson himself, one aircraft was lost on the way to the target; the remainder carried on and breached the Möhne Dam at 00.56 hours. Gibson now led the three aircraft with unused bombs to the Eder Dam, and by 01.54 hours had brought that one down too.

The success of the first wave was equalled only by the bad luck which struck the second. Of the five aircraft which set out two were forced to turn back early after suffering damage, one from flak and the other after hitting the sea and losing its bomb. A further two were shot down, and only the fifth was able to make an attack on the Sorpe Dam. This dam was constructed of hard-packed earth with a concrete core, and so had more 'give' in it than either the Möhne or the Eder Dams. For this reason it was not really a suitable target for Wallis's bouncing bomb, but the importance of the Sorpe Dam had decreed that it should be attacked with the others. The single bomb from the one aircraft remaining in the second wave scored a hit which crumbled away some 50 feet of the parapet; but the dam held. Three aircraft of the reserve force were then ordered to exploit this weakening, but of these one was lost on the way in. By the time Flight-Sergeant Brown arrived at the Sorpe Dam a disconcertingly thick mist was beginning to build up. With great coolness he made ten successive bombing runs until finally, satisfied that all was as it should be, the weapon was released. This bomb also scored a hit but the resilient Sorpe Dam, though cracked, held. When the third of the reserve aircraft arrived the mist had closed right in. There could be no question of a further attack.

The two remaining aircraft in the reserve wave were ordered to attack the secondary targets, the Eneppe and Lister Dams. The Eneppe was hit but not brought down; the aircraft bound for the Lister Dam was shot down before it could attack.

So it was that 617 Squadron, by a brilliant feat of arms, smashed the Möhne and Eder Dams and damaged the Sorpe Dam. There were to be no further attacks using Wallis's dam-busting bomb, for within days the shocked Germans had moved ▷

Top: Winching a 'Tallboy' up to a Lancaster B-III
Above: A Lancaster's bomb aimer in his position

Above: What the 'Grand Slams' did to the U-boat pens: 15 feet of concrete, drilled clean through. *Below:* RAF bomb selection, 10-tonner to 40-pounder

AA defences into position round all their important dams, to prevent any repetition of the attack.

Of the 19 Lancasters and 133 men which had set out to attack the dams, nine planes and 56 crewmen failed to return. For his part in leading the attack, and drawing away the enemy fire while other aircraft in the force ran in to bomb, Guy Gibson received a well deserved Victoria Cross. Some 33 other members of his squadron were also decorated.

When the Möhne Dam was breached there was severe flooding in the valleys of the Möhne and Ruhr rivers. Some 1,200 people were killed, half of them women workers from the east' held in a forced labour camp near Neheim. Nearly a hundred dwelling houses were destroyed or severely damaged, as were six small electricity works. Railway links passing through the valleys were disrupted, and one of the main lines running through the Ruhr area was rendered useless for some time. Several bridges were destroyed, a few cattle and pigs were drowned, and a considerable area of agricultural land was flooded. But there was no long-term effect on production.

Sixty miles away the Eder Dam broke, with similar results. The flood reached as far as the important arms producing centre of Kassel, and the inundated Bettenhausen suburb had to be evacuated. But, here again, the long-term effect on production was negligible.

The Sorpe Dam seemed to bear a charmed life during the attack. Had it burst as well—and the total of eight aircraft sent out to strike at it had been sufficient to smash both the Möhne and the Eder Dams—the Germans would have been in really serious trouble. The Möhne and Sorpe Dams together held the greater part of the vast pool of water vital to production in the area, and in the words of Reichsminister Albert Speer, had they both been broken 'Ruhr production would have suffered the heaviest possible blow'.

The most important effect of the dams attack was the diversion of labour for their repair from Hitler's pet Atlantic Wall project. Within days the number of men thus engaged had topped the 20,000 mark; by the use of such drastic methods both the Möhne and Eder Dams were repaired and back in use in time for the autumn rains.

A bomb called 'Tallboy'

The success of Wallis's bouncing bomb in May 1943 meant that he now had a ready ear for his original scheme, the earth shock bomb. There still existed no aircraft capable of lifting a 10-ton bomb to 40,000 feet. But a suitably modified Lancaster could lift such a weapon almost to 20,000 feet and could carry it for up to 140 miles. For aircraft based in Britain this limited the use of the weapon to a few targets in France and Belgium, but none in Germany. Wallis therefore suggested a scaled-down deep-penetration weapon, weighing 12,000 pounds or almost 6 tons. The Lancaster could carry such a bomb to almost any part of Germany; it would not meet Wallis's 'original conception' of a full earthquake bomb, but if it worked it would certainly come close to it.

In the summer of 1942 the RAF already had a 12,000-pound 'blockbuster' bomb in service. But this weapon had only a very thin casing, and was incapable of pene-

trating the ground without breaking up. Wallis's bomb, on the other hand, was to be strong enough to withstand the shock of smashing into the ground at a velocity greater than the speed of sound; this was the new departure. On July 1 Wallis received the go-ahead to produce the Tallboy, as the 12,000-pound deep-penetration bomb became known.

During the autumn of 1943 a number of further scaled-down 4,000-pound test models were used in the preliminary trials, which initially went quite well. But when the bombs came to be dropped from 20,000 feet over the range at Crichel Down in December, they proved to be extremely unstable in flight. On one occasion the tail broke off in mid-air, and was later found on the ground some 500 yards from where the nose had impacted.

The cause of this instability was one long known to the designers of high-speed projectiles: as the weapon neared the speed of sound the airflow over it became turbulent and pushed the bomb off course. To stabilise the bomb during this critical period, Wallis offset the tail fins so that they spun the weapon along its axis, rather in the same way as a dart with twisted flights will spin when thrown. There were other problems. In some of the trials the bombs crumpled on impact with the ground. The answer lay in a stronger casing, using an improved casting technique and carefully heat-treated to the required hardness. By the spring of 1944 Tallboy was ready for operations. It was first used against the important Saumur railway tunnel in France on June 8, when 617 Squadron put down 19 of these formidable weapons. Most of the bombs were very accurately dropped, but one in particular struck the high ground exactly over the tunnel, and punched its way deeply into the chalk hill before going off. The explosion literally picked up a slice of the hill, and shook it so violently that one end of the tunnel disappeared altogether. The bombs left craters on the surface averaging 84 feet in diameter and 25 feet in depth.

Shortly afterwards the large underground V-weapon stores and bunkers in northern France were caved in by Tallboys. After the attack on the last-named site a German civil engineer reported plaintively to his superiors in the Reich Research Council that '. . . the installations were not designed to withstand bombs such as these'.

Just as noteworthy was the success of Tallboy against the previously invulnerable U-boat pens. Conventional bombs had done little more than scratch the tops of the massive 16-foot-thick reinforced concrete roofs. In quick succession the shelters at Brest, La Pallice, and Ijmuiden, at Rotterdam, Bergen, and Poortershaven were all pierced by the new bombs.

On November 12, 1944 some 32 Lancasters of 9 and 617 Squadrons set out with Tallboys to attack the mighty battleship *Tirpitz*, lying off Tromsö in the north of Norway. Two of the bombs penetrated deeply into the ship then, after a programmed delay of one-fourteenth of a second, detonated. The combined force of nearly 5 tons of explosive, confined within the ship's stout shell of armour, wreaked fearful havoc. *Tirpitz* was literally disembowelled. When the spray from the near misses settled, the battleship looked as if she had been through the rollers of some enormous mangle; one eye witness recalls

that she had the appearance '. . . rather like an unfinished construction on the stocks'. Five minutes later the fierce fire started inside the ship reached the after magazine. The exploding ammunition tore a rent 120 feet long down the 12-inch-thick armour on the port side; as the torrent of water flooded in, the ship heeled over and capsized.

A mammoth 10-ton bomb

The success of Tallboy in its turn led to the decision to push ahead with Wallis's 10-ton giant bomb: 'Grand Slam'. Here experience gained with the Tallboy proved extremely useful, but there were still a few problems to be solved. To obtain the necessary strength for penetration of the heaviest reinforced concrete targets, Wallis asked for a steel with a tensile strength of 50 to 55 tons per square inch. For such a strength oil hardening was necessary and only one manufacturer, the Sheffield Steel Corporation, had a furnace and bath suitable for such large steel castings. The firm went into full production, but alone it could not have produced sufficient Grand Slams to meet all Bomber Command's needs. Therefore other firms were called in to produce the bombs, using a special air-hardening process which was somewhat simpler and produced steel almost as good, with a tensile strength of 48 to 53 tons per square inch. In the event the air-hardened bombs proved successful.

Grand Slam was first used operationally against the Bielefeld Viaduct on March 14, 1945. Thirteen Tallboys and one Grand Slam were dropped during the attack, and as a result it became impossible to differentiate between the effects of the individual types of bomb. Not that it mattered all that much. Six arches of one viaduct and seven of the other were destroyed. Some 20,000 tons of concrete and masonry were brought down by three very near misses, one of them the Grand Slam. Wallis had always said that with his sort of bomb a near miss was better than a direct hit, and so it proved.

All told, 854 Tallboys and 41 Grand Slams were dropped operationally before the war ended. In aggregate Wallis's deep-penetration bombs proved considerably more effective, if somewhat less spectacular, than his bouncing mines. For the fact was that the use of the latter could be rendered impossible by the simplest of defensive measures at the target, and so it could be used only in a single attack. But the Tallboy and Grand Slam bombs were used again and again to smash massive targets.

Although Wallis's deep-penetration bombs were tremendously successful, it should be emphasised that their potential was never exploited to the full. At the time no aircraft existed which could release them from the 40,000-foot altitude which the scientist had reckoned necessary for a really deep penetration. Only when it was planted far beneath the surface could the weapon devote its entire energy to produce an earthquake-like disturbance. Today a modern jet medium bomber could easily lift a Grand Slam to 40,000 feet or even higher. With the opprobrium attached to the use of nuclear weapons nowadays, is it beyond the bounds of possibility that we may yet see Barnes Wallis's brainchild used to its full capability?

At 0245 hours, August 6, 1945 (local time), the Superfortress *Enola Gay* lifted off the specially lengthened runway at North Field, Tinian, with just a few yards to spare—she was 7 tons overweight—and headed for Japan. She carried a crew of nine, with four passengers, all of them scientists, and a single bomb which bore the incongruous code name of *Little Boy*. 'General Bombing Mission 13' was under way. Her captain, Colonel Paul Tibbets, had been training his hand-picked crew for over a year and now, as the spearhead of 509 Composite Group of 20th Air Force, they were preparing to launch the first atomic bomb—though only Tibbets himself, of the crew members, had any accurate idea of the type of bomb it was.

Electronically complex enough to require its own dashboard and wiring system, the bomb had already posed one problem before the plane left the ground. Some B-29s had already crashed when taking off from Tinian on conventional bombing missions, and if the *Enola Gay* had a similar accident, the whole island might well disappear in smoke. Could the bomb be rendered harmless for the take-off and then armed during the flight? Captain William Parsons thought it could. A naval ordnance expert who had been associate director at the Los Alamos bomb laboratory, and who was flying with Tibbets as one of the scientific observers, he spent some hectic hours on August 5 practising the insertion of the conventional explosive trigger. By the time he had finished, his fingers were bleeding from the sharp edges of the bomb's components, but he was confident he could repeat the process in flight. When the plane reached 8,000 feet, Parsons went down into the bomb bay and reported to Tibbets, less than half an hour later, that they were now carrying a 'final bomb'.

They were not the first plane to take off. At 0130 hours three weather planes had left Tinian to report visibility over the possible targets, Hiroshima, Kokura, and Nagasaki. The bomb had to be dropped visually. Hiroshima was the primary target, but if there was too much cloud cover Tibbets was to select one of the other cities. Washington had already provided him with a long-term weather forecast; four months before, a meteorologist had confidently predicted that the most suitable period would be between August 6 and August 9. Understandably, Tibbets had been taken aback by his assurance, but the event justified it.

Major Claude Eatherly, in the weather plane *Straight Flush*, 32,000 feet above Hiroshima, saw a rim of cloud round the edge of the city, but there was a clear gap 10 miles wide which gave perfect visibility. He radioed to the *Enola Gay* the Morse code message which sealed the fate of Hiroshima: 'Y2.Q2.B2.C1'. In cloud terms this meant '2/10 lower and middle and 2/10 at 15,000 feet', so visibility was good over the primary target. At 0809 hours, Hiroshima time, the city was in sight and the crew put on their arc-welder's goggles to protect their eyes from the flash. At 0811 Tibbets started the bomb run and 2½ minutes later handed over to his bomb-aimer.

Major Thomas Ferebee knew by heart the shape of Hiroshima, with the fingers of the Ota river delta reaching out into the sea, and he soon had the aiming-point in

his bomb sight: a bridge over the widest branch of the Ota. The orders were to drop the bomb at 0815 hours, local time, and Tibbets' skill and the excellent conditions had brought the *Enola Gay,* now travelling at 285 mph, over the target within a margin of seconds. At 17 seconds past 0815 hours, the bomb bay doors opened, and *Little Boy* fell out, from a height of nearly 6 miles. As the B-29 and its accompanying observation plane streaked away in a turn of 150 degrees, to put as great a distance as possible between themselves and the explosion, the crew counted. Fifty-one seconds later, *Little Boy* exploded, 1,850 feet over the city, and only 200 yards from the target point.

Purple clouds, seething flames
As the plane turned, the crew saw a flash, and then felt a double shock wave hit the aircraft. They were 15 miles away by this time, and suddenly below them was a ball of fire, with a temperature, for an imperceptible fraction of a second, of $1,000,000°$, changing to purple clouds and seething, boiling flames which swept upwards. A turbulent cloud of dense white smoke, mushrooming at the top, shot up and up into the sky, reaching a height of 40,000 feet in a matter of minutes. The crew could still see it 360 miles away on their flight back to Tinian. The whole city, except for the dock areas on its fringes, lay under a pall of dark grey dust 3 miles across, in which they could make out flashes of red and orange fire.

But there was no appreciable sound, and accounts differ as to the sound heard by those in the city. Dr Hachiya, of the Hiroshima Communications Bureau Hospital, recalled a strong flash of light, and his colleague, Dr Tabuchi, saw a blinding white flash. Those who survived inside the city referred to the bomb as the *Pika* ('flash'). Those outside called it *Pikadon* ('flash-boom'), for there seems to be more agreement about the sound of the explosion many miles away than in Hiroshima itself. An army officer boarding the train at Iwakuni heard a huge *Don* and saw a great mass of smoke as he looked east to Hiroshima; and a fisherman in his sampan 20 miles away in the Inland Sea near Tsuzu saw the flash and heard a tremendous explosion.

Then Hiroshima began to die. In a matter of seconds, the thermal radiation from the fireball in the centre of the city vaporised thousands of people. Others some distance from the epicentre were fearfully burned, and the blast which followed, like a typhoon, whipped clothes and skin from their bodies as they screamed and writhed in agony. The shock wave, lasting about a second, flattened factories, offices, and houses, burying thousands more under the débris. Trains were overturned in Hiroshima station 2,000 yards away, trams were hurled into the air with their grisly load of already charred corpses. One or two reinforced concrete buildings in the centre remained standing, otherwise the whole of the commercial and residential core of the city was simply annihilated in an instant. Trees and grass burned like straw, and as the overturned *hibachis* or charcoal stoves in the devastated houses ignited the walls and partitions, the fire spread rapidly, fanned by a violent wind that swept through the city.

The people of Hiroshima had been caught unawares. Apart from four or five bombs

THE NUCLEAR RAIDS

Louis Allen

earlier in 1945, their city had been spared the raids which had reduced nearly every other major city in Japan to ruins in the past few months. But they had no illusions. As a big military base, containing the headquarters of the II Army Command, the V Division, and many other units, they felt they must be a target sooner or later, and plans had been drawn up and partly carried out to evacuate useless mouths and knock down houses to make east-west firebreaks through the city. Some 70,000 houses had been demolished, and the peak population of 380,000 was now less than 300,000.

There was a nightly exodus from the city, too. Towards sunset people would form up with their belongings in carts, and make their way to the outskirts, to return the following morning. In fact this 'unplanned' evacuation had reached such proportions that the Army HQ and the Prefectural Office were seriously concerned lest a heavy raid find the firebreak programme incomplete and the streets possibly blocked with streams of people, horses, and carts.

Like the rest of the Japanese cities, Hiroshima had an air-raid warning system, an alert on the approach of aircraft, and a rapid alarm if the city itself was threatened. At 0731 hours on August 6, the alert had been sounded as *Straight Flush* was spotted coming in for its weather observation flight. As the plane turned out to seaward again, 22 minutes later, the 'all clear' sounded. Few people paid any attention when two more planes were sighted, but some cheered when they saw parachutes break from one of them. The crews, they thought, must be bailing out. Most people were either in their offices, or on their way to factories in the industrial outskirts. Men unfit for military service and school children who had been mobilised for the firebreaks were already at work. So the estimate of probable casualties—20,000—made by J. R. Oppenheimer, on the assumption that the bomb would be dropped in a city whose population had already taken shelter, bore no relation to what actually occurred.

Men vaporised, shredded, charred
There were innumerable ways of dying. Those close to the epicentre were vaporised, burned to nothing, in less than an instant. All that remained of them, if they had been standing near a concrete wall, was the imprint of their shadow upon it. The whole centre of Hiroshima, 2 miles across, became for a brief moment of time a lethal oven. Then it disintegrated, and what had been an industrial and commercial city of a quarter of a million people was a dust cloud made up of millions and millions of splinters of wood, glass, metal, and flesh, blown outwards and upwards with tremendous force. More than 2 miles from the explosion, bare skin was burned, telegraph poles were charred. Nearly 400 yards from the epicentre, the mica on granite gravestones—melting point 900°C—had fused. Grey clay tiles—melting point 1,300°C—had melted at a distance of 600 yards. The bomb's heat at ground zero, immediately beneath the epicentre, was later believed to have been around 6,000°C. The force of the blast reached a pressure of 8.0 tons per square yard.

But the bomb had other deaths in store. Thousands of those who survived the burns and shock from blast had been bombarded by neutrons and gamma rays. Nearly all those who survived within half a

Central Press

mile of the epicentre died later from the effects of radiation.

Major-General Shuitsu Matsumura had been in Hiroshima just one month. He had been transferred from GHQ Tokyo as Chief-of-Staff to the Hiroshima Military District, and it was a pleasant change to come from the incinerated metropolis to Japan's almost untouched seventh city, where some of the comforts of life were still obtainable. He lived with a Mr and Mrs Kurota, and on the morning of August 6 had taken tea with them, and was about to change into his uniform to make his way to the District HQ in Hiroshima Castle. Hiroshima had been the site of the Imperial GHQ in the Sino-Japanese War, and since 1941 thousands of troops had left its docks for the campaigns in the South Pacific and South-East Asia.

As General Matsumura went into his room, he was suddenly aware of a brilliant flash, followed by a huge PHWATT!! He was hurled through the roof and found himself floating in the air above a Chinese lotus-tree. He saw a dazzling, glowing ball of fire, and then, in what seemed the same instant of time, he was lying in the garden, bleeding from cuts all over his body, with his clothes in tattered shreds. The house collapsed round him, chunks of timber, roof-beams, and pillars came hurtling down. He thought at first that a bomb had exploded directly on top of the lotus-tree, then, as a red glow shone over the house, he feared he was going to be burned alive and covered his head with his hands. Oddly enough, he felt no heat. He spied a crack in the roof above his head, and scrambled out through broken planks and tiles to find himself outside in the street, naked save for a loincloth.

All around, houses were falling down, people were crawling out from cracking roofs, bathed in blood. His first thought was to bring the army in to help, and, oblivious of his own wounds, he decided to fetch troops from the Castle. Unfortunately he did not yet know the town well, the collapsing houses had filled the streets with débris, and he lost his bearings. He came out in front of the blazing radio station where two people lay in a state of shock in the entrance, one of them with blood pouring from a huge wound in the thigh.

An announcer, whose face Matsumura vaguely recognised, dashed out of the building, and Matsumura called out 'Do you know Hiroshima well?' 'I was born here,' was the answer. 'Take me to District HQ,' asked Matsumura, but the announcer found it hard to get his bearings too, so they began to clamber on the roofs of collapsing houses to see where they were. On every side were visions of catastrophe, cars overturned and burning, horses bucking in their death-throes, people screaming with agony, or dazed from shock and loss of blood. When they finally reached the corner of the West Parade Ground, tongues of flame were licking up from the buildings on every side, the C-in-C's residence was already surrounded by fire, and the infantry, artillery, and medical barracks were ablaze. The five-storey castle was not there any more.

But the most horrifying sight was the centre of the parade ground. The troops had just come out to do drill or PT, and the blast had blown them down and crushed them to death. Those whose sleeves were rolled up

or who had taken their shirts off were covered with fearful blisters. The groans of wounded men came from the air-raid shelters. Matsumura turned along the moat towards the castle gates, while troops ran screaming out of the hutments, all with burned hands or forearms raised above the level of the heart to lessen the pain of the burns. Collecting a few men, he made his way towards the Asano Sentei Park. They noticed how badly he was bleeding, and prevailed on him to let them roughly bandage his wounds with their puttees. Using the tramlines as guides they moved along, in the stream of naked or half-naked people with bodies raw-red from burns, or crippled from the blast.

Apart from groans of pain the endless procession went forward in silence. They passed houses where they could see frantic parents scrabbling at tiles and timber to reach children whose voices could still be heard from within, before the devouring flames reached them. The regional governor's house was near Matsumura's. Trapped by a beam and unable to move, the governor screamed to his wife to cut off his legs, then realised it was hopeless. As the flames came nearer, he called to her 'I'm done for, get away as fast as you can!' At the time of the explosion General Fujii, of the District GHQ, had just put on his uniform, and was about to leave the house, carrying his sword. The burned sword was found beside his black charred remains, with the general's gold fillings. His groom, waiting by the side of the porch, had been calcinated in an instant, along with the horse he was holding.

A strange, viscous rain . . .
When they reached the pinewoods by the river, Matsumura could go no further, and sat down among a group of wounded, exhausted from fatigue and shock. The whole front of his body by this time was covered with a sheet of dried blood, and he peeled it off like a sheet of cellophane. There were scores of badly wounded soldiers lying everywhere. Many of them had been drafted into Hiroshima from the surrounding country, and they were begging people to take messages for their relatives. There were still men who kept their heads: one warrant-officer, with his back torn to pieces, pulled a pocket-book from his map-case and began scrupulously noting down the messages.

Then the fire moved on to the pines in the park, and as the wind changed direction, Matsumura's shelter was covered with thick black smoke. He saw the Nigitsu Shrine begin to burn. As both river banks were now alight, boats went back and forth ferrying people to the island in the middle. Then the convection from the intense heat brought a whirlwind whistling along the banks, spreading the fire further, but those who were lying along them were too far gone to move. Many of those who survived the flames were drowned by the rising waters. Matsumura made towards a bridge. As he paused, leaning against a pillar, rain began to fall—a strange, viscous rain, full of the aspirated dust of the city—and the rising tide reached up to his waist.

It occurred to him that it might be possible to contact other units, in Yamaguchi or Shimane prefectures; and perhaps the Akatsuki Unit in the port of Ujina had not been affected. So he made his way up the Ushita hillside, to contact Lieutenant-

General Yamamoto, commanding the Ordnance Depot, reached Yamamoto's house and collapsed on the verandah. He did not notice the passing of time, but was vaguely aware that someone cooked some rice for him, which tasted full of sand. But Matsumura had been in the Canton campaign and sand in his rice was the least of his worries. You simply had to eat from the top. Yamamoto went down the hillside and came back with some nurses and a naval medical officer, who had just reached Hiroshima from the base at Kure. By candle light the ferreted out the splinters of broken glass from 36 places in Matsumura's body, and stitched a deep wound in his neck, using mercurochrome as disinfectant. It was all they had.

Matsumura later learned he was not the only survivor of his staff. Most of them had been killed at once by the blast, but one, Lieutenant-Colonel Kigi, had been standing at the foot of a flight of stairs, and had come off with only light wounds. Kigi's house happened to be near the epicentre and his wife, her sister, and their two children had been annihilated. The sister had been washing the children's clothes and had died face downwards in the wash-tub. Curiously enough, the clothes themselves had remained intact, and Kigi wandered round the charred remains of the HQ, clutching this solitary reminder that he had once had children.

Later the troops from Ujina moved in. Roads had to be cleared of rubble and opened, and the innumerable corpses removed from beneath collapsed buildings and walls. With the summer heat, the stench had become unbearable, and mass cremations took place, but since it was feared the fires from the cremation pyres might be seen and used by enemy bombers, they had to be restricted to the hours of daylight. So the cremations went on, day after day. At Kure, once the news of the Truman broadcast filtered through and put an end to the various rumours about the type of bomb which had been used, the Army Medical Service began to carry out examinations of the blood of casualties. On August 10, the Atomic Bomb Observation group arrived from Tokyo, and by triangulation measurements determined the epicentre of the explosion to be about 1,000 yards from Matsumura's house. The height of the explosion they estimated to be about 500 yards, and the ground temperature immediately beneath it as 5,000°C.

Tortured, melted features
Asano Sentei Park, where Matsumura, with thousands of others, had sheltered from the flames, was the scene of countless strange and horrible incidents. In his book *Hiroshima* John Hersey tells how Father Kleinsorge, a German priest from the Jesuit mission house, himself cut and bleeding from splinters, answered a call for help from a soldier who could not move and begged for water. As Fr Kleinsorge came up to give him some, he saw the soldier was not alone. Behind a row of bushes lay other soldiers, with their faces completely burned, and hollow eye sockets from which the melted eyes had run, liquid, down their cheeks. Their mouths were mere suppurating holes. One of the boatmen ferrying casualties across the river to the Park stopped in midstream to help a girl out of the water. As he pulled her up, he saw her nose and eyes had been burned away; her ▷

It has frequently been pointed out that the casualties from the Tokyo fire-raid on the night of March 9/10, 1945, were greater than those from the atomic bomb, but comparison of overall casualties is not the best way to show the effectiveness of the atomic bomb. If the (rounded) figures are shown in relation to the density of population per square mile destroyed, a different picture emerges: the rate of casualties per square mile is shown to be four times greater in Hiroshima than in Tokyo.

The original Japanese figures for Nagasaki were based on verified cases only, and were considered too low by the US Strategic Bombing Survey. On the other hand, the Japanese themselves later began to raise casualty figures. The Nagasaki Prefectural Office later proposed a figure of 87,000 for the dead alone, and a municipal publication *Hiroshima Today* (1953) declared that the total figure for that city was 260,000. This is lower than the figure of 306,545 given in Toshikazu Kase's *Eclipse of the Rising Sun,* where it is pointed out that the original death roll in

Hiroshima took no account of the military casualties, which must have been high, the estimate being half the military population of the city.

For this particular figure the American Air Force historians give 6,769 troops killed or missing of a total of 24,158. A broadcast early in 1968 by the Japanese Broadcasting Corporation gave a figure for Hiroshima of 240,000 to 270,000 killed outright or from radiation sickness within five years. On the other hand, the same broadcast put the population of the city at the time as 400,000, which is far higher than usual estimates. Over 4 square miles of Hiroshima were obliterated. Within a 2-mile radius of the epicentre, 10,000 buildings were annihilated by blast and 50,000 by fire. In Nagasaki, nearly 2 square miles were destroyed, a figure smaller than that of the average area for incendiary raids on Japan (2·97 square miles). But the Hiroshima bomb fell into a commercial and administrative area. At Nagasaki, *Fat Man* hit a much more heavily industrialised zone, nearly 70% of which was destroyed.

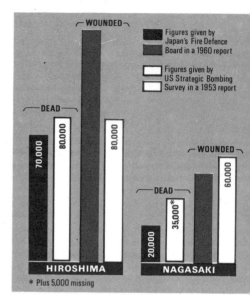

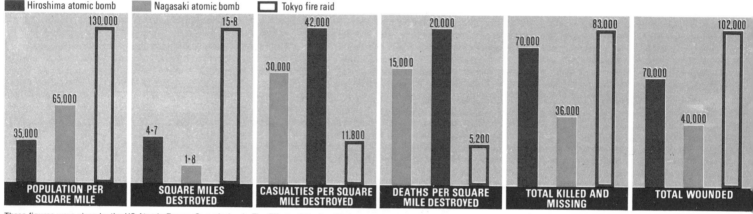

These figures were given by the US Atomic Energy Commission in *The Effects of Nuclear Weapons*

ears looked as if they had melted. Then the round, featureless face fell back into the water, to drown with thousands of others.

Perhaps the strangest incident that day, and one which sheds light on the mood of wartime Japan, was one related by Dr Hachiya in his *Hiroshima Diary.* A portrait of the Emperor was kept in a special place in the Communications Bureau, and Mr Yasuda, the employee responsible for the safe keeping of the picture in emergencies, was on a tram going to work when the bomb fell. His first thought was for the portrait, and he left his shattered tram and made his way on foot through the burning streets, the corpses, and the dark clouds of fiery dust. Running up to the fourth floor, he forced open the iron door behind which the picture was kept. His colleagues thought the Castle would be the safest place for it, so with four of them (one in front, one behind, one on either side), Yasuda carried the picture on his back out of the grounds and made for the Castle. At the Castle gates, a sentry warned them fire was spreading everywhere, so they turned towards the Asano Sentei Park.

As the little procession made its way through the dense crowds of dead and wounded, the cry 'The Emperor's picture!' went up, and those who were still on their

feet, however badly burned they might be, saluted or bowed low. Those who were too seriously wounded to stand clasped their hands in prayer. When the party reached the river, the crowds made way and the picture was entrusted to Mr Ushio, a senior Bureau official, who climbed into a boat with it. As the boat drew away from the shore an officer drew his sword and rapped out an order. The burned and bleeding troops lining the banks stood to attention and saluted. Just after Ushio reached the opposite bank with his precious charge, the whole river bank he had just left turned into a maelstrom of flames. The great pine trees of Asano Park caught fire too, and thousands tried to escape the flames by jumping into the river, where they drowned. But the Emperor's portrait was brought to safety.

Hiroshima was not the only city in Japan to report damage that day. On August 5, USAAF bombers had raided a number of cities, among them the port of Kobe, and reports from these were coming into the capital when the news from Hiroshima arrived. But it was soon evident that what had happened there was exceptional both in the scale and speed of the catastrophe, and the number of aircraft involved. Telephone communication between the city and the Japan Broadcasting Corporation in

Tokyo was cut; the telegraph line to Hiroshima had ceased to function, according to the Tokyo railway signals centre; and Army GHQ could not contact II Army HQ.

Finally a message came through from the Army Transportation Office at Ujina: Hiroshima had been annihilated by a single bomb (Tokyo Radio, in spite of this, was to refer on August 7 to 'a small number of bombs'). The city itself had been full of rumours: a plane had sprayed petrol from the sky and ignited it by dropping incendiaries; the city had been sprinkled with magnesium powder which exploded when it came into contact with the electric tram wires. To many of the Japanese on the ground, as to the navigator of the *Enola Gay,* the first effect had been that of an enormous photographic flash.

A rapid realisation

But there were those in Japan who had a shrewd idea of what was involved. As early as February 1944, the nuclear physicist Yoshio Nishina, the constructor of Japan's first cyclotron in 1937, and a former pupil of Niels Bohr, had been introduced to the Prime Minister, Tojo, by the head of the Second Bureau (Intelligence), General Seizo Arisue. Nishina had proposed the manufacture of a bomb employing the priniple of nuclear fission. Tojo refused: there ere simply not enough funds available for he industrial installations such a bomb vould require. Arisue remembered Nishina's roposal when he was told to go down to liroshima with an investigation team on ugust 7, and he asked Nishina to go with im. Arisue had received a message from he naval base at Kure which referred to new weapon of unprecedented destruc-veness, and the following day his monitors icked up the phrase 'atomic bomb'.

An air-raid siren sounded as he was about o take off from Tachikawa airport outside okyo, and he told Nishina to follow later. t 1800 hours he was flying at 4,500 feet ver devastated Hiroshima. Arisue was no tranger to bombed cities, but this cal-inated desert with its few blackened trees ave no sign of life at all. He landed in a eld close to the port, about 2½ miles from round zero, and as he jumped down, he oticed the mud-coloured grass was all ent seaward, as if it had been pressed at by a gigantic iron.

An officer ran to meet the aircraft, sword n hand. The right side of his face was per-ectly normal, the left was a hideous mass f deep burns. Arisue made his way by aunch to the Army Transport HQ in Ujina, vhere he was met on the quayside by General Baba. There was no light, no elec-ricity, no water, and the staff was working y candlelight in a backyard. General Baba egan to tell Arisue what had happened, hen burst into tears. He had seen his laughter leave for school that morning, nd a few minutes later found her dead ody lying in the street, cut to pieces by lying glass. Baba's own personal agony ad not prevented him making observa-ions: people in reinforced concrete build-ngs or deep shelters had survived; shade nd white clothing had provided some pro-ection from burns.

The next day, August 8, Arisue went round liroshima. Corpses of men and horses ay everywhere, and after two days in the ummer heat, they were already decompos-ng. In the afternoon Nishina arrived with iis team of scientists and declared at once hat a bomb using uranium had been used. Arisue arranged an interservices conference t Kure for the following day, but on hearing f the Russian declaration of war he re-urned to Tokyo, bidding farewell to the 70-year-old Field-Marshal Shunroku Hata t his command post on a hillside outside liroshima. Arisue could see that the old Marshal had no hope left.

The second bomb
At least two Americans—Admiral Purnell and General Groves, who had been the military 'midwife' of the atomic bomb pro-ject—were convinced that a rapid 'double dose' of atomic warfare would end the war; and some of the Los Alamos scientists who had tested another type of bomb, using plutonium, wanted to know if the device would work in battle. August 11 had been fixed as the date for dropping this second bomb, then the weather reports showed good weather could be expected for August 9, with bad weather for the following five days, so it became imperative to bring the date forward. Of the three targets remaining, Kokura, Nagasaki (put on the list when Kyoto was removed because of its cultural and religious associations), and Niigata, he last was deleted because of the extra distance involved. Now part of the in-dustrial complex known as Kitakyushu, Kokura was a large war arsenal extending over 200 acres.

Nagasaki was a big shipbuilding and re-pair centre and a major military port, but considered less suitable as a target both because it had been bombed five times in the previous 12 months and because its topography would limit the blast effects and make the damage harder to assess: it was broken by hills and valleys, where Hiroshima had offered a relatively smooth, flat surface.

Instead of being a gun-type bomb, trig-gering off a Uranium 235 reaction, the second bomb—*Fat Man*—employed the implosion method, a circle of 64 detonators to drive pieces of plutonium together into the supercritical mass. There was no question of arming it in flight.

Where Tibbets had had a smooth run, everything seemed to go wrong with Major Sweeney's trip. Just before take-off at 0349 hours his strike plane, *Bockscar*, was found to have a faulty fuel pump, which meant that the bomb bay could not pump its 800 gallons of fuel to the engines. The plane would not only be deprived of the use of the fuel, it would have to carry a use-less load to Japan and back.

The strike plane and observation planes flew separately, and one of the latter (carry-ing two British observers who had obtained last-minute authorisation from Washington to accompany the flight, William Penney, the scientist, and Group Captain Leonard Cheshire) muffed its rendezvous over the island of Yakushima. Sweeney waited over Yakushima at least 15 minutes, then made for the primary target, Kokura, where it was obvious that visual bombing was impossible. Sweeney made three runs over the city, shortening his fuel still more, but the bomb-aimer could find no break in the cloud. It was Nagasaki's bad luck.

On the way to the secondary target, they worked out what fuel they had left: enough for one run only, and even then they would not be able to return to Tinian, but would have to drop short at Okinawa. Com-mander Ashworth, operations officer of 509 Group, and a naval atomic weapons expert, was Sweeney's weaponeer and took the responsibility of cancelling the Washington order that only visual bombing be permitted. He told Sweeney to go ahead on radar, if Nagasaki was covered with cloud. It was. There was 8/10 cloud cover when they reached it, and most of the bomb run was made by radar. At the last moment, the bomb-aimer found a break in the cloud, lined up on a race-track, and let go the bomb from 28,900 feet. It was 1058 hours, Nagasaki time.

A second holocaust
Nagasaki was different in several ways from other Japanese cities, with a longer history of western contacts. Founded by a local Christian *daimyō* ruler in the 16th century and then presented by him to the Society of Jesus, it was a port to which Spanish and Portuguese ships had brought traders and missionaries, and was later the scene of the martyrdom of thousands of Japanese Catholics during the persecutions under the Shōgun Hideyoshi. Nagasaki still had a large Catholic population, centred chiefly round the industrial and residential district of Urakami. Wide of its aiming point, *Fat Man* fell on Urakami.

As in Hiroshima three days before, Naga-saki had sounded the alert when Sweeney's weather plane was spotted at 0745 hours, and the alarm went five minutes later. But the alert had often been sounded when planes were attacking other targets in Kyu-shu, and the citizens had grown sceptical and careless. When the second alert was sounded at 1053 hours, after the strike plane had been observed, very few people bothered to take shelter. As it happened, Nagasaki was well off for shelters: tunnels had been dug into the surrounding hill-sides, and these would have been very effective. In the event, the casualties from fire were less than in Hiroshima, as the large water areas prevented the fires spread-ing so ruthlessly. A firestorm, which had terrorised Hiroshima, did not occur in Nagasaki.

On the other hand, the plutonium bomb was more efficient than *Little Boy*, and the blast was greater. Because of the bowl-shaped terrain, the damage extended roughly in an oval 2·3 by 1·9 miles, and it was uneven, as the buildings in Urakami were less congested and more irregularly spread. Within the oval nearly every build-ing was destroyed or made uninhabitable, and minor damage occurred up to 16,000 feet from ground zero. On the other hand there was not the same total disorganisa-tion of medical services which had so increased the Hiroshima casualties, al-though some of the finest hospitals in the Far East—Nagasaki University and Naga-saki Medical College—were destroyed. Oddly enough, the train service was not interrupted. But the individual tragedies were very much like those of Hiroshima.

Matsu Moriuchi, an elderly woman, was in Yamazato Grade School air-raid shelter when the bomb fell. Many people in the shelter were killed, and almost all those in the immediate area outside it. When she peered out, she saw half-naked people, lying around the mouth of the shelter, their bodies swollen to a monstrous size, and the skin peeling off like pieces of torn rag. She realised they were the school teachers who had been outside digging a new shelter. They were not dead and moaned pitifully for water. Sadako Moriyama was in the same shelter and was petrified with horror when she saw two foul, croaking, lizard-like monsters crawl into the shelter mouth. She was even more terrified when the light revealed them to be human beings, their skin stripped to the raw flesh by burns and their bodies shattered where the blast had hurled them against a wall.

In a pathetic heap on a sand-pit outside the shelter lay four children who had been chasing dragon-flies a few minutes before, now naked and burned, the skin hanging from their fingertips like gloves turned inside out. Then she saw the yard was covered with the still twitching bodies of other dying children. On the Koba hillside, 3½ miles away, Fujie Urata saw a flash of red then blue light of intense and unbear-able brilliance, but she was separated from the explosion by a mountain and so felt no blast and was exposed to no radiation.

As she watched the black smoke boiling up into the sky, the wounded began to file past her from Urakami, young children with black and swollen faces, workers from the Mitsubishi Urakami Ordnance Plant, naked too, sobbing with shock, faces, necks and hands bleeding or covered with blisters, the skin peeling off in great sheets that flapped in the black dust. On her way to

Urakami she saw a woman's head lying grotesquely by itself in a pumpkin field, with a single gold tooth gleaming in the open mouth, and burned black holes where the eyes had been. A mile from Urakami her sister Tatsue came upon a woman lying in the road with two babies, her face one huge blister, her hair burned to the roots, begging passers-by to take her dying children with them.

From the mountain tops, St Francis' Hospital could be seen blazing, and the hills around Urakami were stripped bare of foliage—the trees had been blasted down to the stumps. About 30 nuns from the Urakami Orphanage who had been working outside on the orphanage farm lay in a huddle behind some rocks, saying the Rosary. They had been burned all over, and the blast that followed the heat had whipped both clothing and skin off their bodies.

Some 'double' survivors
In the hospitals, the scenes from Hiroshima were repeated, living and dead lying together in heaps of burned and mangled flesh, blood, and skin everywhere, uncontrollable diarrhoea cases pouring excreta over hospital floors and down stairs covered in filth and blood. By what must seem the most tragic of coincidences, there were even a number of people in Nagasaki who had survived the Hiroshima bomb, and who lived through the terror of Nagasaki as well. A newspaper publisher, a naval architect, an accountant, an engineer, a dock labourer, and, most improbably, four kite-makers, were 'double' survivors, and there were no doubt others. They were all born in Nagasaki or had family connections there, and all worked in Hiroshima, with the exception of the newspaper publisher who had stopped in the city on his return from a business trip to Tokyo. Within three days of the Hiroshima bombing they were back in Nagasaki. Their experience warned them and their families to take shelter when the B-29s were spotted approaching the city, and so they escaped death a second time.

Perhaps the most poignant story is that of Kenshi Hirata, the accountant, who had only been married a few weeks and had brought his new bride to Hiroshima ten days before the bomb fell. He had been on duty in his office throughout the night August 5/6, and after the bomb fell began searching for his wife, only to find their house crushed flat and her dead body inside. Sadly bearing his wife's ashes back to the city of her birth, he arrived in Nagasaki just in time for the second atomic bomb.

Apathy, defiance, despair, and joy
The reaction of the people of Hiroshima to the bomb did not follow a straightforward pattern. Immediately after the first terror, they made for the suburbs and hills, broken in spirit, unable to think of anything except following the silent, mournful files moving along the railway lines, footpaths, or river-beds out of the doomed city.

Then life began to re-assert itself. When the news of Nagasaki arrived, the rumour began to spread that Japan too had the atomic weapon but had refrained from using it. Once the Americans had dropped it, a special naval squadron of six-engined bombers had crossed the Pacific and delivered it on San Francisco and Los Angeles. As this rumour spread, it cheered up those suffering from wounds and sickness, patients in hospital began to laugh and sing,

and prayers were offered for the pilots who were supposed to have made the gallant suicide flight.

On August 15, those listening in to the Emperor's broadcast at Hiroshima Station or in the Communications Bureau could hardly make out what he was saying, and not everyone realised at first that he was telling them the war was over. The shock made some of them almost faint, and Dr Hachiya felt cold sweat running down his back as he returned to his bed with the words 'Haisen da!' ('We've lost the war') ringing in his ears. The other patients in his ward were weeping in despair. Then suddenly their tears gave way to anger, and even those who had been hoping for peace were shouting that the war must go on, that it was better to die for Japan than live in disgrace. The following day, when news came that a Japanese air force unit from Kure, 25 miles away, was dropping leaflets encouraging resistance to the surrender, some of the patients shouted for joy.

But side by side with this passionate rejection of the unendurable, radiation sickness and moral disintegration made their way. No one in Hiroshima knew the symptoms or treatment of radiation sickness, a hazard brought by no other weapon of war, and which struck at those who had lived through blast and fire. Those who had been within 500 yards of the epicentre began to show a low blood platelet count, leading to fatal haemorrhages. Two to 15 days after the explosion, many of those who had been within 500 yards of it, but had been shielded by buildings from flash burns and the shock wave, began to develop the fatal signs: loss of appetite, vomiting, spitting of blood, abnormally low white blood cell counts. Those nearest to the epicentre developed *petechiae* (subcutaneous haemorrhages of tiny blood vessels). In the next 500-yard zone the death rate was high, but the symptoms developed later. Even many of those who were up to 3,000 yards from ground zero fell ill and died.

American historians attribute 7 to 20% of the deaths to radiation sickness, but point out that thousands of those who were vaporised or burned to death must have been so close to the explosion that they would have been among the severest radiation casualties had they not died in some other way.

Years after the bomb, there were several cases involving scientists and doctors which gave the Japanese furiously to think. Three men had come to Hiroshima and Nagasaki to examine the after-effects: the nuclear physicist Yoshio Nishina, an expert on the medical aspects of radiation, Masao Tsuzuki, and a radiobiologist, Koichi Murachi. Nishina died in 1951 of liver cancer, Tsuzuki in 1960 of lung cancer, Murachi in 1961 of leukemia. All these men had handled radioactive substances for many years during their researches, but they undoubtedly were exposed to exceptionally high doses of radiation in the bombed cities, and whatever the causality involved in the three cases, they seemed more than coincidental to the ordinary Japanese and pointed up the concealed dangers of lingering radiation sickness decades later.

The damage was not merely physical. The huge dumps left by the Japanese army in the hills behind Hiroshima were soon raided when the surrender was announced,

and in the disordered state of the city in the following months, looting, gangsterism and black marketeering flourished. Later still, the reconstruction of the city and the focussing upon it of a rather gruesome tourist industry brought to the town many thousands of people on the make, so that the survivors gradually found themselves to be a minority in a city that had once been theirs.

Spiritual wreckage beyond repair
On the individual plane, there were many who had not only suffered unspeakably but had also, they obscurely felt, let down some deeply loved person in a moment of great need. The sufferings inflicted by the bombing and the state of utter despair it left behind had drawn men's courage up to—and frequently beyond—the extremes could bear, and the best of wills had often snapped. Those who stayed in shelters, fearful of what might happen if they emerged to look for parents or brothers and sisters felt later a remorse they would never overcome.

Dr Nagai, the author of *We of Nagasaki*, who slaved in a hospital for days after the explosion while his wife died, unattended, from burns, accused himself not only of her death but also of creating a gap or 'fissure' between himself and those of his *tonarigumi* ('neighbourhood group') who —he knew—had relied on him to help them during air raids, and to whose help he had not come. All those who survived, he claimed, were like him: those who ignored calls for help, those who could not bear to stay and care for the horrible, twisted charred sub-human objects which had once been their sons and daughters, their fathers and mothers, those who had failed in their duty, were not merely lucky, they were selfish, driven by a savage instinct of self preservation.

Dr Nagai later wondered whether those who decided the fate of nations and who seemed already to have classified the atomic bomb as merely one weapon among others, if slightly more frightful and effective, realised what the bomb had done, not just to the bodies, but to the hearts and minds of those who had survived. Those who visited the incinerated wastelands of Hiroshima or Nagasaki and later saw fine modern cities growing there may have marvelled at the power of recuperation the communities had shown in rebuilding their shattered surroundings.

But they did not see the stubborn spiritual wounds in the hearts of those who could not look their neighbours or friends in the eye because, in the last extremity, they had failed them. These were the victims of a spiritual wreckage which was, he believed, quite beyond repair.

LOUIS ALLEN was born in Yorkshire in 1922, educated at the Universities of Manchester, London (School of Oriental Studies), and Paris. He served in Indian Army Intelligence as Japanese language officer in India and Burma, and was mentioned in dispatches. After the surrender, he lived in Japanese army camps in Burma, Siam, Malaya, and Indo-China, interrogating Japanese commanders and staffs on the Burma campaign, and writing divisional histories. Mr Allen is co-translator of a Japanese account of the end of the war and its aftermath in Burma: Yuji Aida's *Prisoner of the British*. He now teaches French literature in the University of Durham.

Allied Strategic Bomber Offensive, 1941/1945/Dr Noble Frankland

Was the strategic bombing of Germany really necessary? Did it help to shorten the war at all? What was its actual effect on the German economy, on German morale, on the effectiveness of the German fighting machine? Dr Noble Frankland, official historian to Bomber Command, puts the RAF case for the strategic bombing offensive, which reached its climax in the still controversial raid on Dresden

Brown Bros.

BOMBING
THE RAF CASE

Smoke markers indicate targets for B-17 Flying Fortresses during a raid on Berlin—a major target, along with Dresden, of Operation 'Thunderclap'

Three underrated factors led to the failure of the early Allied raids . . .

Civilian and industrial resilience

Effective fighter and AA resistance

Dispersal of bombing effort

In the last year of the war the Allied bomber forces possessed and meted out to the Germans a huge destructive power. Between them the Lancasters, Halifaxes, and Mosquitoes of the British Bomber Command and the Fortresses and Liberators of the US 8th and 15th Air Forces knocked out Germany's oil supply by the almost total destruction of her synthetic oil industry, rendered her transport system chaotic by the dislocation of railway, road, and canal systems throughout the Reich, and left many of Germany's cities in utter ruins—especially the Saxon capital Dresden, which in February 1945 suffered a comprehensive disaster greater than anything witnessed in any other European city during the Second World War.

These achievements of strategic bombing had a decisive effect upon the outcome of the war. Obviously Germany could not continue an effective military resistance when there was no more fuel to keep her tanks moving and her aircraft flying in effective strengths. Nor could she look to any future recovery when her industries lay either in ruins or without their essential supplies through the collapse of her transport systems. The ruin of her cities probably helped to signalise at last to the masses of the German people that further resistance was impossible.

Even so this great contribution to Allied victory by strategic bombing came late in the day, and it made itself felt only in combination with the products of military and naval victory. Though the eventual achievement at least approached the estimates of bombing effectiveness which had been made before the war by its advocates, it took much longer to get the results than most of them had expected. For this disappointment there were three main reasons:

● Effective damage by bombing required a much more sustained and greater weight of attack than had been expected. This was because people in general and the Germans in particular proved to be enormously more resilient to the horrors and hardships of bombing than had seemed likely and because the organisation of repair, recovery, and substitution, again especially in Germany, was greatly more efficient than expected.

● Second, the efficiency of bombing was in proportion to the effectiveness of the opposition from anti-aircraft guns and more particularly of fighters to a much greater degree than had ever been envisaged before the war. So much was this so that in fact bombing, though heavy and sustained, had a minimal effect upon Germany's war effort until her air defences were overcome and command of the air won. It then had its maximum effect.

● Third, even when command of the air existed and the Allied bomber forces had reached mammoth proportions, the maximum concentration of effort upon the most decisive targets was prevented not only by weather considerations but by disagreements within the high command as to what were the best targets. Thus, in the final phase of the war, the efforts of the heavy bombers were divided between a variety of aims to an extent which delayed the fulfilment of any of them. In this last phase the combined Anglo-American bombing offensive had three main themes: oil, transport, and general attack on major cities.

Ever since there has been a continuous controversy as to the wisdom or otherwise of the various schools of thought and experience which produced these competing themes and even now, a generation later, w seem to be no nearer the realisation of wha may be the verdict of history than in thos critical days of 1944 to 1945 when the issue were hotly disputed by the great prota gonists upon whom the responsibility fo decision or for command fell: Churchil Portal, Harris, Tedder, Roosevelt, Arnol and Spaatz. In the public eye this contr versy has assumed the appearance of bein crystallised in the issue raised by the bom ing of Dresden, and on this there is still regular and voluminous outpouring explanations, sentiments, judgments, an statistics in the popular press and othe media of publicity.

This crystallisation and the mode debate which has stimulated it are espec ally unfortunate. In the first place the bom ing of Dresden is not an event which can b understood, as so often the attempt to unde stand it has been made, in isolation from th bomber offensive and the war situation as whole. The motives for the attack were con plex and in view of the results produce they deserve to be clearly and objectivel understood before the stage of moral judg ments and the like is reached. Moreover, is as well to remember that sensationa statistics, for example of the deaths cause in Dresden, are liable to leave a profoun public impression long after they have bee withdrawn by their originators; that thos near the centre of government or high com mand in war are as liable as anyone else t have faulty memories or even, perhaps, t have missed the point at the time; and, las but not least, that the partial digestion bits of the documentary evidence is liabl to produce very misleading conclusions. A one particular example of this danger, th recent so-called discovery of a documen gives the implication that Portal relentlessl pursued the destruction of Dresden eve after being warned off it by Churchill. I fact, as will be shown in the course of thi article, this charge against the war-tim Chief of the Air Staff is not only quite un founded but is absolutely contrary to incon trovertible evidence.

These alone, in addition to the Dresde raid's intrinsic interest, are perhaps suffici ent reasons to analyse the course of th strategic air offensive.

'The bomber will always get through'

Before the war the British air staff, o the principle that the bomber will always ge through, had evolved a doctrine of air powe which has since become known as the Tren chard doctrine, suggesting that the onl defence against bombing was counter-bomb ing and that the side which would win th war was that which could first develop an then sustain the heaviest air attack upo the sources of the opposing war strength Trenchard's ideas as to what constituted th sources of enemy war strength were onl loosely defined, but it is certain that h regarded the moral effect of bombing—tha is, of course, the effect upon the people bein bombed—as much more important than th material—that is, the systems such as mar shalling yards and power grids, or the struc tures such as oil plants and factories. It i also certain that he did not regard fighte defence as a major consideration in strategic bombing offensive. If the enemy ai defence, or for that matter his air offence became too strong, the balance, it was sup posed, could be restored by attack upon hi aircraft factories. Thus the heavy bombe was the heart of air power, and in all probability, Trenchard thought, of the war effort. Other elements of air power—such as defensive fighters, or naval and military supporting squadrons—were at worst a waste of effort and at best subordinate and marginal instruments.

When in the last three or four years of peace it became increasingly obvious that the enemy in the next war would be Germany, the Trenchard doctrine was however somewhat watered down. For one thing, by the time that the British rearmament programme began to get into its stride it became apparent that the Germans had built up an important lead in air strength which, especially because it looked more impressive than it really was, rather suggested that a slogging match between the bombers of Germany and Britain might well end rather quickly in a victory or knock-out blow in favour of Germany.

For another thing the British, when they came to the brink, found themselves unwilling to initiate unrestricted bombing—or, to use the jargon of the time, 'to take the gloves off'. Thus Bomber Command's war plans, known as the Western Air Plans, consisted mainly of highly selective attacks which were to be applied with extreme precision against key points in the German war economy such as power, oil production, or transport. Even these were only to be carried out in certain circumstances which it was hoped would not, and in the event did not, prevail at the outset of the war. Even so, the heavy bomber was still regarded as the main weapon with which both to prosecute the offensive and to reduce the scale of the enemy offensive.

This was strange, because the development of techniques in Fighter Command which was going on at the same time began already to indicate somewhat different probabilities. The introduction of high-performance interceptor fighters represented by the Hurricane and later the Spitfire, coupled with the introduction of radar, gave air defence the real prospect, at least in daylight, of getting effectively to grips with air offence. Indeed Sydney Camm who designed the Hurricane, R. J. Mitchell who designed the Spitfire, Sir Robert Watson Watt who evolved the principle of radar, Sir Henry Tizard who seized upon its military application, and Sir Hugh Dowding who commanded the force which received these nourishing reinforcements, released the potential which made possible the first wholly decisive air battle in history: the victory in the Battle of Britain. The victory was one of the British air defence over the German air offence.

But even before this crucial battle began, the British Bomber Command had discovered that its plans for precision bombing of German targets in daylight were impracticable. Sufficient proportions of the Wellingtons and Hampdens simply could not survive the onslaught of the German defending fighters, which also, though less effectively than the British, had the early warning of radar. And so before the war was six months old, Bomber Command had turned for all save exceptional purposes to night bombing.

In the course of 1940 and 1941, rather slowly but nevertheless clearly enough in the end, it became obvious that at night in the face of the enemy defences the Bomber Command crews could not find such precision targets as oil plants or even marshalling yards. If these were to remain as

The defenders take their toll. (Top) A B-24 Liberator receives a direct hit on its way to bomb the Kiel and Hamburg U-boat pens. Of 1,000 bombers in this raid, 9 were lost. (Bottom) A B-17 Flying Fortress scatters smoke and debris as it disintegrates in the sky after being hit by German AA fire. The nose and one engine have been completely torn off

143

'We can smash the German machine by the bomber blitz'

(Air Marshal Lord Trenchard, 1942)

'Our aircraft occasionally killed women and children'

(Air Chief Marshal Sir Arthur Harris: Bomber Offensive)

'In spite of all that happened at Hamburg, bombing proved a comparatively humane method'

(Air Chief Marshal Sir Arthur Harris: Bomber Offensive)

the aiming points, the bulk of Bomber Command's tonnages would continue to fall harmlessly in fields. Since by the end of 1941 Britain's armies had been defeated or driven on to the defensive wherever they had appeared; since her navy was engulfed in a desperate struggle for survival in the Battle of the Atlantic; since the Russians had been driven back almost to Moscow; and since the Americans had hardly recovered from the shock of Pearl Harbor, it was utterly inconceivable that the one and only Allied force which could so much as cast a shadow over Germany should not exert every possible effort to do so.

Thus Bomber Command turned not surprisingly—indeed in the circumstances of the time inevitably—to the attack of targets which at any rate to some extent it could find and hit. These targets were whole German towns. The policy was at the time described, and has since become famous, as that of 'area bombing'.

Though it was the response of Britain to an utterly desperate war situation in which Germany and Japan were everywhere victorious and Russia, America, and Britain everywhere vanquished, it was not simply an emotional outburst of frustrated rage leading to wanton terror bombing. General area attack upon German towns was a carefully conceived strategic plan to undermine the basis of the German war effort by the dislocation of her industries, sources of power, and communications through the general destruction of the towns associated with them. The hope was that the aim would be realised by a combination of the material damage caused in the towns themselves and the moral effect upon the workers who lived in them.

However well- or ill-founded were these hopes, and many of them proved to be based on not much more than wishful thinking, the fact remained that if Bomber Command was to achieve any effects at all, this was the only policy open to it. In war, as Moltke observed, one must do what one can and not what one ought. Here then were the foundations of one of the great elements in the final bombing offensive against Germany: the general area attack upon towns in which by aiming at the centres of the target areas it was intended to cause such destruction and dislocation that one industrial area after another would seize up.

Thus daylight bombing had to be abandoned because the Wellingtons and Hampdens (and later the Lancasters, Halifaxes, and Stirlings) could not survive in the face of the German fighters. The cover of darkness had to be sought. But this meant that small targets such as those offered by particular factories could not be found or aimed at, at least by the squadrons of the main force. So came the attack on the larger areas offered by whole towns.

While these developments took place and while in the course of 1942 Bomber Command began under the leadership of its new Commander-in-Chief Sir Arthur Harris to win its first major successes over Lübeck and Cologne, the Americans were preparing to join in the bombing offensive. But they were not, as the RAF originally hoped, prepared simply to reinforce the Bomber Command squadrons any more than a generation earlier they had been willing simply to reinforce Haig's divisions in France. As Pershing had then resolved to lead an independent American army into the alliance so now Arnold, the Commanding General of the American

Army Air Forces, determined to send an independently commanded American force into the combined bomber offensive.

The Americans in their Fortresses and Liberators were not going to follow the British into the night area bombing offensive, for they were determined to mount a daylight attack which would enable them to launch precision attacks against key points in the German war economy. The British who had, of course, had exactly the same idea before and at the outset of the war, explained that such a plan was impracticable and that it would be better to convert the American aircraft and crews to night work.

The Americans were unmoved. Their bombers could reach much greater altitudes than the British and they carried heavier guns. By the use of highly disciplined formation flying tactics they would be able to provide such concentrated fire-power that their formations would be able to fight their way to and fro between base and target—and, so far as their ranges permitted, they would have the benefit of escorting fighters, Spitfires from RAF Fighter Command and in time their own machines, for the 8th Air Force was to include both bombers and fighters under the command of General Ira Eaker.

Heavier and heavier US losses

On August 17, 1942, the Americans opened their offensive with an attack on the marshalling yards at Rouen. It was carried out by 12 aircraft. All returned safely, and for the rest of the year the Americans continued the working up of their force by attacks on targets in France, picking usually on submarine bases. This was a beginning—but as Churchill hinted to Roosevelt at the time not all that impressive a beginning, especially by comparison with the widespread and increasingly heavy attacks being carried out in many parts of Germany, including three 'thousand' raids by the night bombers of Bomber Command.

Nor did this comparison seem to improve in 1943 when the American bombers, from the beginning of the year, began operations against German targets. While Bomber Command cut a swathe of devastation through the Ruhr valley, Hamburg (the scene of a singular calamity for the Germans), and towards Berlin, the 8th Air Force tried to begin its selective attack upon key industries. The heavy losses which it soon began to suffer from the German day fighter force led it to concentrate its effort more and more upon aircraft factories in the hope that this would reduce the effectiveness of the German air defences. The trouble was that aircraft factories were particularly difficult targets in inaccessible and therefore dangerous places such as, for example, Regensburg and Wiener Neustadt.

The American losses became heavier and heavier and neither the scale nor the effectiveness of the German air defences declined. On the contrary, they steadily increased. Moreover, the German night fighter force, developing upon the basis of primitive beginnings, was now becoming a formidable menace to the night bombers of Bomber Command. The very means which the latter used to reduce the disadvantage of having to navigate and bomb in the dark—such things as radar transmissions, flares, and route and target markers—disclosed the position of the force to the German night fighters, now skilfully directed and scientifically equipped.

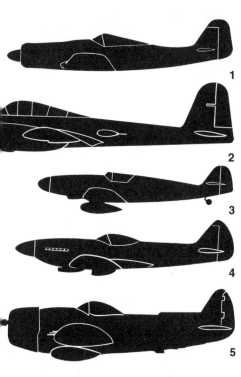

Escorts and defenders

Two of the fighter aircraft that escorted the bombers—and three that flew against them

(1) The FW 109D ground attack fighter was also used to great effect for bomber interception
(2) The ME 410, a high-altitude fighter
(3) The ME 109G was used to 'bomb' Allied formations with a 500-lb bomb slung under the fuselage
(4) The Spitfire, the RAF's only escort, was hampered by very short range
(5) The Thunderbolt, 8th Air Force's high-altitude, long-range escort fighter, was the first airscrew fighter to fly faster than 500 mph

Thus not only the obstacle of the darkness but also its cover was being removed from the night bombers, while the American day bombers, despite their formation tactics, their gunnery, and their high altitude, were, once they had crossed the Rhine, beyond the range of fighter support and all on their own. As the British had feared they were almost sitting ducks for the high-performance German interceptors—the Me-109 and the FW-190—as well as such heavier machines as the Me-110 and the Ju-88.

If Bomber Command could not quickly induce a German collapse under the impact of its area offensive, or if the Americans could not strangle the German fighter force in production, then the combined bomber offensive was heading straight for a crisis of the first magnitude.

Berlin: climax of the offensive

Some specialised crews in Bomber Command who had gained exceptional experience, who had enjoyed statistically unlikely good luck, and who were nourished by extraordinary resources of courage and a specially developed Barnes Wallis bomb, had evolved a technique of night precision attack which had enabled them to breach the Möhne and Eder Dams in May 1943. But although this technique later produced a method of night precision marking which revolutionised the possibilities of night bombing, nothing of this kind was possible for the main force of Bomber Command in 1943 or for much of 1944. The general area offensive remained the only recourse, and in November 1943 Bomber Command opened its greatest and most ambitious assault, the Battle of Berlin, which raged throughout the winter and until March 1944. It was to be the climax of the offensive. It was intended to complete the wreck of Germany from end to end.

A month earlier, in October 1943, the Americans had determined to attempt a rapier blow against Schweinfurt, the centre of German ball-bearing production, whose destruction they believed would cripple the Luftwaffe, and lay the foundation of their selective attack on German industry.

These operations, those of Bomber Command in the Battle of Berlin and that of the Americans against Schweinfurt, were therefore of critical importance. If the Battle of Berlin had ended in the collapse or virtual collapse of Germany the policy of area bombing would have been wholly vindicated and the invasion of Europe would have become a formality required only to collect the surrender. If the American operation against Schweinfurt had caused a seizure of the German aircraft industry and had resulted in the collapse of the German fighter force, the American bombers would then have had the way open to the destruction of such vital industries as oil production.

On October 14, 1943, some 291 Flying Fortresses set course in formation for Schweinfurt. As they neared Aachen their fighter escorts, running out of range, turned about and went home. They were quickly replaced by wave after wave of German fighters. Single-engined aircraft came in firing 20-mm cannon and machine-guns, twin-engined fighters fired rockets, and meanwhile the single-engined aircraft landed, refuelled, rearmed, took off, and attacked again.

The Americans pressed on against hopeless odds with the utmost gallantry and even managed to inflict considerable damage upon the ball-bearing factories in Schweinfurt.

Sixty of their bombers were shot down, 17 more were heavily damaged, another 121 sustained some damage. Nor was this an isolated disaster. It was the climax of a frightful week in which, in four attempts to break through the German fighter defences, the Americans lost 148 bombers and crews shot down.

Operations on such a scale and of such a type could not be continued, for if they had been they would rapidly have led to the strangulation in infancy of the American strategic bombing forces. Whether successful or not, they had to be called off. General Arnold, who had his ear close to public opinion in his country, let it be thought that the attack on Schweinfurt had been so successful that it *need* not be repeated. The harsh truth was that it *could* not be repeated.

Nor had it been very successful. No great harm was done to any vital element in the German war effort. Repairs were quickly made, stocks were drawn upon, and where neither expedient answered the German requirement, substitutes were used. The American plan to strike selectively at German industry by daylight heavy bombing precision attacks had apparently been decisively defeated by the German fighter force. The Battle of Britain seemed to have been refought on a greater scale with the same outcome: the victory of the defence over the offence.

'Strong medicine'

Appearances in war, when so much is on the other side of the hill, are often, as in this case they were, deceptive. From March 1943 great developments in the application of area bombing had taken place. New strengths had come to Bomber Command. Lancasters, the best of the heavy bombers, and Mosquitoes, the best of the light ones, had come more and more into service. The scope of radar had also been enlarged and techniques greatly improved. The Battles of the Ruhr and of Hamburg had demonstrated a new degree of air warfare. For the first time Essen, the home of Krupps, and, on account of industrial haze and especially heavy defences, an exceptionally difficult target, was severely damaged. In Hamburg nearly 50,000 people were killed in a series of attacks to which the Americans contributed but in which the British were predominant.

Surely this medicine would prove too strong. Surely the destruction of Berlin, and the other towns which would go with it, would be the *coup de grâce* for Germany. Even the German Economics Minister Speer thought so at the time. Six more attacks on the Hamburg scale would, he feared, finish the war. Later he realised his fear was exaggerated, but he did fear it at the time.

Success in the Battle of Hamburg had turned not only upon the great weight of the attack delivered but upon the unusually high degree of accuracy achieved and the very short space of time into which the operations were compressed. Apart from some harassing and the light American daylight attacks, Bomber Command completed the Battle in four major operations, each mounted by over 700 bombers, on the nights of July 24, 27, 29 and August 2, 1943. Some 3,095 sorties were flown and nearly 9,000 tons of bombs dropped. In all but the last attack, when the weather was bad, highly concentrated patterns of incendiary bombs, of which about 4,500 tons were dropped, were achieved, with the result that the fires in Hamburg got out of control and built up to such an ▷

New Allied Weapons in the Air War

British doctrine had maintained that the heavy bomber would always be the most important factor in air power— 'The bomber will always get through'. But the unexpected effectiveness of fighter resistance and AA fire dispelled this illusion, and early attempts by the RAF at daylight raids incurred wholly unacceptable casualties. It became obvious that bombers without fighter protection could operate only at night, and also that the RAF's heavy bomber, the Lancaster, was inadequately armed, particular its underside. The US 8th Air Force, with its better armed Flying Fortresses and Liberators, in its turn adopted a policy of unescorted bombing. Though American bombers flew in 'impregnable' formations, they too, like the RAF, suffered heavily and soon realised the vital necessity of an escort fighter. Because of its superior range, the American Mustang, illustrated below, was adopted to fill the rôle

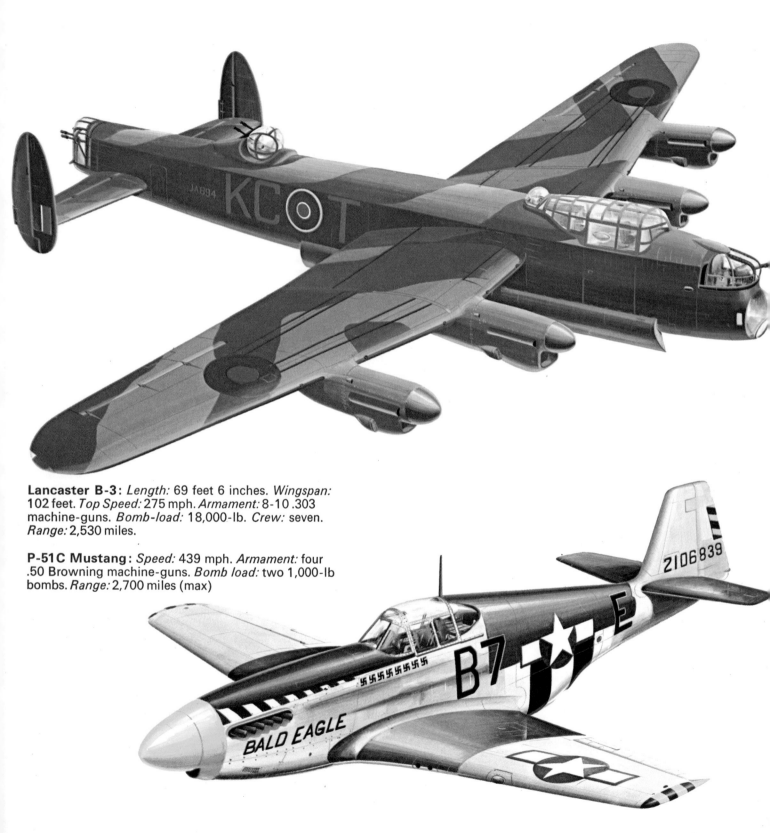

Lancaster B-3: *Length:* 69 feet 6 inches. *Wingspan:* 102 feet. *Top Speed:* 275 mph. *Armament:* 8-10 .303 machine-guns. *Bomb-load:* 18,000-lb. *Crew:* seven. *Range:* 2,530 miles.

P-51C Mustang: *Speed:* 439 mph. *Armament:* four .50 Browning machine-guns. *Bomb load:* two 1,000-lb bombs. *Range:* 2,700 miles (max)

Gen H. H. Arnold, Chief of the US Army Air Force: he urged a sole commander for the joint bombing commands

Air Chief Marshal Sir C. F. A. Portal, Chief of the Air Staff: he favoured selective targets but was ultimately unable to change the area bombing school of thought

Wing Commander Guy Gibson VC: a pilot with Bomber Command from the first days through to the '1,000-bomber' raids, he led the famous 'Dam Buster' raid

Lieutenant-Colonel Lent had a total score of 110 Allied aircraft, only 8 of them by daylight

Major Prince Sayn-Wittgenstein, credited with a score of 83 Allied aircraft, was shot down on January 21, 1944

Colonel Werner Streib was credited with 66 kills over Germany, a remarkable total for a night-fighter pilot

Boeing B-17G Flying Fortress: *Length:* 74 feet. *Wingspan:* 103 feet. *Top speed:* 287 mph. *Cruising speed:* 182 mph. *Armament:* thirteen .5-inch Browning machine-guns. *Bomb load:* 8,000 lb in various combinations. *Crew:* ten. *Range:* 2,100 miles with 5,000-lb bomb load.

The bomber crews—and where they sat
(1) The Lancaster's crew of seven consisted of (from left to right), bomb aimer (who also operated the forward gun turret), flight engineer, pilot, wireless operator, navigator, mid-upper gunner, and rear gunner. (2) The Flying Fortress, more heavily armed, carried a crew of ten: (left to right) bomb aimer, navigator (with two 'window' guns to operate), pilot and co-pilot, flight engineer (also responsible for the top turret guns), wireless operator, belly gunner, two waist gunners, and tail gunner

Liam Butler

extent that firestorms were set up. The result was an exceptionally severe scale of devastation.

Berlin was, however, an altogether more formidable target than Hamburg. It was much farther from England, which meant that the petrol/bombload ratio had to be less favourable, and also that there was a greater problem of navigation and risk of destruction en route. Unlike Hamburg, Berlin gave a very confusing radar response since it was a huge built-up area without the clarifying factor of the contrast given by sea and land. It was also densely packed with anti-aircraft guns and searchlights. Finally, Bomber Command's device for confusing the German radar which guided night fighters and guns, the so-called 'Window', was now familiar to the Germans and therefore less confusing than when it was first used on the opening night of the Battle of Hamburg.

There was never the possibility that the attack could be exclusively concentrated against Berlin. The weather often made operations in one area impossible but left them possible in another; moreover, operations concentrated in one area for too long would enable the German defences to concentrate there too. The concentration of 3,000 sorties against Hamburg in summer time within a week, and with the special advantage conferred by the Window surprise, was one thing; a corresponding concentration against Berlin in the winter was quite another. In fact, the Battle of Berlin can only be understood if it is taken to include not only the 16 major attacks on Berlin itself, but also the 19 major attacks on other German towns which were carried out within the same period between the middle of November 1943 and the end of March 1944.

The main attacks on Berlin involved 9,111 bomber sorties. The other main attacks involved 11,113 sorties. Thus, the Battle of Berlin amounted to 20,224 sorties of which 19,914 were flown by four-engined bombers including 14,652 by Lancasters.

Great damage was wrought in Berlin and in the other towns attacked, but nowhere did it approach the extent of the catastrophe which had been inflicted on Hamburg and at no time did it threaten a fatal undermining of the German capacity to continue the war. Indeed, as events were to show, the Germans continued to fight on an increasing scale for more than a year after the end of the Battle of Berlin, and they then succumbed only to much more grievous blows than they suffered in that battle.

RAF losses become intolerable

Bomber Command, on the other hand, had suffered a severe reverse. Of the 20,224 sorties flown in the Battle of Berlin, 1,047 aircraft failed to return. Another 1,682 returned with degrees of damage varying from minor to complete wreckage. The gravity of these losses and the strain which they imposed upon Bomber Command is made apparent by the realisation that the average daily availability of aircraft with crews in the Bomber Command squadrons during November and December 1943 and January, February, and March 1944 was only 890. Thus in an engagement lasting four and a half months Bomber Command lost substantially more aircraft and crews than it had available for action at any one given moment in the battle. Moreover the longer the battle lasted the worse the casualties tended to become. Indeed, in the final major action on

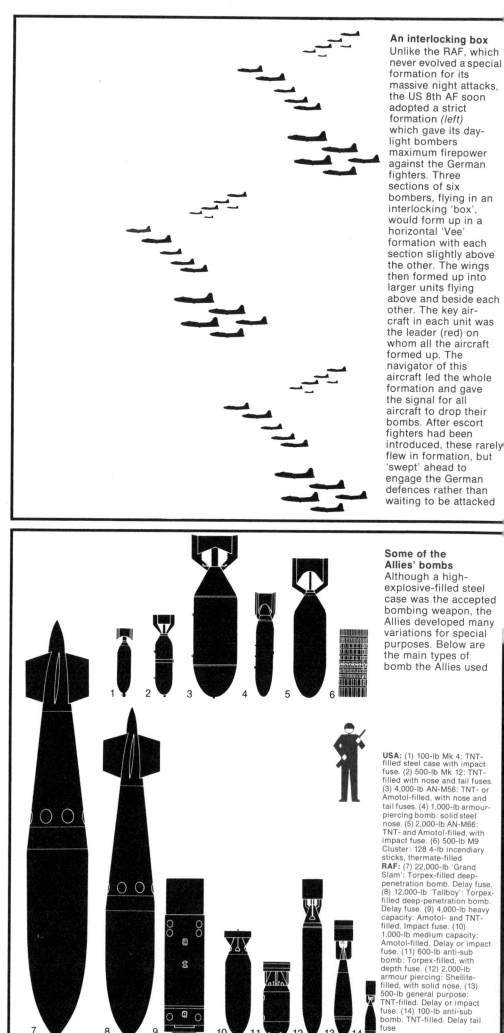

An interlocking box
Unlike the RAF, which never evolved a special formation for its massive night attacks, the US 8th AF soon adopted a strict formation (left) which gave its daylight bombers maximum firepower against the German fighters. Three sections of six bombers, flying in an interlocking 'box', would form up in a horizontal 'Vee' formation with each section slightly above the other. The wings then formed up into larger units flying above and beside each other. The key aircraft in each unit was the leader (red) on whom all the aircraft formed up. The navigator of this aircraft led the whole formation and gave the signal for all aircraft to drop their bombs. After escort fighters had been introduced, these rarely flew in formation, but 'swept' ahead to engage the German defences rather than waiting to be attacked

Some of the Allies' bombs
Although a high-explosive-filled steel case was the accepted bombing weapon, the Allies developed many variations for special purposes. Below are the main types of bomb the Allies used

USA: (1) 100-lb Mk 4: TNT-filled steel case with impact fuse. (2) 500-lb Mk 12: TNT-filled with nose and tail fuses. (3) 4,000-lb AN-M56: TNT- or Amotol-filled, with nose and tail fuses. (4) 1,000-lb armour-piercing bomb: solid steel nose. (5) 2,000-lb AN-M66: TNT- and Amotol-filled, with impact fuse. (6) 500-lb M9 Cluster: 128 4-lb incendiary sticks, thermate-filled
RAF: (7) 22,000-lb 'Grand Slam': Torpex-filled deep-penetration bomb. Delay fuse. (8) 12,000-lb 'Tallboy': Torpex-filled deep-penetration bomb. Delay fuse. (9) 4,000-lb heavy capacity: Amotol- and TNT-filled. Impact fuse. (10) 1,000-lb medium capacity: Amotol-filled. Delay or impact fuse. (11) 600-lb anti-sub bomb: Torpex-filled, with depth fuse. (12) 2,000-lb armour piercing: Shellite-filled, with solid nose. (13) 500-lb general purpose: TNT-filled. Delay or impact fuse. (14) 100-lb anti-sub bomb. TNT-filled. Delay tail fuse

he night of March 30, 1944, some 795 ombers were dispatched to Nuremberg. Ninety-four of them failed to return and another 71 returned damaged, including 12 totally destroyed at or near their bases.

Such losses could not of course have been sustained for much longer. Bomber Command would soon have consisted almost exclusively of new and inexperienced crews. Those who argue that this great campaign, the Battle of the Ruhr, the Battle of Hamburg, and the Battle of Berlin, would have proved decisive if there had been less diversion from it and if it had been continued in the spring of 1944, reckon without the fact that at the end of March 1944 Bomber Command, like the Americans in October 1943, had reached the point at which the casualty rate could no longer be sustained. Thus, as Schweinfurt had seemed to mark the failure of the American daylight precision bombing offensive, so the Battle of Berlin, culminating in the Nuremberg operation, seemed to do the same for the British night area bombing offensive.

A plan laid before these sombre events had disclosed themselves, however, now led Bomber Command to shift the centre of its attack from Berlin and the great German towns, to the railway system of northern France. This was part of the direct preparation for the invasion of Europe by the Anglo-American armies, which was to follow in the summer. Though the casualties in these attacks on French installations presently began to result in severe losses as the Germans redeployed their fighter defences, they did give Bomber Command a breathing space. They also produced most impressive results, which had very important military effects when General Eisenhower's invading armies, working on exterior lines of communication, engaged the Germans working on destroyed interior lines of communication. This, in turn, had another important result. It re-emphasised the possibilities which had long been considered of transport bombing as a main air strategy.

These possibilities were especially impressed upon the mind of the Deputy Supreme Commander, Sir Arthur Tedder. It was he who had adopted the plan for railway bombing in France and who presently foresaw that an extended application of the same principle to Germany herself might be the quickest and most effective way of assisting the advance of the Allied armies while at the same time bringing about the destruction of the German war economy.

The 'Oil Plan'
Meanwhile, however, the possibilities of another air strategy were also being heavily underlined. This was the attack upon German synthetic oil production. Throughout the war and before it, Britain and the United States knew that oil was among the weakest links in the German war machine. Its limited availability made Germany critically dependent upon a relatively small number of rather delicate synthetic oil plants and the Rumanian supplies. Clearly if their production could be drastically reduced and stocks diminished the effect would be reflected in a seizure of mechanised armed forces and much of war industry as well. To General Carl Spaatz, who on New Year's Day 1944 assumed the overall command of the 8th Air Force in England and the 15th in Italy (henceforth known jointly as the United States Strategic Air Forces in Europe), oil was the target *par excellence*. He foresaw

that the main target must be one which the Luftwaffe would be compelled to defend against all odds and one whose destruction would immediately and directly lead to the downfall of the Luftwaffe. For General Spaatz, the destruction of the German air force in being was a preoccupation.

To Sir Arthur Harris, the now famous Commander-in-Chief of Bomber Command, most arguments about so-called key targets were unconvincing. Nor was his scepticism without reason. Near the coat tails of the Air Staff and all the other staffs were large bodies of apparent experts. Much of the advice they gave was inappropriate or too clever by half. Harris believed that what would tell in the end was the destruction of the great towns of Germany themselves.

These beliefs, that of Tedder that the way ahead lay in transport bombing as the common factor between the military requirements of the armies and the strategic potentialities of the air forces, that of Spaatz in the attack on oil as the means of bringing down the Luftwaffe and Germany in turn, and that of Harris that general area attack would capitalise on the past efforts of Bomber Command and crown its future, were highly influential. Tedder, though not Churchill's favourite air commander, had the prestige of success won as the air commander in the Middle East and now enjoyed the full confidence of the Supreme Commander, General Eisenhower. Spaatz, commanding the greatest volume of air power yet seen in history and backed to the last ditch by Arnold from Washington, was in a position to make his opinions count. Harris, redoubtable, resolute, and convinced, had already demonstrated his status as one of the greatest leaders of men in the Second World War. Bomber Command without Harris was virtually inconceivable.

Moreover, as the last year of the war began, these different and even conflicting views assumed a real strategic importance. This was because in the American pause after Schweinfurt and the British one after Nuremberg, new factors arose or were injected into the situation which immensely, almost unrecognisably, increased the effectiveness of strategic bombing. Thus the options were increased and the importance of choosing the right ones enhanced.

A new Allied fighter
Among many, there were two principal factors bringing about this change. The first arose from the introduction of a highly effective long-range fighter, the P-51 Mustang, an American airframe now fitted with a Rolls-Royce Merlin engine. Between December 1943 and March 1944 this aircraft was worked up in the 8th Air Force until by the end of that period it could engage anything German as far afield from its British bases as Berlin. Now there was almost nowhere in Germany where, at least in daylight, any German pilot could enjoy any real security. Wherever he was, whether training or operating, he was liable to encounter increasing numbers of more and more aggressive Mustang pilots.

The result was that in a short time the daylight air over Germany was American dominated. Not only did this have a generally disruptive effect upon the Luftwaffe but it had a particularly favourable one upon the daylight bombers which, up to Schweinfurt, had taken such a hammering. Their ambitions became greater; their casualties became lighter; their attacks became more

accurate. These favourable tendencies set in in February 1944 and developed steadily thereafter, and in March 1944, operating on an ambitious scale, the percentage loss rate of the Americans fell to a third of what it had been in October 1943.

The second great factor was the advance of the Allied armies from the Normandy beach-head across France and eventually towards the Rhine. In August 1944 the armies over-ran the front line of the German fighter defence and their radar early warning posts, so that Bomber Command, already enjoying the symptoms of air superiority in daylight, now had the way at night opened as well. In the course of August 1944 the German air defences more or less folded up and an effective command of the air passed to the Americans and the British. The weather was still an obstacle, however, and anti-aircraft guns remained in action. Occasionally the remnant of the German fighter force concentrated to gain a temporary and local superiority. But the conditions of bombing were now unrecognisable by comparison with what they had been throughout the war up to then. In September 1944 Bomber Command flew more than three times as many sorties against major German targets as it had done in June 1944, but it lost only about two-thirds as many aircraft.

And so it seemed in September that the strategic air forces were poised for a final knock-out blow against Germany. They had already made substantial progress with the destruction of her oil production and her transport system, and the general area offensive against her towns had been resumed on a major scale. The military situation too looked good, for the Anglo-American armies were at the Rhine and the Russians also were on the way. There was hope that the war would be over by Christmas.

One reason for the disappointment of this hope was the failure of the Arnhem operation, which might have got the military advance going again. Another was the continuing failure of the strategic air forces to concentrate their immense potential effectively enough to produce immediately decisive effects. The competing claims of oil, transport, and general industrial dislocation, though theoretically given their order of priorities in the bombing directives, could not, in practice, be adequately adjusted.

Knowing how well the oil offensive was going and seeing from Intelligence appreciations (which in this case were remarkably accurate) how critical the German oil position was becoming, the Chief of the Air Staff, Sir Charles Portal, weighed in on the side of the oil advocates. He pressed Harris strongly to increase his effort against oil targets, even if it did mean a reduction in the area offensive against towns. Though Bomber Command, which carried much heavier bombs than the Americans, did play a major role in the oil offensive, it was, so far as Harris was concerned, rather a reluctant one. The eventual almost complete oil famine in Germany might have come earlier if Portal had been more insistent. But if he had been, he would probably have had to find a replacement for Harris. This, not surprisingly in the circumstances, he was unwilling to do. The resulting spread of bombing between oil, cities, and transport (as well as some other target systems) produced in the end perhaps a more certain and a more comprehensive collapse in Germany than any other method could have done. But it may all the same have delayed the moment ▷

The Key Raids against Germany

[Statistics compiled by the IWM.]

1940, May 15/16: RAF Raid on the Ruhr
Night precision raid on oil plants and marshalling yards. Of 99 planes involved, 1 lost. Amount of damage unknown but probably negligible. This raid opened strategic air offensive against Germany. (RAF had previously confined itself to raids on coastal targets and military communications, and to dropping leaflets.)

1940, December 16/17: RAF Raid on Mannheim
Night area raid on city centre. Of 134 planes involved, 3 lost. Only scattered damage inflicted: many bombs fell outside target area. First RAF 'area' raid. Lacking means to carry out effective precision attacks, Bomber Command bombed main industrial cities. Object was to disrupt German war production and break civilian morale.

1942, March 28/29: RAF Raid on Lübeck
Night area raid on town centre. Of 234 planes involved, 12 lost. Some 1,500 houses destroyed, much damage to factories. But production nearly normal one week later. First large-scale incendiary raid.

1942, April 17: RAF Raid on Augsburg
Daylight precision raid on MAN diesel engine factory. Of 12 Lancasters involved, 7 destroyed, 5 damaged (no fighter cover). Main assembly shop and other buildings damaged but production hardly affected. Raid showed that it was impractical for heavy bombers to make precision attacks in daylight, and reinforced RAF's faith in the night offensive.

1942, May 30/31: RAF Raid on Cologne
Night area raid on city centre. Of 1,046 planes involved, 40 destroyed, 116 damaged. Nearly half of city devastated, 474 people killed, over 40,000 homeless. But Cologne made a surprisingly rapid recovery. First of the 'Thousand Bomber' raids.

1942, August 17: 8th AF Raid on Rouen
Daylight precision raid on Sotteville marshalling yards. Of 12 B-17s involved, no losses. Some damage to rolling stock and rails but only temporary. US 8th AF's first attack. US firmly committed to daylight precision raids.

1943, March 5/6: RAF Raid on Essen
Night area raid on Krupp works. Of 442 planes involved, 14 destroyed, 38 damaged. Heavy damage to Krupps, 160 acres of Essen devastated. But British estimates exaggerated effect of raid on production. First use of 'Oboe' radar device helped to overcome industrial haze in the Ruhr area.

1943, May 16/17: RAF Dams Raid
Night precision raid on Möhne, Eder, and Sorpe dams. Of 19 Lancasters involved, 8 destroyed, 6 damaged. Möhne and Eder dams breached; Sorpe dam only damaged. Some 1,000 people drowned and severe flooding, but raid had no appreciable effect on German war economy. Landmark raid in development of precision bombing techniques.

This map shows the main Allied bombing targets in Europe between 1942 and 1945. Unless otherwise specified, the cities listed below were general industrial targets.

- Allied airbase
- Industrial target
- Rail target
- Oil target
- Operation Thunderclap

Allied fighter ranges

0   50   100   150 miles

Key Allied Airbases
A. Sunninghill Park (HQ US 9th Air Force)
B. High Wycombe (HQ RAF Bomber Command/HQ US 8th Air Force)
C. Bushy Park (HQ US Strategic Air Force)

Key Bombing Targets
1. Bordeaux (U-boats)
2. La Pallice (U-boats)
3. Lorient (U-boats)
4. St Nazaire (U-boats)
5. Nantes (aircraft)
6. Brest (U-boats)
7. Le Mans (aircraft)
8. Paris
9. Rouen
10. Martinvast (V-bombs)
11. Sottevast (V-bombs)
12. Siracourt (V-bombs)
13. Lottinghem (V-bombs)
14. Mimovecques (V-bombs)
15. Watten (V-bombs)
16. Wizernes (V-bombs)
17. Lille
18. Brussels (aircraft)
19. Rotterdam
20. Amsterdam (aircraft)
21. La Rochelle
22. Cherbourg
23. Le Havre
24. Boulogne
25. Dunkirk
26. Metz
27. Emden (U-boats)
28. Wilhelmshaven (U-boats)
29. Vegesack (U-boats)
30. Bremen (aircraft)
31. Hamburg
32. Flensburg (U-boats)
33. Kiel (U-boats)
34. Lübeck
35. Hannover
36. Brunswick
37. Magdeburg
38. Oschersleben (aircraft)
39. Dessau (aircraft)
40. Essen
41. Dortmund
42. Duisburg
43. Düsseldorf
44. Cologne
45. Bonn
46. Möhne Dam
47. Wuppertal
48. Eder Dam
49. Sorpe Dam
50. Kassel (aircraft)
51. Leipzig (aircraft)
52. Dresden
53. Liegnitz
54. Berlin
55. Rostock
56. Peenemünde (V-bombs)
57. Stettin
58. Danzig (U-boats)
59. Erfurt
60. Gotha (aircraft)
61. Schweinfurt (ball-bearings)
62. Fürth
63. Nuremberg
64. Regensburg (aircraft)
65. Augsburg (aircraft)
66. Munich
67. Ulm
68. Stuttgart
69. Ludwigshafen
70. Saarbrücken
71. Bochum
72. Karlsruhe
73. Friedrichshafen
74. Chemnitz
75. Prague
76. Wiener Neustadt (aircraft)
77. Frankfurt
78. Hanau
79. Aschaffenburg
80. Koblenz
81. Oberlahnstein
82. Giessen
83. Siegen
84. Schwerte
85. Soest
86. Hamm
87. Löhne
88. Osnabrück
89. Rheine
90. Bielefeld
91. Altenbecken Neuenbecken
92. Seelze
93. Lehrte
94. Hameln
95. Paderborn
96. Bebra
97. Stendal
98. Halle
99. Gera
100. Breslau
101. Oppeln
102. Heydebreck
103. Bohumin
104. Minden
105. Mulhouse
106. Freiburg
107. Offenburg
108. Rastatt
109. Karlsruhe
110. Heilbronn
111. Treuchtlingen
112. Pasing
113. Munich
114. Rosenheim
115. Salzburg
116. Strasshof
117. Würzburg
118. Mannheim
119. Darmstadt
120. Mainz
121. Bingen
122. Vienna
123. Münster
124. Wesseling
125. Reisholz
126. Dülmen
127. Gelsenkirchen
128. Salzbergen
129. Nienburg
130. Farge
131. Heide
132. Hitzacker
133. Dollbergen
134. Derben
135. Pölitz
136. Salzgitter
137. Lützkendorf
138. Leuna
139. Ruhland
140. Böhlen
141. Rositz
142. Mölbis
143. Zeitz
144. Brüx
145. Deschowitz
146. Blechhammer
147. Auschwitz
148. Neuburg
149. Freiham
150. Linz
151. Moosbierbaum
152. Korneuburg
153. Floridsdorf
154. Schwechat
155. Lobau
156. Budapest

Aug/Dec 1942
Dec 1942/Jul 1943

1943, July 24/25: RAF Raid on Hamburg
Night area raid on city centre. Of 791 planes involved, 12 destroyed, 31 damaged. Over 2,200 tons of bombs dropped. Widespread damage to residential areas. Fires still burning 24 hours after raid. Major success for Bomber Command. German radar confused by 'Window'—strips of tinfoil used for first time. This raid followed by mass attacks on nights of July 27, 29, August 2. Hamburg left in ruins. Over 42,000 people thought to have been killed.

1943, October 14: 8th AF Raid on Schweinfurt
Daylight precision raid on ball-bearing works. Of 291 planes involved, 60 destroyed, 138 damaged. Most damaging of the 16 Schweinfurt raids but caused only temporary setback in production. Germans reorganised ball-bearing industry before next attack 4 months later. Bombers escorted only part of way to target. Crippling losses caused by German fighters exploded theory of self-defending bomber formation, forced US to curtail daylight bombing offensive.

1943, November 18/19: RAF Raid on Berlin
Night area raid on city centre. Of 444 planes involved, 9 lost. Some 1,500 tons of bombs dropped. Damage unknown but probably considerable. First of 16 mass raids on Berlin, involving over 9,000 planes in all. These raids less effective and more costly than ones on Hamburg and the Ruhr, owing to distances, strength of defences, weather.

1944, March 8: 8th AF Raid on Berlin
Daylight precision raid on Erkner ball-bearing works. Of 590 planes involved, 37 lost. Heavy damage to works (75 direct hits). Production at standstill for some time. Third US raid on Berlin. Bombers escorted by large force of P-51s. Beginning of US daylight air command.

1944, March 30/31: RAF Raid on Nuremberg
Night area raid on city centre. Of 795 planes involved, 95 destroyed, 71 damaged. Some 2,500 tons of bombs dropped but raid too dispersed to cause serious damage. Heaviest defeat suffered by Bomber Command in war. Nuremberg was to RAF night raids what Schweinfurt was to US day raids. Both showed that without command of the air long-range bombing could not be kept up indefinitely. After Nuremberg RAF broke off mass raids on distant targets.

1944, September 23/24: RAF Canal Raid
Night precision raid on Dortmund-Ems Canal, inland waterway linking Ruhr with other industrial areas. Of 141 planes involved, 14 lost. 11 'Tallboy' bombs (12,000 lb each) dropped. Canal breached, 6-mile section drained.

1945, February 13/14: RAF Raid on Dresden
Night area raid on city centre. Of 805 planes involved, 8 lost. Immense damage to old town and inner suburbs: 1,600 acres devastated. Incendiaries kindled worst firestorm of war. Estimates of killed range from 35,000 to 135,000 (latter figure almost certainly too high). Most destructive—and most controversial—European raid of war. Dresden, whose strategic importance is questionable, was crowded with refugees and virtually undefended. Bombed again next morning by 400 planes of US 8th AF.

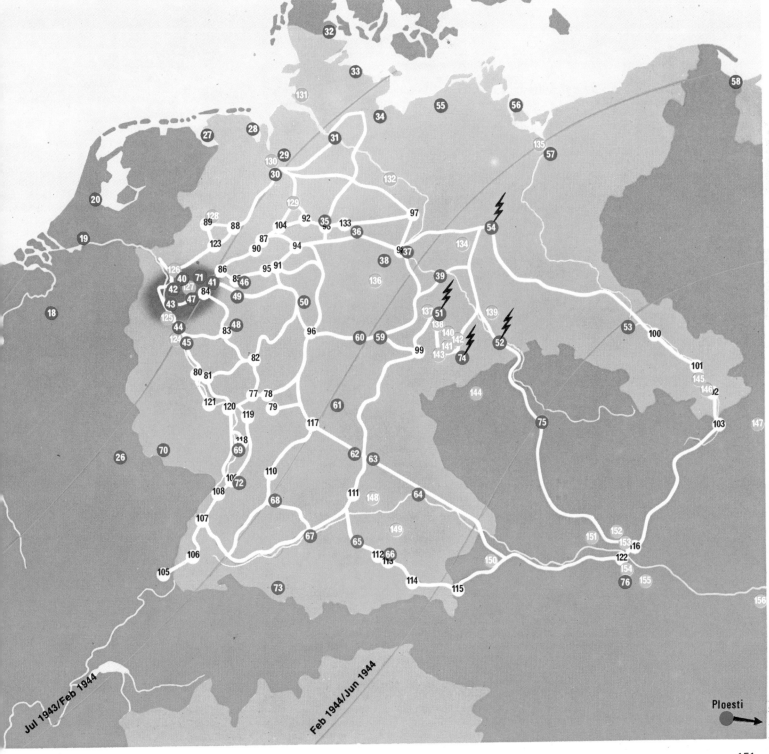

at which collapse occurred by comparison with what might have happened if there had been a greater concentration against oil, especially in the last four months of 1944. This, however, is a speculative conclusion of which the probable validity is easier to assess now than it was at the time.

The war drags on

Thus the Anglo-American offensive of all arms against Germany lost its momentum in the autumn of 1944 and the war, after all, was to drag on into 1945. Indeed, for the Western camp of the Grand Alliance, 1945 opened in a distinctly depressing atmosphere. Discussion in the councils of strategic bombing left all—Portal, Tedder, Spaatz, and Harris —with a feeling of frustration. Nor was it only the air force high command which suffered this frustration, for Eisenhower's plan for the final advance into Germany had received a rude check from the German counteroffensive in the Ardennes.

These delays may now seem inconsequential. The Allies had a vast preponderance of military power, the Russians were about to resume their offensive, the damage done in the Ardennes was soon repaired, and the bombers now had Germany at their mercy.

But the prospect did not appear quite in that light in January 1945. The Germans had shown an alarming ingenuity in the development of new weapons. Schnorkel breathing threatened to give their U-boats a new lease of life. In the development of high-speed flight they led the world. Jet-propelled aircraft might yet unmake the Allied command of the air. The V-weapons (and the V-2 was no less than a partly guided missile) might portend even more alarming possibilities. There could be no certainty that Germany would not produce an atomic bomb.

Moreover, the support given by the German people to Hitler was still very real. Hitler survived all attempts at assassination or deposition; his armed forces fought on with courage and determination despite the odds; the civil population endured with a stoicism which is one of the wonders of history. Even when Hitler had been disposed of, there still remained the problem of Japan, so it was hardly strange that the Allies were urgently seeking a means of accelerating their victory over Germany.

In January, with the Anglo-American armies temporarily halted, there seemed to be two main possibilities. One was that the Red Army would advance rapidly into the heart of Germany; the other was that the heavy bombers might strike a mammoth pulverising blow at a German city, or group of cities, which would amount to the last straw.

The Chiefs-of-Staff of Britain and America had had such an idea (given the codename of 'Thunderclap') in mind for some time, but they had not found any specific plan sufficiently convincing to be worth attempting, for an air strike of this character, it seemed, would in itself be insufficient to cause the collapse which was sought. But, as occurred to them in January, such a blow might, if aimed at Berlin and timed to coincide with the westward flow of refugees fleeing before the Russian advance, have at least a markedly helpful effect upon the Russian advance.

On January 25, 1945, the Deputy Chief of the Air Staff, Sir Norman Bottomley, discussed these ideas on the telephone with Sir Arthur Harris, and the next day he reported Harris's suggestion to Portal: that the main attack on Berlin should be supplemented by operations of a like nature, against Chemnitz, Leipzig, and Dresden. These cities, with Berlin, would be trying to house refugees fleeing from the Russians and were, also like Berlin, focal points in the German system of communications behind their eastern front.

Churchill demands action

On the same day as this telephone conversation, January 25, 1945, Churchill spoke to the Secretary of State for Air, Sir Archibald Sinclair, about the same possibilities. In particular, as he explained on the following day in a minute to Sinclair, he wanted to know whether Berlin and other large cities in east Germany should not now be considered especially attractive targets. In a somewhat peremptory manner he indicated that what was now required was not consideration, but action.

Portal, however, was somewhat doubtful of the wisdom of the whole idea. He did not think that Thunderclap, even on the heaviest scale, would prove decisive. He feared that the bombers might suffer heavy losses over Berlin. He firmly believed that the oil offensive should continue to have absolute priority. He also insisted that attacks on U-boat and jet aircraft factories should be kept up, but subject to all those considerations, and if the Americans would join in, he was prepared to agree that one big attack on Berlin supported by severe blitzes on Dresden, Leipzig, and Chemnitz and perhaps some other places would cause confusion in the evacuation from the east, and hamper the Germans in moving their troops from the west.

On January 27, Sinclair sent a minute to Churchill telling him that the Air Staff had now arranged to make attacks on Berlin, Dresden, Chemnitz, and Leipzig or other cities where severe bombing would destroy communications vital to the evacuation from the east and would also hamper the movement of troops from the west. He made it absolutely clear that this would be done only subject to the over-riding claims of the oil offensive and other approved target systems.

Such was the plan, its origin, and its motive; and thus, a little reluctantly, because he feared that it might detract from the oil offensive, Portal assented to it.

The plan, then, arose from the application of the Thunderclap idea to the particular situation created by the Russian advance. The actual targets selected came from the telephone conversation between Bottomley and Harris and the urgency with which the idea was pressed forward proceeded directly from the very insistent prodding administered by Churchill.

Perhaps these facts will serve to make clear the development of events up to this stage which has been so widely misunderstood in so many places. But now there is a new misunderstanding which has to be cleared up. This is the extraordinary suggestion that on January 28 Churchill tried to call off the Dresden attack but that Portal nevertheless persisted with it. In fact on January 28 Churchill only told Portal in a minute that he felt doubtful about the wisdom of so much *transport* bombing when oil was meant to be the first priority. Portal assured him that oil was still the first priority, though he put in a reminder that there would shortly be heavy attacks on certain eastern towns including Dresden.

This of course merely confirmed what had just been arranged and agreed.

General Spaatz was now consulted about the plan. Though the severe sudden damage required was thought to be especially appropriate to heavy night attacks by Bomber Command, American daylight operations were also required and, in the event, forthcoming. The plans were also touched on at the Yalta Conference, which followed immediately upon these events, and though the Russians did not specifically call for the bombing of Chemnitz or Dresden, they did ask for the paralysis of Berlin and Leipzig as centres of communication behind the German front against which they were about to speed up their advance.

The plan was now nearing execution, but it could not be initiated until the moon had waned and until the weather was right. On the night of February 13, 1945, Bomber Command set course in two waves over 800 strong for Dresden. In daylight on February 14 the American 8th Air Force followed, more than 400 strong. The Americans went again, about 200 strong, on February 15 and finally 400 strong on March 2. Meanwhile, on the night of February 14, Bomber Command made a major night attack on Chemnitz and the Americans carried out other related attacks including one on February 26 on Berlin by over 1,000 bombers.

These were the operations designed to speed up the Allied victory by causing confusion behind the German line, urged upon the Air Staff by the Prime Minister and, in their generality, asked for by the Russians. If they had not been carried out people would no doubt now be wondering why the strategic air forces had not exerted their power against these targets at this critical moment in the war. They fitted the general conception of the area bombing offensive now more than four years old, they fitted the immediate military situation, and they were executed without undue prejudice to the main priority, the oil campaign.

Most of these attacks, like so many others carried out by Bomber Command, have long

Ullstein

The crucial equation: bombs dropped against German production

The ultimate justification for the Allied bomber offensive was that it struck directly at the German war machine and could thus cripple her forces at the front. The graphs below, taken from figures published in the British Official History, show the mounting total of bombs dropped, and the output of three key German industries

◁ Part of the Krupp Works (Essen) in ruins

BOMBS DROPPED

It was not until the war ended that the Allies were able to take stock of the effect of the vast weight of bombs which they had hurled at Germany, and realise that in almost all types of production German output had risen almost as swiftly and steadily as the weight of bombs. The massive rise of bombs dropped during 1944 reflects the achievement of a continuous day-and-night offensive co-ordinating the attacks of RAF Bomber Command and the USAAF

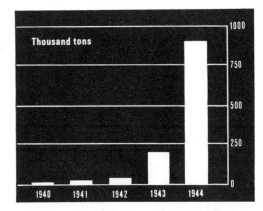

AIRCRAFT PRODUCTION

One way in which the attacking forces were to gain air supremacy over their targets was by smashing the air frame and aero engine factories of the defenders. This the Allies tried, but German countermeasures proved so successful—dispersing the large factories into small units scattered all over the country which were difficult to locate and attack—that their aircraft production rose steadily, and it was not until the Allies were able to introduce long-range escort fighters for their daylight raids that they were able to achieve a reasonable level of superiority

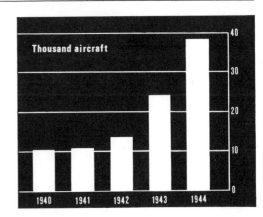

TANK PRODUCTION

During the years before D-Day while the Russians had complained that they were bearing the whole brunt of the war, the British and American strategic bombing offensive had been the great symbol of what the Western Allies were doing to strike directly at Germany. But in tanks, as in aircraft, the German production totals continued to rise—although this is not to say that they would not have risen considerably faster had the bombing not taken place

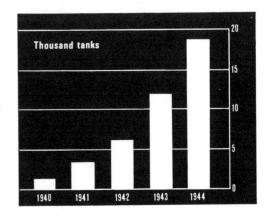

OIL PRODUCTION

The assault on German oil production was one of the fields in which the Allied bomber offensive was shown to be conspicuously successful. The Germans had long realised the threat which hung over this most vital and vulnerable part of their economy, but, except for two raids on Ploesti, it was not until October 1943 that US bombers were unleashed in concentrated attacks on the plants in the Ploesti and South German areas. At first the damage to production was slight, but during the summer of 1944 German oil output collapsed and her forces were condemned to near immobility during their most vital battles

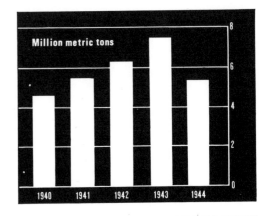

since been forgotten, but not so the Dresden one. The conditions proved to be virtually perfect and the defences nil. The success of the raid, unlike that of the following night against Chemnitz, was overwhelming. Huge but uncertain numbers of Germans were killed. In all probability the death roll was even greater than that caused in Hamburg in July to August 1943. By far the greater part of the damage was done by Bomber Command in the night attack.

Some newspaper men at the time thought it represented a change of policy and referred to it as terror bombing. This caused embarrassment in America, where bombing was thought to be a different sort of thing to what it was, and even in Britain, where at least some had deluded themselves into thinking of bombing as surgery instead of what it was: an element in nearly total war.

Perhaps it may suffice to say that Dresden was the logical climax of the strategic air offensive against Germany, which as a whole played a major part in the defeat of Nazi hegemony; that it was dramatically more successful than could reasonably have been anticipated; and that, while it seemed to be urgently necessary at the time of its execution in the middle of February, it was possible to wonder as soon afterwards as the end of March how the Germans, then visibly and rapidly crumbling, could have merited such an ultimate punishment.

NOBLE FRANKLAND was born in 1922 and educated at Sedbergh and Trinity College, Oxford, where he was a Scholar. During the war he served as a navigator in Bomber Command and was awarded the DFC. After a period as a Narrator in the Air Historical Branch of the Air Ministry and after taking a doctorate at Oxford, he was in 1951 appointed, jointly with the late Sir Charles Webster, as official historian of the *Strategic Air Offensive Against Germany*. The History was published in four volumes in 1961. Dr Frankland is the author of several other works. From 1956-1960 he was Deputy Director of Studies at the Royal Institute of International Affairs. Since then he has been Director of the Imperial War Museum.

The JU 287: The first heavy jet bomber to be flown successfully, the Germans had intended to have 200 operational by 1946. *Span:* 66 feet. *Length:* 60 feet. *Performance:* 527 mph at 16,400 feet. *Range:* 985 miles (loaded). *Max load:* 9,900 lb. *Armament:* Two tail mounted 13-mm machine guns

The Gloster Meteor 1: Britain's first jet fighter. *Span:* 43 feet. *Length:* 41 feet 3 inches. *Performance:* 385 mph top speed. *Range:* 1,346 miles. *Armament:* Four 20-mm cannon

BRAINCHILDREN OF THE AIR WAR

The last year of the war lent enormous impetus to two major aspects of aeronautics, jet powered flight and rocketry. All the major powers made advances in these fields, and though the Germans had a lead in both, their overall military situation was by that time so bad that they were unable to exploit this advantage. The Allies, more interested in producing overwhelming numbers of proved conventional aircraft, were under less pressure than the Germans to produce a completely revolutionary 'war-winning' aircraft. Nonetheless, the appearance, albeit fleeting, of German rocket and jet powered aircraft over the Western Front in 1945, forced the importance of this development on the Allies' attention. In many respects their knowledge, if not their initial enthusiasm, was in advance of the Germans'. We show here the aircraft that were the direct result of these developments, and though not all of them were participants in the wars (the Shooting Star, for example, did not see combat till Korea) all were the direct result of knowledge and techniques acquired during the war

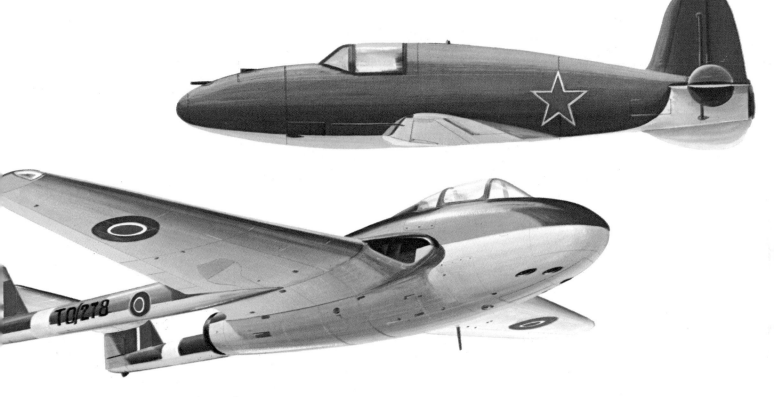

The de Havilland Vampire: Britain's second jet fighter incorporated a raised tail, and twin tail booms to cut down turbulence from the jet outflow. It was the first pure jet aircraft to operate from a carrier. *Span:* 40 feet. *Length:* 30 feet 9 inches. *Performance:* Max speed 531 mph. *Range:* 730 miles. *Armament:* Four 20-mm Hispano cannon

Top: **Berezniak-Isaev BI-1:** A liquid-fuel, rocket powered fighter aircraft developed by the Russians. The 1,100 lb bi-fuel motor proved heavy and rather erratic. *Span:* 23 feet 7½ inches. *Length:* 22 feet 11½ inches. *Performance:* 8-15 minutes powered endurance. *Armament:* Two 20-mm ShVAK cannon

The Lockheed XP-80A Shooting Star: The most successful jet fighter to come out of the war. *Span:* 39 feet. *Length:* 34 feet 6 inches. *Performance:* Top speed 558 mph. *Armament:* Six .50 calibre machine guns, and 1,000 lb of bombs (or drop tanks). *Range:* 540 miles (normal), 1,200 miles max

The first jet aircraft, Hitler's last hope

As early as 1942, the Germans had developed a thorough practical twin-jet fighter, the ME-262. In this field they years ahead of the Allies, but their higher authorities slow to realise the potentialities of the discovery, and at the end of 1943 was a production line started. Even the first jet fighter group had been formed in November 1944, Hitler refused to give jet fighters production pr it was not until 1945 that he gave the order. Of the ty shown below, the ME-262s saw the most combat, bu were too late and too few to be decisive. Nearly 1,400

Bachem BA-349B Natter. *Crew:* One. *Span:* 13 feet 1¼ inches. *Length:* 21 feet 3 inches. *Weight:* 4,800 lb. *Top speed:* 620 mph. *Armament:* 24 55-mm rockets

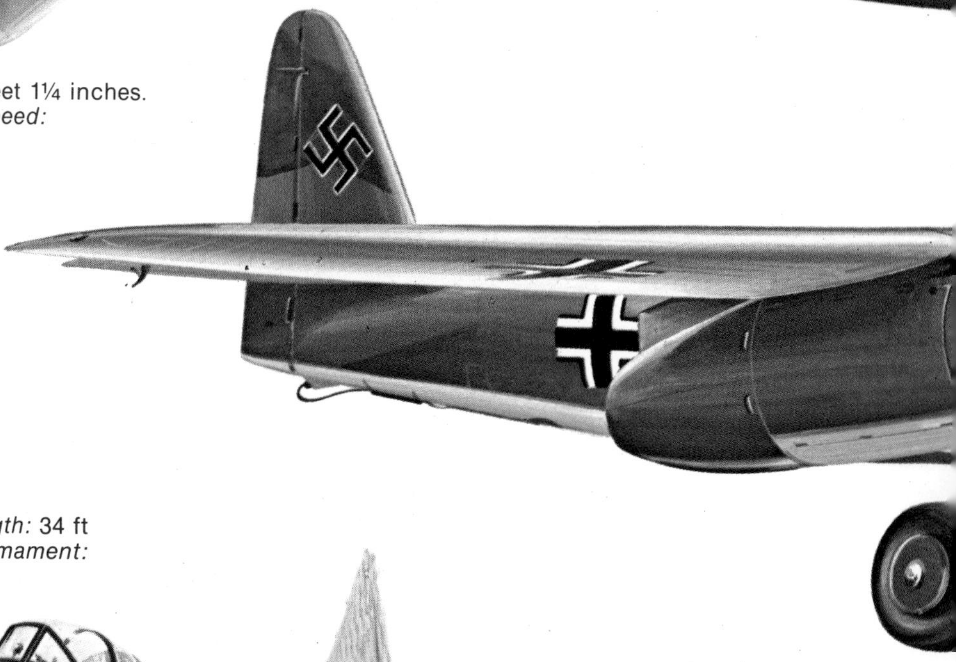

ME-262A-1a. *Crew:* One. *Span:* 40 ft 11½ in. *Length:* 34 ft 9½ in. *Weight:* 14,101 lb. *Top speed:* 538 mph. *Armament:* Four 30-mm cannon and 24 50-mm rockets

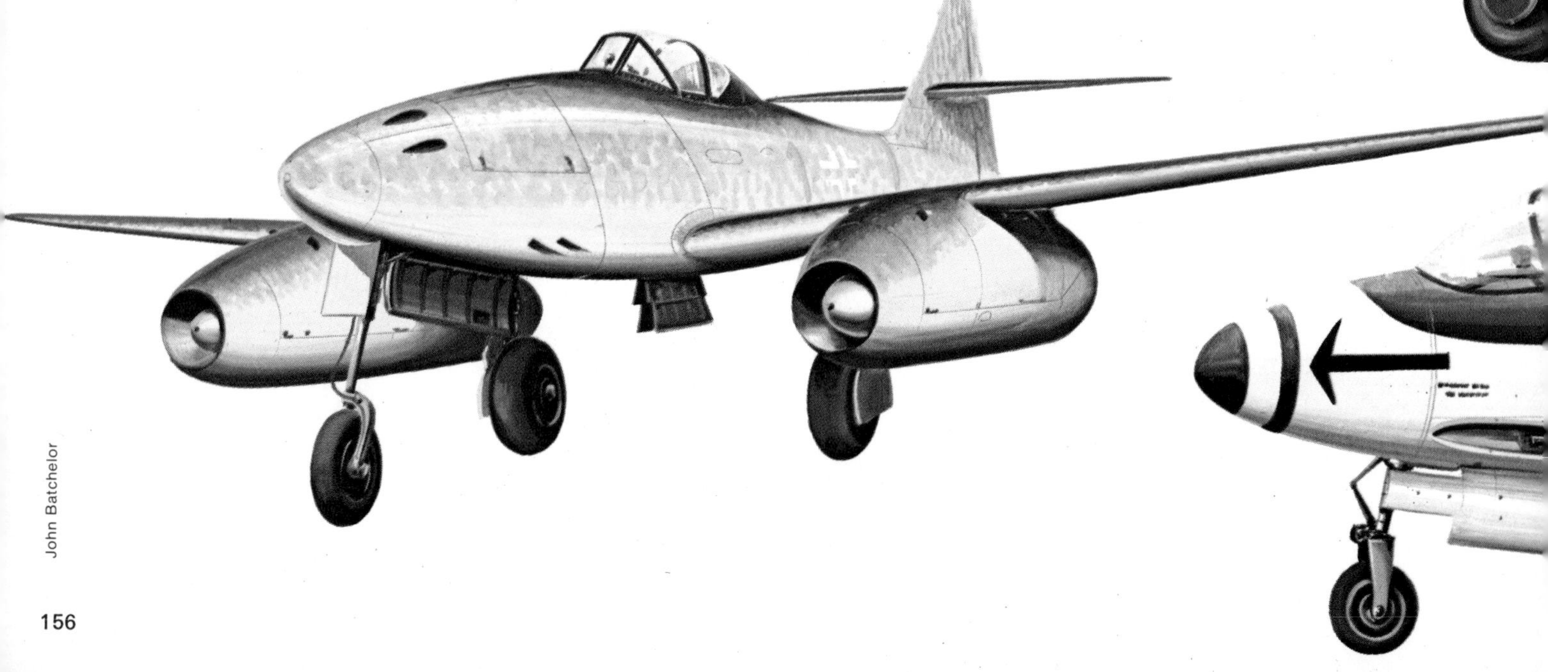

John Batchelor

...craft of this model were made, but only 200 were ever ...ed in combat. The results that these few achieved against ...ylight bombing formations, however, leave no doubt ...at, produced earlier in sufficient numbers, this aircraft ...uld have wrested command of the air from the Allies. The ...d story of too little and too late applied to all German ...t aircraft production. The Arado 234, the first jet bomber, ...as used only in small numbers, and the Natter was never ...ed operationally. The Messerschmitt 163 'Komet', a rocket-...wered fighter, had striking success against Allied bombers

ME-163. *Crew:* One. *Span:* 30 ft 7 in. *Length:* 18 ft 8 in. *Weight:* 9,500 lb. *Top speed:* 596 mph. *Armament:* Two 30-mm cannon and 24 55-mm rockets

Arado 234B. *Crew:* One. *Span:* 46 ft 3½ in. *Length:* 41 ft 5½ in. *Weight:* 18,541 lb. *Top speed:* 461 mph. *Armament:* Two 20-mm cannon

HE-162A-2. *Crew:* One. *Span:* 23 ft 7½ in. *Length:* 29 ft 8 in. *Weight:* 5,480 lb. *Top speed:* 522 mph. *Armament:* Two 20-mm cannon

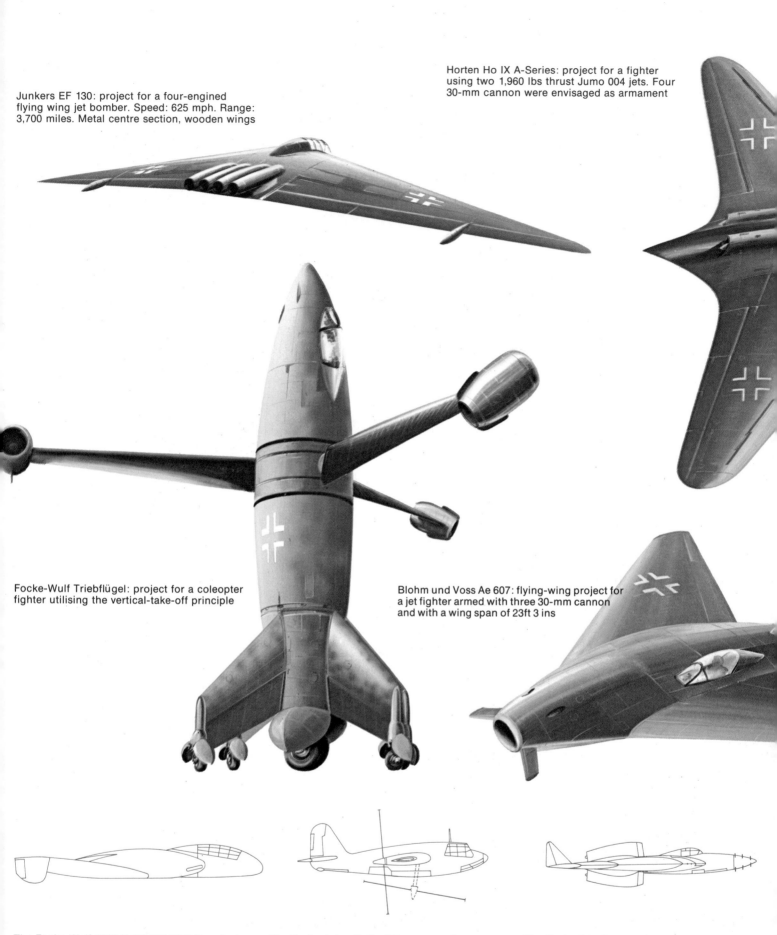

Junkers EF 130: project for a four-engined flying wing jet bomber. Speed: 625 mph. Range: 3,700 miles. Metal centre section, wooden wings

Horten Ho IX A-Series: project for a fighter using two 1,960 lbs thrust Jumo 004 jets. Four 30-mm cannon were envisaged as armament

Focke-Wulf Triebflügel: project for a coleopter fighter utilising the vertical-take-off principle

Blohm und Voss Ae 607: flying-wing project for a jet fighter armed with three 30-mm cannon and with a wing span of 23ft 3 ins

The Focke-Wulf 1000 X 1000 X 1000 B project was for a bomber capable of carrying a 1,000 kilogram bombload (2,200 lbs) at 1,000 kilometres per hour (625 mph) for 1,000 kilometres (625 miles). Span was to be 41 ft 6 ins and length 47 ft 3 ins. There were three designs to the same specification, two being conventional in layout. This version, of near-delta layout, appeared to possess better flying characteristics, but would have been hard to maintain

The Focke Achgelis Fa 269 was a project originated in 1941 for an aircraft able to take off and land vertically by means of swivelling propellers mounted in each wing. These would swivel to a vertical position to lift the aircraft off the ground, then turn to the rear to drive the aircraft along at an estimated 375 mph in level flight. Long undercarriage legs were provided to give ground clearance to the propellers when the aircraft was on the ground

The Gotha P.60C was a project for a large fighter equipped with Morgenstern radar in the nose for night fighting. The most unusual feature of this aircraft was the arrangement of the powerplants, two BMW 003 turbojets giving 1,760 lbs of thrust each, in a tandem mounting above and below the rear fuselage. This aircraft was another German attempt to produce a tailless, swept-wing design, a field in which Germany led the world

Lippisch DM 1: experimental glider to test the pure delta-wing shape. It had great influence on the development of US delta-winged aircraft

Blohm und Voss P.208: projected 500 mph fighter armed with three 30-mm cannon. It was to use swept wings and a divided tailplane carried on short booms on the outboard edge of the main wing panels. No fin or rudder was necessary because of the anhedral on the tail-plane

Daimler-Benz 'A': projected long-range bomber combination. The larger aircraft carried the smaller towards the target and released it when this was relatively close, this giving the combination great range as the bomber aircraft did not waste fuel on take-off and cruise

John Batchelor

The Messerschmitt P.1101 was designed as a jet fighter in 1944, but the structure proved to be very heavy as a result of the complicated engine attachment, so the aircraft was dropped as a fighter though Messerschmitt intended to use the prototype as a research aircraft. It was, however, destroyed by bombing just before it was completed. Estimates of its performance had been speed 608 mph; ceiling 46,000 ft; span 27 ft 0¾ ins; and climb rate 4,380 ft/min

The Messerschmitt P.1110/II fighter project of 1944 featured two unusual ideas. The more obvious of these was the V-shaped tailplane. but no less interesting was the other oddity. the air intake for the Heinkel HeS 011 turbojet. This intake was arranged the whole way round the fuselage toward the rear of the sharply-swept wings. Armament was to be three 30-mm cannon; speed 630 mph; span 21 ft 6 ins; length 31 ft; and range 940 miles

The Focke-Wulf 0310225 was a project for a long-range bomber carrying 6,600 lbs of bombs for 5,625 miles. The aircraft had a large central fuselage with the divided tailplane carried on booms attached to the wings so that the rear gunner had a good field of fire. The speed estimate was 360 mph at 28,400 ft with four BMW 801D engines giving 1,600 hp each. Armament was to be four 30-mm, one 20-mm and four 15-mm cannon, and four 13.1-mm machine guns

John Batchelor

The Focke-Wulf 0310251 project for a bad-weather and night-fighter was originally conceived in late 1944. The aircraft was designed to utilise a combination of two BMW 003A-1 turbojets of 1,760 lbs thrust each and one Junkers Jumo 222 pistol engine of 2,500 hp driving a pusher propeller. Armament was to comprise four 30-mm cannon mounted in the nose. Span was 68 ft 6 ins and the length 54 ft

The Blohm und Voss P 202 was a project for a single-seat fighter, in which the most unusual feature was the arrangement for swinging the wings. Instead of variable sweep wings, this aircraft's wings swivelled on the centre line of the fuselage, giving an angle of sweep of 35°, with the left wing leading in the configuration for high speed flight. Power was to be provided by two Junkers Jumo 004 turbojet engines providing 1,960 lbs thrust each

The Lippisch P 01.116 was first conceived in April 1939 as a rocket driven interceptor fighter for the Luftwaffe, a role that was eventually to be filled by the Messerschmitt 163 Komet. The basic idea behind the design, that of a small tailless aircraft, was common to both, but whereas the Messerschmitt featured swept wings, the Lippisch used stubby wings of large chord. Later Lippisch designs, however, were nearer to those of Messerschmitt

The Junkers EF 09 project was for a vertical takeoff fighter designed to take off under the power of ten small jets mounted on the nose. After climbing vertically, it turned to the normal attitude and flew like an ordinary fighter. The landing was made on skids. Top speed was estimated to be about 600 mph, the span 13 ft, and the length 16 ft 6 ins. The pilot adopted a prone position to alleviate the acceleration forces at take off

The Focke-Wulf 0310.025 project was conceived in 1944 in answer to a request for a high altitude fighter. Armament was to have comprised two 30-mm cannon and two MG 213 cannon of 20-mm calibre. The powerplant was to have been one Argus 413 of 4,000 hp driving contra-rotating propellers. Weight was to be 21,600 lbs loaded for normal flight. Span was 53 ft 9 ins and length 46 ft 6 ins

The Messerschmitt P.1102 project of 1944 for an unarmed bomber features variable sweep wings (sweep was 20° for take off and landing, 50° for high speed flight). Power was provided by three BMW 003 turbojets of 1,760 lbs thrust each, two being mounted under the nose and one in the tail. The aircraft was carried on a tandem bicycle type undercarriage under the fuselage, balanced by outrigger wheels beneath the wings

proost Turnhout (Belgium)